MW00792023

Susan,
Keep shining
God's light to the world!
Love you,
La Vonne

Praise for *Loved into the Light*

"**I** meet too many people that have stopped going to church altogether because they got hurt for one reason or another. This is very sad to me. This book, 'Loved into the Light', addresses this problem with hope and healing. It not only exposes so many of the issues that can enslave a person emotionally and spiritually, but also describes the Biblical steps to freedom in Jesus Christ. It is a must read—for anyone, of any faith."

Pastor Greg Baker
Greeley, CO

"**T**his inspiring book comes from the heart of a truly remarkable woman whose insights run true and deep. Looking back and sharing her own experiences of hope and healing, LaVonne uses Scripture to present clear corrections to false principles and presents a Biblical path for the healing of spiritual and emotional struggles. With sensitivity and caring, this book helps us understand biblical truth in a way that will help you discover firsthand the freedom to walk in God's truth and grace."

Karen Shadrack
Marriage, Family Therapist

"**B**y interweaving her personal experiences as a former member of the Church of Jesus Christ of Latter-day Saints with documented statements from LDS leaders, LaVonne Earl offers the reader a fascinating look at an organization that craves acceptability despite its historical inability to escape controversy. She energetically defends the biblical text, and by doing so, extends a message of hope to the struggling Latter-day Saint who may have erroneously assumed that, "if Mormonism is wrong, nothing is true.""

Bill McKeever
Mormon Research Ministry

"This book is a must read for anyone who is enslaved to the false teaching of the Mormon Church; however, it is also a very helpful read for people who are Christians and are seeking to be more like Christ experiencing a greater measure of freedom, joy and healing than ever before in their lives."

Harold Cameron- Moscow, Pennsylvania

"This book exposes the truth on religion, legalism and rituals that has blinded many from experiencing the true Love of God......a must read for anyone who has been led to believe that our works, actions, or lack thereof will earn us God's love, forgiveness, and salvation, ...If you are looking for truth to set you free from your own works and bondages of religion this book is for you!"

Flunda Youil –CA

"In her work, 'Loved into the Light' Mrs. Earl becomes an amazing guide for the journey of those whose nagging conscience tells them something is not right with Mormonism. She provides a Biblically accurate, clearly documented, concisely written, and yet engagingly personal doorway into the truth of the Bible as compared to the teachings of Mormon Theology. With a special blend of accuracy and gentleness Mrs. Earl neatly avoids the heated offensive polemics of so many others, and instead simply holds out a hand to say, "I was there, let me help". This is an awesome book for those who want to know Jesus. I wholeheartedly recommend it! "

Dr. James Johnson, Ph.D.

"What a powerful book! I came from a legalistic Mormon upbringing and though I have been walking in freedom with Christ for about eight years, I still found deeper insight about the power of unearned grace by reading this book. I love the compassionate tone the author takes. She is completely free of judgment for those still a part of the LDs community. I know this book will be a blessing not only to those recovering from legalism but also to those seeking to minister in this area."

Erika Ulrich- Former Mormon

"'Loved into the Light' is a refreshing read that offers the reader a clear understanding of Mormonism and the struggles one experiences (as a member) within the church. The author, a Mormon for eighteen years, helps the reader view the faith as an insider who truly loves people and desires their freedom in Christ. She exposes the problems and deception within the church without diminishing the worth of those who practice its teachings."

Russ Wise, Vice-President, Christian Information Ministries, —Apologist

"As a former Mormon, having recently left the Mormon church, I didn't realize how much I did not know about the Mormon religion until I started reading Loved into the Light. I was truly blind! I suffered with emptiness, confusion and a lack of connection with God.

Thank you for this priceless gift of knowledge, wisdom and love. I am finally free from guilt and confusion! I am happier having left the heavy weight I had been carrying for years. The door has been opened for me to reach out to Jesus Christ directly without the need to go through a load of rituals. Thank you for showing me the truth, and lighting my path to Him!"

In His Love, Diva L.

"It has been very enlightening reading your book! I have found it not only fascinating, but it has also helped me to understand some of your struggles. You are so much more at peace and you seem more connected with God now than you ever were. I am happy for you that He has shed clarity in your life, it shows, you are more content with yourself and others..... this must be the amazing grace and glory of God at work!!!"

Your sister, Susan S.

"'Loved into the Light' has left a beautiful and lasting impression in my spirit. The book truly captured La Vonne's passion for lighting the path to a most loving God and in the process freeing those who have been bound to man's rules. This exemplifies her compassion to preserve God's truth. Her knowledge and experience in the Mormon religion has encouraged me to break the bonds of religion in my own life, drawing me even closer to God and His living Word."

Wendy Ann- former Catholic

"My voice had been silenced for years due to the oppression of being a third generation Mormon. I went through all the motions out of duty and love for my family.

Now that my chains have been broken I am free to love God in a way that has brought me not only peace and happiness, but also a closer relationship to God and others.

Thank you La Vonne for giving a voice and an understanding to what was once an inner turmoil and a resentment towards God. I am prayerful that many others will read your book, search out the truth and come to experience the Freedom and Joy I have found."

Your husband- Michael Earl

Loved into the Light

Shining God's Light
on Mormonism

La Vonne Earl

Loved into the Light
Shining God's Light on Mormonism

by
La Vonne Earl

Publisher: Kingdom Press Publishing

First Edition

Copyright © 2012 La Vonne Earl

ISBN: 098553821x
ISBN-13: 9780985538217
Library of Congress Control Number:: 2012904534
Kingdom Press Publishing, Laguna Niguel, CA

Cover design by Zakr Studios

*Unless otherwise stated, all scripture quotations are from
the New International Version of the Bible.*

All rights reserved. No part of this publication may be reproduced or
transmitted in any form or by any means, electronic or mechanical,
including photocopy, recording, or any information storage retrieval
system, without permission in writing from the copyright owner.

Dedication

I dedicate this book to the One has who saved me,
the one that gave up His life for mine.
I am eternally grateful and
will sing praises to Him all my days.

My Lord, Jesus Christ.

Acknowledgements

I would like to first thank my daughter, Erika, for being brave enough to come to me, a very Mormon mother at the time, and tell me she did not believe Mormonism to be true. That takes incredible courage! If it were not for her, not only would this book not have been written, but I would still be living a life of religious bondage in the Mormon faith. Thank you, Erika, for encouraging me to search for truth! I also thank her for allowing me to use some of the experiences she had while a Mormon.

I would like to thank my best friend and husband, Michael, for standing by me through all the craziness, for supporting me throughout this entire book, for reading and helping me edit, and for listening to me talk about this book constantly. I would also like to thank him for allowing me to use his perspective and some of his experiences.

I would like to thank my sweet son, Nicholas, for giving me insight and feedback on God's great love. His heart for God and desire to serve Him is one to emulate. I also thank my son, Matthew, for being supportive and giving me his feedback as he has a great heart for all people.

I am thankful to my friend Tiffany Colter who believed in this project. Her godly insight and guidance is much appreciated. I also would like to thank all those that supported, encouraged me and cheered me on throughout this process.

I am thankful to Greg Baker, my amazing editor. He not only encouraged me, he was constantly attentive providing relative concepts along with proper theology. His pastoring experience was tremendously valuable.

I am also so thankful to Anthony Antenucci for tirelessly working with me on the cover design to make it perfect!

Contents

Purpose for this Book xv

Introduction   Journey to Freedom xvii

Chapter One   Who Is To Blame for the Fall of Mankind? 1

Chapter Two   Can We Trust God's Word? 15

Chapter Three   What is the True Church? 29

Chapter Four   What Makes a True Prophet? 45

Chapter Five   The Dangers of Polygamy 63

Chapter Six   What Happened to My Sexy Wife?—Garments . . . 77

Chapter Seven   Rules, Rules, Rules—Losing the Connection . . . 105

Chapter Eight   Baptism, a Necessary Ordinance? 119

Chapter Nine   Temple Ordinances, a Roadblock to God 135

Chapter Ten   Who Can Be Forgiven? 159

Chapter Eleven   Do You Trust God? 179

Chapter Twelve   Freedom versus Control 195

Chapter Thirteen   Transparency 209

Chapter Fourteen   Identity 225

Chapter Fifteen   Does God Love Everyone the Same? 239

Chapter Sixteen   Is the Church Safe or Judgmental? 255

Chapter Seventeen   Your Calling and Outreach 269

Chapter Eighteen   Will I Ever Be a God? 289

Chapter Nineteen   His Great Love 303

About the Author   xxx

Purpose for this Book

It is my prayer that each and every individual will come to know as his or her Lord and Savior, Jesus Christ. To really know Him is to practice His gospel of Grace, to do as He has commanded, and to go and make disciples of all nations. Why is this important? Because there are people everywhere that need to experience the love and compassion that our Savior has for all men. True and perfect religion is to care for the poor, sick and needy.

As humans, we truly act the way we believe. If we believe we are better than others, we will act that way. If we believe we are to be servants to our neighbors, we will serve. If we believe we are to be generous with the poor and needy, we will supply their need. If we believe we are to love as Jesus loved, then love will become as natural to us as breathing.

It is my life's mission to see everyone become a vessel through which God can work for the good of all men, to teach all men to love God with all their heart, mind and soul, and to love their neighbor as himself.

Thy kingdom come, Thy will be done on earth as it is in heaven! Amen!

"I do believe; help me overcome my unbelief!"

— Mark 9:24

Introduction — Journey to Freedom

"Then you will know the truth, and the truth will set you free."

— John 8:32

I was born in Phoenix, Arizona, and raised in Las Vegas, Nevada. I lived a pretty sinful life growing up and was introduced to the Mormon religion when I was 19 years old. Some of the girls at the beauty college I attended sent the women missionaries to my home to teach me about the Mormon faith. I didn't know it at the time, but my soon to be husband was a Mormon.

The gospel they introduced me to was not the Gospel I know now. I was taught very little about Mormonism, but I was taught that Jesus loved me—which was enough for this sinful, spiritually hungry girl. I wanted His love and forgiveness, and so I was quickly baptized into the Mormon Church.

What started out as my love for Jesus, and His love for me turned into a continuous battle of trying to be good enough to earn salvation, all through a set of rules imposed upon me. I would continually try to perfectly adhere to these rules, thinking it the only way to maintain this love and forgiveness that I had found. Soon, the Church made it necessary that I change my lifestyle even more—not that the way I was living was bad (according to God's Word) during that time; it just didn't conform to their worldview. I had to adapt to these new laws and rules that I never even knew existed before I was baptized. For a while, it seemed that each new member that came into my life, whether they were a leader or just a member of the congregation, had a new rule to offer me. I continued to obey these rules and encouraged my family to do the same.

I remember vividly a time when my husband wanted to take our 10-year-old daughter out on a Harley ride and get a Jamba on a Sunday. I got so upset with them because this was not honoring the Sabbath—a rule I was told to keep in order to keep me on the path to salvation. Additional rules began to affect my marriage and family in ways I had not expected. Without realizing, my family began to suffer.

The fruits of living this oppressive lifestyle were adding up quickly. Our family looked really good on the outside. We all appeared happy and looked very nice. What remained hidden from everyone else were the guilt, oppression, anger, captivity and fear that began to dominate everyone's life in our home. I didn't understand where this was all coming from at the time, but now that we have all been set free from religious captivity I know. The fruits of Christ's True Gospel are very different and apparent in our home and our lives now. There is so much peace, tranquility, love, happiness, and joy it is hard to explain, but makes me ache to do so. I know God desires this happiness for everyone!

I would like to make it clear that my separation from the Mormon Church had nothing to do with unworthiness or transgression. For 18 years, I was 100% devoted to the LDS Church.

During those years, I never once questioned the truthfulness of their gospel. My faithfulness was clearly demonstrated by my service in the Church, and anyone who has ever served with me can attest to my wholehearted dedication and commitment. We held weekly family home evening, daily personal/family prayer and scripture study, regular church attendance, temple attendance, and gave generous tithes and offerings. I was a very faithful member.

The turning point for me came because the fruits of living this way began to destroy my family. I could no longer deny the truth of what was happening. My family was falling apart and I needed God more than ever. I went out alone and fell to my knees crying, "Jesus, what do you want me to do? I do not want to betray you by leaving the Mormon Church and yet my family is falling apart. Tell me, Lord, what to do." I felt a peace come over me about leaving the Mormon Church. It became a peaceful conviction that I could do this and Jesus would walk with me. I could not have left the Mormon Church otherwise, because leaving God's "true" church was not something I ever wanted to do.

I went to my husband and told him what I had experienced. After much prayer, we decided we would go to our community Christian Church. Each lesson from the podium was as if God was answering every question I ever had about the Mormon Church, and the pastor never once mentioned Mormons. But God was doing something wonderful in my heart. He was setting me free.

I began my search. I wanted to know everything. For years, I was warned not to read anything contrary to the Mormon Church, that just the act of doing so would be apostatizing and demonstrating a lack of faith. So at first, I was scared to do it. I never knew how much fear had been instilled within me.

But because of my walk with Jesus, He gave me the strength to carry on and search. I learned that Jesus wants us to search out truth. He wants us to know everything about Him. He is not afraid of anything! Wow, it has been great overcoming my fear.

I know that Mormons are generally really great people. They love God very much. I sure did then and still do. But I must tell you; there is so much they do not know.

I invite you to take a walk with me through this book and discover how you can be freed from *any* religious captivity you might be in. Whether Mormon, Muslim, Catholic, New Age, or whatever it may be, there is a God that wants to set you free—free to live the most amazing and adventuresome life you could ever imagine!

— La Vonne Earl

Who is to Blame
for the Fall of Mankind?

"And the result of God's gracious gift is very different from the result of that one man's sin. For Adam's sin led to condemnation, but God's free gift leads to our being made right with God, even though we are guilty of many sins."

— Romans 5:16

An interesting question arises from out of the ashes of the Garden of Eden. Did Adam really sin when he ate of the Tree of the Knowledge of Good and Evil? Strangely, the question exists in some religious circles, and by its very existence, it seems to cast the entire blame for the fall of mankind squarely on the shoulders of Adam, or was it the woman—Eve?

The result hints at peculiar consequences. For example, if Eve is to blame, could it be that the woman and not the man passed the sin nature to mankind? Perhaps a curse has been placed on all women making them subservient to men? Better yet, maybe a woman's role in Heaven is somehow in servitude to men, instead of God?

To many people, putting things just this way seems strange and rather sexist. Yet this is not an uncommon belief regarding Adam and Eve. Teaching that Adam made a tough but correct choice to follow the woman in a form of martyrdom is another approach to this subject within the Mormon Church. With many different approaches to this very critical piece of the puzzle, I myself was rather confused and needed clarity. I wanted to understand, so my longing for more information continued. I yearned to have a closer walk and fellowship with God. My life before Mormonism was filled with confusion and guilt, and I wanted freedom from these spiritual chains, but the more I studied Mormon beliefs, the more confused I became as I tried to reconcile what I read in the Bible with Mormon Doctrine.

I imagine this is true for many different religions—not just Mormonism. Thankfully, we have an incredible God that reveals truth through His Word and Holy Spirit. Spiritual chains of confusion, whether of our own making or of man's, do not have to bind us. We can have freedom and clarity through truth.

"Then you will know the truth,
and the truth will set you free."

— John 8:32

For me, the contradictions of Mormon teaching and in supposed *inspired* books led to confusion and an unnecessary questioning of God—and what He has said. For those following anything but God's Word, there will be contradictions and confusion that will only continue to bind you in the spiritual chains of confusion, stunting your spiritual growth.

"For the LORD gives wisdom, and from his mouth
come knowledge and understanding."

— Proverbs 2:6

Mormon Doctrine brought these chains of confusion into my life. On one hand, the second of the Mormon thirteen Articles of Faith says, "Men will be punished for their own sins and not for Adam's transgression."[1] Yet in other writings, we find that Adam did not so much as sin, but ate of the tree in an effort to fix what Eve did. For example, Marion G. Romney, a Mormon apostle and member of the First Presidency in the Mormon Church wrote the following: "I do not look upon Adam's action as a sin. I think it was a deliberate act of free agency. He chose to do that which had to be done to further the purposes of God."[2]

It appears that, according to Mr. Romney, Adam needed to disobey God in order to fulfill His command of multiplying. This is a catch-22 in that it sets a contradictory precedent that sometimes it is necessary to walk in opposition to God in order to obey God. It is as if they are saying God sometimes needs us to do wrong in order to assist in fulfilling His will. How can an individual ever have a sense of what is right and what is wrong if even the foundational belief of their faith contradicts itself?

And without doubt, the story of Adam and Eve in the Garden of Eden is foundational to everything we believe. It gives the reason for Salvation, sets the tone for Redemption, and provides understanding of our purpose and for God's creation. It is not something we should meddle with.

But meddling is the main reason why we have such problems to begin with. In Genesis, God very clearly stated His command to Adam. Adam was told not to eat from the tree of the knowledge of good and evil. There was no debate or misunderstanding:

> *"And the Lord God commanded the man,*
> *'You are free to eat from any tree in the garden;*
> *but you must NOT eat from the tree*
> *of the knowledge of good and evil,*
> *for when you eat of it you will surely die.'"*
>
> — Genesis 2:16-17

1 http://lds.org/scriptures/pgp/a-of-f/1?lang=eng

2 Marion G. Romney, *Look to God and live: Discourses of Marion G. Romney* (Deseret Book Co, 1971), 251.

As parents we understand the need to provide clear expectations and boundaries to our children. We need to let them know what we want them to do, the rewards for obedience, and the consequences of disobedience. God did exactly that with His children—Adam and Eve. He offered them everything man would ever need. He provided abundant resources. He gave man a purpose to live for. Man walked with God in perfect fellowship.

However, to have the relationship with man that God desired, he needed man to voluntarily choose to love Him. In order for love to be love, it must be freely chosen; therefore it was necessary to provide man with a choice. He could continue to walk with God, or he could eat of the tree of the knowledge of good and evil. God's perfect plan and desire was to live in eternity with Adam and Eve in Eden. Scripture makes this clear (1 John 1:7, Psalms 9:10). God is not the author of confusion. He makes His commandments perfectly clear. He does not want His children to fall and commit sin. The Tree of the knowledge of good and evil allowed Adam and Eve to continually demonstrate their love for God by their choice not to eat of the tree and to obey God.

"Jesus answered and said unto him, If a man love me, he will keep my words: and my Father will love him, and we will come unto him, and make our abode with him."

— John 14:23

Mormon Doctrine, however, muddies this call from God. The end results are confusion and double speak. They don't give a clear answer to the question of whether Adam sinned or not—despite the fact that Scripture clearly indicated that he did. Mormons teach that Adam made the correct choice to eat of the fruit offered to him by Eve. They don't see it as a sin. They see it as necessary to correct Eve's sin and replenish the earth.

To explain this, the Book of Mormon says in 2 Nephi 2:25, "Adam fell that men might be; and men are that they might have joy." The logic suggests that Adam didn't sin, but rather stepped up to the plate and bailed God out of a tenuous situation as a direct result of Eve's sin.

In this case, Adam was the savior—not of Mankind or even of Eve, but of God's plan.

In the Temple ceremony—an important step in a Mormon's eternal progression and status within the church community—you watch a movie in which God speaks to Adam and Eve saying, "Nevertheless you may freely choose." In the Mormon book, *The Pearl of Great Price*, you can clearly see how they add to God's word in order to justify Adam's actions. It says in Moses 3:17, "But of the tree of the knowledge of good and evil, thou shalt not eat of it, *nevertheless, thou mayest choose for thyself, for it is given unto thee*; but, remember that I forbid it, for in the day thou eatest thereof thou shalt surely die." God certainly wanted them to choose correctly, but He never *said* that they had the freedom to choose to eat of the tree. The opportunity to choose does not make all available options right.

This is obviously not God's word. This is injected scripture! God never says this anywhere in the bible! Remember, God's Word was clear. They could freely eat of any tree—except one. Of that one tree, they were *not* to eat of it! This is why God commands us not to add to the Bible. When we add or subtract from God's Word under the guise of inspiration, the only thing that ultimately results is more confusion.

According to Genesis 1:28, God commanded man to be fruitful and multiply the earth. Unfortunately, Mormon doctrine teaches that this command was somehow in jeopardy as a result of Eve's sin and it was up to Adam to preserve it. Mormon's teach that it was necessary for Adam to partake of the forbidden fruit in order to produce the necessary children for the ongoing goal of eternal progression—the belief that every person has the potential to become their own god of their own planet in the hereafter. Thus Adam is left with fear and his own bizarre choice. If he refuses to eat, he would remain in the garden, Eve might be exiled, and he could remain in close relationship with God. But there would be no children. There would be no means for the spirits in Heaven to continue on their eternal progression. The other choice for Adam would be to eat of the forbidden fruit, leave the garden with Eve, bear children and so in his mind fulfill the will of God.

Mormons believe that Adam chose the latter in order to preserve God's plan.

However, it is not necessary for Man to bail God out. Adam never gave God a chance to rectify the situation. Instead he took matters into his own hands resulting in a sin, not a solution.

What Really Happened in the Garden?

To put it simply, both Adam and Eve sinned. There is no other way to look at this. We can't blame the fall of mankind on just Eve, nor on just Adam—although Scripture indicates that Eve was deceived, and Adam was not (1 Timothy 2:14), Adam's decision to eat of the tree was indeed a deliberate act, but it was still an act of sin.

> *"When Adam sinned, sin entered the world.*
> *Adam's sin brought death, so death spread to everyone,*
> *for everyone sinned."*
>
> — Romans 5:12

Adam's decision to eat of the tree may indeed have been done for some altruistic reason—a reason that probably had more to do with his fear of losing the only other human on the planet to exile or death than from a desire to fulfill the will of God. Nevertheless, it is always a mistake to circumvent God and take things into your own hands.

When King Saul tried to do this in 1 Samuel 13, God's disappointment became immediately apparent. Saul offered a sacrifice to God. That in of itself seems like a good thing. The problem was that Saul wasn't allowed to actually perform the sacrificial ceremony—that was a job for a Levite. His disobedience to God brought a staggering reaction:

> *"You have done a foolish thing," Samuel said.*
> *"You have not kept the command the LORD your God*
> *gave you; if you had, he would have established your*
> *kingdom over Israel for all time. But now your kingdom*

*will not endure; the LORD has sought out a man after
his own heart and appointed him ruler of his people,
because you have not kept the LORD's command."*

— 1 Samuel 13:13-14

Saul tried to take things into his own hands and even trying to do a good thing in a wrong way was considered to be a sin in the eyes of the Lord. Later, Saul did the same thing with similar results. In the second case, Samuel pointed out that obedience is better than sacrifice, and to listen to God is better than an offering to Him (1 Samuel 15:22). Samuel went on to explain that rebellion is equivalent to the sin of witchcraft and stubbornness to the sin of idolatry (1 Samuel 15:23).

With this very direct Scripture, it cannot be construed that Adam did anything other than sin against God. His sin and the sin nature have now passed upon all men (Romans 5:12).

The idea that Adam did not sin as put forth by the Mormon Church has allowed others to likewise justify their sins under the guise of doing God a favor. This is unacceptable to God. To Him, it is the same as witchcraft and idolatry!

We are commanded to obey Him. Adam and Eve's sin and the direct and indirect consequences of their actions is a valuable lesson that we need to take to heart. Neither Adam nor Eve tried to confess their sins. In fact, they tried to pass it off onto someone else—an action that too many of us are guilty of. If Adam and Eve had tried to confess their sin, instead of justifying it, perhaps an alternative could have been found other than exile from the Garden of Eden. We will never know, but we do know what the Scriptures say:

*"If we confess our sins, he is faithful and just and will forgive
us our sins and purify us from all unrighteousness."*

— 1 John 1:9

Instead of trying to justify our sins, perhaps we ought to try confessing them. A loving and faithful God has more power to make things right than a sin committed with good intentions does. Taking things into our own hands is always a mistake. Trusting God, obeying him, and casting all our care upon him is what brings lasting peace with Him.

Dangers of Justifying Sin

One of the more peculiar dangers to justification of sin is a demotion of the holiness of God. If sin can be right, then God is less holy than Scriptures indicate. Mormons, who do have a hunger for God, are being taught that the God they're following is a cruel taskmaster that once possessed all the human fallibilities and capacity for mistakes as they do. They are taught that the Mormon god of this world, Elohim, was once a man like us living on a different planet. He was a sinner like us, but eventually attained godhood. What's more, under this belief, immortality and God status is fully attainable by any perfect Mormon able to follow the same pattern as Elohim did—a peculiar belief considering that Scripture repeatedly tells us that there is only one God (Isaiah 44:6, 8; 45:5-6) and that we are to worship one God only (Exodus 34:14, Matthew 4:10).

This idea of becoming a god can appeal to our sense of pride while undermining the holiness and ultimate perfection of God. Although Mormons now believe God to be perfect and sinless, they believe that he wasn't always like that. Thus justifying of Adam's sin sets the stage for justifying the sins of mankind, including prophets and leaders, all in the name of a greater good.

This belief suggests that the ends justify the means—a notion that is abhorrent to God.

Sin stabs at our souls and pulls us away causing us to hide from the very God we all seek to know. When I was a Mormon, I never got what I had most desired—clarity of God's will and therefore a closer relationship with Him. The teachings set up a system where it was nearly impossible for me to hear His direct command and follow Him.

This is another one of the dangers of attempting to justify sin. It creates the illusion of a double minded God that either can't make up His mind, or has a somewhat whimsical sense of bizarre humor. Any time you attempt to justify a sin, you must make changes to the prevailing thought, current belief, or understood command. The immediate result of this double-speak is an open door to question anything God said.

This was Satan's very first tactic...to get us to question the Word of God.

"Did God really say, 'You must not eat from any tree
in the garden'?" The woman said to the serpent,
"We may eat fruit from the trees in the garden,
but God did say ,'You must not eat fruit from the tree
that is in the middle of the garden, and you must not
touch it, or you will die." "You will not surely die,"
the serpent said to the woman. "For God knows
that when you eat of it your eyes will be opened,
and you will be like God, knowing good and evil."

— Genesis 3:1-5

Eve justified her actions by allowing Satan to question what God said. This created a question in her own mind that led her to consider what she never before even thought of doing. This led to both Adam and Eve's sampling the forbidden fruit, which led to their exile from the Garden and the condemnation of sin. Any time there is a direct contradiction to what God said, there is an opportunity to justify a sin. Mormon doctrine is rife with contradictions that provide many opportunities to justify a sin. Direct contradictions of what God supposedly said leaves us with several uncomfortable choices in regards to God's Word—and even God Himself:

1. God changed His mind—contrary to Numbers 23:19.

2. God forgot what He originally said.

3. God's got a strange sense of humor and likes to see us confused—this is not what a loving Father does.

4. God is testing our ability to read His mind—despite Isaiah 55:9.

Not a one of the choices inspires hope. Fortunately, not one of these is true; God meant what He said, and it is man or Satan that has contradicted God, not God. The other options leave God's Word susceptible to hijacking by evil men who claim to speak on behalf of God. He has never changed His mind about who He is, the nature of sin, or the nature of holiness.

God hasn't changed (Numbers 23:19, Malachi 3:6, Hebrews 13:8). God won't change, either. Thank God for that. We can always count on His love. We can always rely upon His grace. We can always appeal to His mercy. And we always have access to His salvation.

A third danger of justifying sin is that you begin to glorify the wrong choice. This is a form of self-righteousness and embodies all the dangers listed. Self-righteousness, as we already explored in the life of Saul, is contrary to God.

> *"All of us have become like one who is unclean,*
> *and all our righteous acts are like filthy rags;*
> *we all shrivel up like a leaf,*
> *and like the wind our sins sweep us away."*

> — Isaiah 64:6

When compared to God, our righteousness is an unclean thing. So how does God look upon our efforts to glorify a sin in the name of righteousness? We can tell from His Word, not very well. Yet any attempt to justify a wrong is in essence an attempt at self-righteousness. The sin itself must be glorified in order to accomplish this. I was astounded that the Mormon Church venerated Adam's decision as wholesome and right. This led me to question areas in my own life where I wondered if doing a wrong was the right thing to do.

When we begin this process of glorifying a sin, holding it up as some kind of example of righteousness, we steal from God's Word, reduce God's holiness, and blur the lines between right and wrong. Blurring the lines or even saying that wrong is right and right is wrong, puts us in the precarious position of trying to play God. Invariably, we no longer demonstrate trust in God, but fall back on our own base reasoning to determine right from wrong.

"he saved us, not because of righteous things we had done,
but because of his mercy. He saved us through the washing
of rebirth and renewal by the Holy Spirit,"

— Titus 3:5

Only the righteousness of Jesus Christ can save us. His righteousness, not ours, is our only hope.

Healing from the Wounds of Self-righteousness

We are all guilty of self-righteousness. It seems to be part of our very nature. No one likes to look bad. No one likes to even think of himself or herself as a terribly bad person. We justify our sins in order to feel better about ourselves. Unfortunately, this leaves behind a cancerous guilt that gnaws away at our consciousness. This results either in insecurity and spiritual injury or a seared conscience (1 Timothy 4:2). You will not find the joy of the Lord as you begin to believe your own lies.

You can heal from this. Here are the steps to follow:

1. Accept sin for what it is—sin.

2. Repent, meaning turn from your sin.

3. Realize that you are never separated from God's love—except by choice.

4. Place your complete faith in God's Word.

5. Seek the Fruits[1] of the Spirit.

To begin with, it is important that we never try to justify sin. The more we attempt to do this, the more we play God, resulting in an insensitivity to sin.

---

1 Galatians uses the singular word fruit in scripture-the author has chosen to use the plural form of fruit to demonstrate the many benefits or 'fruits' that the Holy Spirit brings into our life.

This is known as a seared conscience (1 Timothy 4:2). Sin separates us from God. When Adam and Eve sinned, they were separated from God when they were kicked out of the Garden of Eden. This is the natural result of sin. To believe that sin is in some way justifiable only separates us further from God in the sense that we don't even believe we need forgiveness. This separation is one of fellowship—your communication with God is impaired.

Imagine a child who disobeys his father. Does the father continue to love his son? Yes! But how is their communication? Until this disobedience is resolved, there is an issue in the relationship that prevents it from being all that it can be. The father still loves the son—which is why the relationship can be repaired, but there is still a separation in fellowship. The child must go to his father to repair the relationship. His isolation, so to speak, from the father lasts as long as he decides not to make it right. The moment he tries to make it right, the relationship is repaired (1 John 1:8).

This leads me to the next point. Peace comes from love (1 John 4:18). It is not necessary to justify your sin to find peace of mind. It is only necessary to envelop yourself in the love of God. According to Romans 8:38 and 39, there is nothing in this universe that can separate you from God.

> *"For I am convinced that neither death nor life, neither*
> *angels nor demons, neither the present not the future,*
> *nor any powers, neither height nor depth, nor anything*
> *else in all creation, will be able to separate us from the*
> *love of God that is in Christ Jesus our Lord."*
>
> — Romans 8:38-39

However, we can *feel* like we've been separated from God, but this is the result of what we do to ourselves. It is a choice we make. As with all sin, God will forgive us if we ask. In order to repent of our sin, we first have to recognize it as sin, be remorseful of it and ask for that forgiveness from God. It would be wrong to glorify our sin and let everyone think we made the right choice (1 John 1:10). Only then can we feel like we have access to God's love.

We want to be certain we are obeying all of God's commands found in His Word. Until we have complete faith in His word, we are prone to add to it and subtract from it. All of this additional false doctrine creates confusion and blurs the line between right and wrong. If we cannot see sin clearly, then Satan will pervert our minds to believe that what we are doing is right or justified as the Galatians begin to do in Galatians 1:8.

It is essential to understand that God's commands are given to protect us. God wasn't trying to restrict Adam and Eve, He was trying to keep them from the pain and suffering that followed their sin. You may ask, "Why didn't God remove the tree then and take away temptation?" Because a walk with God must be made freely, of our own will, for it to have meaning. One choice is not a choice. The tree gave Adam and Eve that choice. God, in His love and desire to protect them, clearly outlined the consequences of eating of the Tree of the Knowledge of Good and Evil. God wanted to protect them. So too, does God want to protect us by giving us commands and laws to follow. We must go to God and His Word and seek to be in His will for our life. If we begin to think that God's concept of sin is not really sinful, or if we believe that God is double minded, we are merely issuing ourselves a license to sin and calling it good!

This is an insane way to live our lives!

The Fruits of the Spirit, interestingly enough, begins with love. Love comes before joy and peace! If we wrap ourselves up in God's love, grace, mercy, and forgiveness, then we will find joy and peace. This is the means God created to give us the joy and peace we crave while keeping sin forbidden.

> *"But the fruit of the Spirit is love, joy, peace, patience, kindness, goodness, faithfulness, gentleness and self-control. Against such things there is no law. Those who belong to Christ Jesus have crucified the sinful nature with its passions and desires."*
>
> — Galatians 5:22-23

The fruits of Satan's spirit are death, manipulation, oppression, depression, confusion, hate, and sin. Being trapped in Satan's lies never brings the joy and peace you want. But Satan's grasp can be loosened—yes shattered, by turning to Christ again, refusing to justify your sin, and surrounding yourself in the love of God.

A Prayer of Healing

"Lord, thank You that Your Word, the Bible, is perfectly clear, and that you give us commandments for our protection, because you love us. I thank You for Your clarity. I ask that You continue to make my path straight and clear. I will listen to You alone through Your Word, the Bible. Thank You that You forgive me of my sins. Lord, thank You that You came to redeem the fall of Adam. I am grateful for Your grace and love that is never ending. I want to walk in the fruits of Your spirit Lord. I shall have no other god but You Lord. In Your mighty Name, I pray, amen."

Can We Trust God's Word?

"The very essence of your words is truth;
all your just regulations will stand forever."

— Psalm 119:160

The Bible.

Can we trust it? Is it reliable? With so many 'learned scholars' out there pointing out the problems and loopholes in the Scripture, it is hard to think of the Bible as an authority for our faith and religious practice. Yet at the same time, these 'learned scholars,' while pointing out the errors, also claim that their belief in God is predicated on the very Scriptures they hold to as having errors. This presents a problem.

The Bible is the foundation of the Christian faith. From it we are to learn what God has instructed us to do, how He wants us to live, and the promises God offers. Just like a building, a solid foundation is crucial to supporting the structure above it.

Jesus Himself spoke of the importance of this solid footing when he told the story of the wise man and foolish man in Matthew 8:

*"Therefore whoever hears these sayings of Mine, and does them,
I will liken him to a wise man who built his house (remember
we are the temple of Christ) on the rock: and the rain
descended, the floods came, and the winds blew and beat on
that house; and it did not fall, for it was founded on the rock.
But everyone who hears these sayings of Mine, and does not
do them, will be like a foolish man who built his house on the
sand: and the rain descended, the floods came, and the winds
blew and beat on that house; and it fell. And great was its fall."*

— Matthew 8:24-27

For Christians, Jesus is our example and God's Word is our instruction manual. Without it there is not a solid belief system. Cracks in a foundation weaken the entire structure, destabilizing the building that rests upon it. Cracks in the foundation of someone's faith put their very soul in peril. That is why it is crucial for a person seeking to know God to have a rock solid foundation in something that they can turn to with the utmost confidence—a final authority that has the power to direct their faith.

You must first determine your belief in the Bible, whether it is corrupt or not before you can determine what your beliefs are. Christianity rests on the assurance that the Bible is 100% accurate. If there are any errors in Scripture the book can no longer be our standard of truth. You either believe the Bible is the Word of God or you don't. You either believe God when He said His Word will stand forever or you don't.

If I or any other person, even one claiming to be a prophet, can decide individually which statements in the Bible are corrupt and which are accurate then that person—not the written text—becomes the final authority and standard of truth. I become the standard of truth, as I determine which Bible statements are corrupt and which are not. If I can't trust God when He says that His Word will stand the test of time, how can I trust Him with other areas of my life like salvation, and the place that He is preparing for me in His kingdom?

Unfortunately, some religions do just that. They take the word or declaration of an individual to be the same as—or better than—the Bible. These extra-biblical decrees and texts open the door for confusion and abuse. Suddenly the foundation of a person's faith isn't standing on the solid rock of God's eternal Word. Instead it becomes the shifting sand of man's doctrine.

*"Heaven and earth will pass away, but my
words will never pass away"*

— Luke 21:33

If the Bible is not true or if it is filled with errors, Christianity would only be a "blind faith"—something people believe without any evidence to support it—a faith built more on superstition and personal flights of fancy than on a concrete authority that molds our lives to the Word, rather than molding His words to us. However, Christianity is *not* a blind faith. It is not superstition. It is the *only* religion that can prove itself, and the source of that proof is the Bible. There is solid evidence that supports the validity of the Bible.

However, when I was a Mormon I was taught that the Bible was not pure anymore and that through interpretation and translation much was lost and distorted. This is exactly the argument Satan used in the Garden of Eden. He had to first convince Eve God didn't really mean what He said. He had to discount God's Word in Eve's eyes. Only then would Eve consider Satan's words over God's words. With God's Word being invalid, Eve was able to sin.

The Mormons teach that the Book of Mormon is the only book that has not lost its purity through translation since Joseph Smith was the only one to translate it. Joseph Smith states, "I told the brethren that the Book of Mormon was the most correct of any book on earth, and the keystone of our religion, and a man would get nearer to God by abiding by its precepts, than by any other book."[3] But since Smith's work so obviously contradicted the Bible, he had to discredit the Bible in order to make his work more acceptable to others. He sold his work as something 'purer' than the Bible. I had never been exposed to true Christianity and had not learned to recognize the authentic gospel.

---

3 Joseph Smith, *Documentary History of the Church* (DHC, vol. 4), p. 461.

Therefore, when I was taught something that looked like Christianity it was easy to fall prey to a cult.

The Bible Versus the Book of Mormon

In comparing the Bible to the Book of Mormon (BOM), we must concede that one has to be right and the other wrong. God said His Word would stand forever and yet Joseph Smith states that his book is more pure. There can only be one true authority. Which one is it? How do we determine which is right and which is wrong? And just how different are they?

To begin with, a very blunt example can be found in diametrically opposed teachings that begin so similarly but end so differently. The Book of Mormon teaches in 2 Nephi 25:23, "...that it is by grace that we are saved, after all we can do." The Bible, beginning in a similar manner teaches a different conclusion altogether in Ephesians 2:8-9, "For by grace are ye saved, through faith, and that not of yourselves: it is the gift of God: not of works lest any man should boast." So according to this, the BOM teaches salvation is by grace plus works while the Bible teaches us that salvation is by grace alone.

Clearly, only one can be right. The trouble here is that the teaching is about salvation and the different teachings are mutually exclusive. Whichever one is correct means the other is *not* teaching salvation, but damnation.

Truly a troubling thought.

This becomes even clearer when we read from one of the Quorum of the Twelve Apostles, Bruce R. McConkie. He writes in a treatise about the Bible: "But we do not believe, as does evangelical Christianity, that the Bible contains all things necessary for salvation; nor do we believe that God has now taken upon himself the tongue of the dumb which no longer speaks, nor reveals, nor makes known his will to his children.[4] Indeed, we know that the Bible contains only a sliver, a twig, a leaf, no more than a small branch at the most, from the great redwood of revelation that God has given in ages past."

---

4 Bruce R. McConkie, *The Bible, a Sealed Book*, (BYU, 1984).

His very statement has made the Bible irrelevant—and by extension, the BOM as well. If the Bible contains only a sliver of revelation, then how much does the BOM, which in size and scope is actually less than the Bible, contain? If all we have is two slivers of revelation from God then what is to say that we aren't missing something vital? How do we know that somewhere, something essential to our salvation is now lost? And if that is true, then are we all damned? This is the ultimate dilemma that arises when you begin to question the Bible. You must, by extension, believe that your salvation is always in jeopardy, that there is always the risk that something important, something vital has somehow slipped through the fingers of an Almighty God, and we are living on in ignorance.

The BOM, interestingly enough, has entire passages that are word for word exact duplicates of the King James Version of the Bible that was available in the early 1800's. This is interesting, because Smith purportedly translated the Book of Mormon from a hither to lost language that he called 'Reformed Egyptian.' Yet the KJV was translated from Hebrew and Greek—nothing even remotely similar to any known Egyptian writings. How then is it possible to translate a language from Egyptian into old Victorian era English exactly as the King James Translators did from Hebrew and Greek back in 1611? It stretches credulity—especially since the plates Joseph Smith claimed he used for his translation were 'taken to heaven by an angel' and are now unavailable for inspection!

While we have multiple manuscripts from which the Bible is translated from, we must take a single man's word that he was divinely inspired to—all alone—translate the Book of Mormon. In comparison of the two works, the Bible not only has the historical record to back it up, but it has mounds of textual documents to support every single word. The Book of Mormon has the word of one man and not a shred of historical evidence to back it up.

The Truth of the Book of Mormon

The *Book of Mormon* (BOM) teaches that an Israelite family fled Jerusalem in 589 BC and sailed to America. The father had a number of sons including Nephi and Laman. Nephi and Laman started two nations called the Nephites and Lamanites. As you'll see, these nations present a foundation for racism in addition to the fact that their existence cannot be proven.

The Lamanites were miraculously made black, or dark skinned, and were presented as being the more primitive people, while the Nephites were 'white...and delightsome' (2 Nephi 5:21). These two families are claimed to have spread throughout all of North America (Helaman 3:8). So much did they spread that the BOM lists around 40 cities that the Nephites built. Not one of these cities has ever been found—unlike the Bible where archeology has overwhelmingly supported the Biblical record. The BOM teaches that Jesus Christ went to America in 34 AD after his resurrection to preach to the Jewish descendants and then ascended to heaven again.

Then, in 385 AD the Lamanites exterminated the Nephites and became the Indians. Mormon, one of the last Nephites, wrote the BOM on gold plates in 'Reformed Egyptian' (Mormon 9:32). His son, Moroni, completed the Book.

In 1823-1827, Moroni, now an angel, (the angel on all the current temples) visited Joseph Smith and gave him the gold plates. Smith translated them, producing the English BOM in 1830. The angel Moroni then took the plates from Smith. Mormons believe that the Lamanites and even the Israelites are the main ancestors of the American Indians.

With no proof for the BOM's authenticity, Mormons hoped the new science of DNA research would link the Indians to ancient Israelites and prove that the BOM is a translation of an ancient document. The DNA method had been used by other groups to support various historical records, so the Mormon Church hoped it would support their claims as well.

The opposite happened, however.

DNA research confirmed what anthropologists concluded long ago—Native Americans originated in East Asia over 10,000 years ago, not in Israel 2,600 years ago.[5] In his documentary, "DNA Evidence

---

5 For an extensive look into the DNA evidence get a copy of the DVD entitled DNA Evidence of The Book of Mormon - Produced by Living Hope Ministries of

of the Book of Mormon", Dr. Murphy concludes, "It is genetically, archaeologically, historically and linguistically impossible for American Indians as a whole to be descendants of Lamanites who came from Israel."[6]

Furthermore, no remains of the about 40 American cities named in the BOM have ever been found. Of about 180 ancient American people named in the BOM, not one has archaeological verification. No event in the BOM has archaeological support. No object mentioned in it has been found—no coins, armor, Egyptian writings, swords, gold plates, chariots, steel or copper, nor remains of domestic animals such as cows, oxen, asses or horses mentioned in 1 Nephi 18:25.

In fact, to add confusion to mystification, there are at least two versions of the BOM. Mormons actually use a revised version with almost 4,000 alterations and corrections to Joseph Smith's 'perfect' translation! The Reorganized Church, which split off after Joseph Smith died, still uses Smith's first version of the BOM.

You need to decide if the BOM is true. Aside from all the evidence that it is not true, the most important truth to consider is how the BOM has changed the Gospel of Jesus Christ.

> *"But though we, or an angel from heaven, preach any other*
> *gospel unto you than that which we have preached unto you,*
> *let him be accursed."*
>
> — Galatians 1:8 (KJV)

The Truth of the Bible

One of the strongest arguments for the truthfulness of the Bible is its 100% accuracy in predicting the future. The Old Testament was written between approximately 1450 BC and 430 BC. During that time, God's prophets recorded many predictions of the future in the

---

Utah

6 Thomas W. Murphy, *Lamanite Genesis, Genealogy, and Genetics*

Bible. Of the events that were to have taken place by now, each and every one happened just the way the prophets predicted it would.

"Above all, you must realize that no prophecy in Scripture ever came from the prophet's own understanding, or from human initiative. No, those prophets were moved by the Holy Spirit, and they spoke from God."

— 2 Peter 1:20-21

Now if God gave us His Word through His prophets, do you really think it would be in God's nature to let His book get corrupted? The Bible has stood the test of time. It is 100% accurate. No one has ever been able to disprove the Bible, and the Bible will never get corrupted. God will not allow it!

If faith alone isn't sufficient to prove the validity of the Bible, the discovery of the Dead Sea Scrolls found between 1947 and 1956 have proven that the Bible has been almost completely unchanged since it was written down. The few minor differences between the accepted text and the scrolls do *not* change the meaning of the text. The Word has remained intact. The discovery itself is verification of the truth Jesus spoke of in Matthew:

"I tell you the truth, until heaven and earth disappear, not even the smallest detail of God's law will disappear until its purpose is achieved."

— Matthew 5:18

The most important prophecy contained with Scripture is of the coming Messiah as laid down in the Old Testament. Messiah means, 'Anointed one.' His coming was to change everything, and His coming, His life, and His very presence is what the entire Bible is centered around. Since these prophecies were written down at least 400 years before they happened, there is no doubt that the Bible's writers were inspired supernaturally—by God. These very texts were being read in the Temple when Jesus was born. The predictions were astoundingly accurate, down to minute details that no one could have manipulated or duplicated.

Yet, it is this miracle of prediction and beauty that Joseph Smith challenged when he claimed that many "plain and precious parts" were removed from the Bible thereby demeaning the whole. By casting a shadow of doubt on the completeness of scripture, it opened the door for a variety of interpretations and new edicts.

This is by no means a new tactic. Still, by challenging the truth and accuracy of the Bible, it allowed Mormonism the room it needed to incorporate aspects they deemed important such as the law of polygamy known as 'The New and Everlasting Covenant of Marriage.' This is something we will cover in greater detail later. Needless to say, this, among other things, allowed Joseph Smith to add his own doctrine—doctrines that deviate greatly from anything found in the Bible.

The Bible has proven that it can stand-alone. It needs not any assistance, and it surely does not need any help in bringing us to God. Alone it can take us to God. Alone, it can bring us to salvation. Alone, it can teach us to have a dynamic relationship with Jesus Christ. Alone, it is sufficient. Since no one alive today, or in Smith's day, was present when the Bible was written, no one can bear witness to the complete or uncompleted Scriptures. Thus, we must ask ourselves if the Bible, as a work of God, can stand-alone. Is it sufficient for my faith? For nearly two thousand years it was for millions of people. Then comes one man who claims it is not.

For me, this deception kept me confused and did not allow me to find my faith in the inerrancy of the Scriptures alone until I was able to break away from Smith's claims and put the Bible to the test for myself. Searching the Scriptures has brought the truth and clarity of God's Word to my life. It has brought me the peace of knowing I am saved by grace alone. Because of God's grace I have grown more in my faith and I am filled with the love God has promised me. This has strengthened me and allowed me the opportunity to develop my ministry in loving others to Christ. God's Word alone saves and transforms. I pray you will search the scriptures for yourself and allow God to transform your life with His Word.

Jesus Christ Himself constantly quoted from the Old Testament Scriptures and showed full confidence in their completeness and accurate transmission as they had survived down to His time. When Satan came to Jesus in the wilderness and sought to twist the meaning of scripture to meet his own ambitions, Jesus was not swayed. He knew what the Word said and understood it in perfect context.

But, take a verse alone outside of its context, or claim a verse should not be there, or better yet, add any number of verses that say what you like and you can support any position you like. A careful study of the Bible as a completed work, however, will keep you from falling for these distortions.

Jesus declared in Mark 13:31, "heaven and earth shall pass away, but my word shall not pass away." Later in John 14:26, He promised His disciples (who would pen much of the New Testament) that the Holy Ghost "shall teach you all things, and bring all things to your remembrance, whatsoever I have said unto you." In John 15:6, Jesus further promised the apostles that they would "bring forth fruit, and that your fruit should remain." These promises clearly imply that the fruit of the apostles, which are the New Testament Scriptures and the Christian church, would endure forever.

It seems strange that we would believe in a God capable of miraculously penning the Word for man and then think that He lacks the power or the wherewithal to preserve His word through each and every generation.

"The words of the LORD are pure words: as silver tried in a furnace of earth, purified seven times. Thou shalt keep them, O LORD, thou shalt preserve them from this generation for ever."

— Psalms 12:6-7 (KJV)

If the Bible is missing things, if the Bible is inaccurate, then it casts a cloud on other verses that teach us of God's character, truthfulness, power, and wisdom. If any part of the Bible is wrong than, by default, the entire thing is a lie. Why? Because God said that His words would never pass away. He promised to preserve them.

- <u>Hebrews 6:18</u> – "It is impossible for God to lie."

- <u>Proverbs 1:7</u> – "The fear of the LORD is the beginning of knowledge."

- <u>Psalms 19:7</u> – "The law of the lord is perfect."

- <u>Psalms 19:9</u> – "The judgments of the Lord are true forever."

- <u>Psalm 119:43</u> – "The word of truth."

- <u>Psalm 119:142</u> – "Thy law is the truth."

- <u>Psalm 119:160</u> – "Thy word is true from the beginning."

- <u>John 17:17</u> – "Thy word is truth."

- <u>Galatians 2:5</u> – "The truth of the Gospel."

- <u>2 Timothy 3:7</u> – "The truth."

- <u>John 14:6</u> – "I am the way, and the truth."

If the Bible is wrong, then our faith is in vain. But it is not.

The Power of the Bible to Change Lives

The Bible can change your life. If you would get into it, learn from it, memorize it, study it, and meditate on it, <u>you will discover a rich resource that will never be tapped out. It has</u> answers for every conceivable situation. It has guidance for anyone who finds himself or herself cut off and adrift.

Trust in the Word and you won't be steered wrong.

- It is holy, inerrant, infallible, and completely authoritative (Proverbs 30:5-6; John 17:17; Psalms 119:89).

- It is profitable for teaching, reproving, correcting and training me in righteousness (2 Timothy 3 :16).

- It matures and equips me to be ready for every good work (2 Timothy 3:17).

- It is a lamp to my feet and a light to my path (Psalms 119:105).

- It makes me wiser than my enemies (Psalms 119:97-100).

- It brings me stability during the storms of my life (Matthew 7:24-27).

- If I believe it's truth, I will be set free (John 8:32).

- If I hide it in my heart, I will be protected in times of temptation (Psalms 199:11).

- If I continue in it, I will become a true disciple (John 8:31).

- If I meditate on it, I will become successful (Joshua 1:8).

- If I keep it, I will be rewarded and my love perfected (Psalms 19:7-11; John 2:5).

- It is the living, powerful, discerning Word of God (Hebrews 4:12).

- It is the Sword of the Spirit (Ephesians 6:17).

- It is sweeter than honey and more desirable than gold (Psalms 19:10).

- It is indestructible and forever settled in Heaven (2 Corinthians 13:7-8; Psalms 119:89).

- It is absolutely true about God (Romans 3:4; Romans 16:25, 27).

- It is absolutely true about man (Jeremiah 17:9; Psalm 8:4-6).

- It is absolutely true about sin (Romans 3:23).

- It is absolutely true about salvation (Acts 4:12, Romans 10:9).

- It is absolutely true about Heaven and Hell (Revelation 21:8; Psalms 119:89).

- Every word of God proves true (Titus 1:2).[7]

---

7 List used by permission – Excerpt taken from *The Love Dare Day by Day* by Stephen Kendrick and Alex Kendrick, c. 2009 B&H Publishing Group.

As we continue to look at the truth of God's Word through these chapters and discover the freedom of knowing the God of the universe personally through His Word, I hope that you'll continue to reflect on these scriptures. God gave His word so He could walk in relationship with us. Jesus said that His burden was easy and His yoke was light. Step out from under the weight of religion and step in to the freedom of faith in God.

A Prayer of Healing

"I thank You Lord for Your word, the Bible. Please forgive me for even one moment thinking that You were not powerful enough to preserve Your Word. You are a good Father and Your desire is to guide us and save us. I pray for Your wisdom and discernment Lord. I pray You will walk with me through the Bible, giving me great wisdom. I will read only Your Word, the Bible, to know You, and I will have faith in Your Word alone. Amen."

What is the True Church?

"Religion that God our father accepts as pure and faultless is this: to look after orphans and widows in their distress and to keep oneself from being polluted by the world."

— James 1:27

eligion has taken on so many different tones and aspects through the centuries that the exact meaning has been diluted or even changed, resulting in confusion and division. Often well-meaning people that really do not understand the Gospel in its entirety are unknowingly preaching false doctrine. In other instances, religion has been corrupted becoming a tool for power and domination.

True religion should reflect what James spoke of in the verse above. He made it perfectly clear what God expects His church to look like. We are to nurture relationships and care for those in need while keeping our eye on God.

Unfortunately, religion and church has come to mean something other than fellowship and an action of love towards others. It has been twisted to mean a series of rules and regulations dictated to us by earthly authorities.

Authority definitely has its place in society and is structured by God himself, but since by nature man is fallible we need to make sure our teaching is directed by the right motives. Church should lead to God, not force one into submission through ungodly tactics such as guilt, control and manipulation. Impure motives and lack of grace often leads to an attempt to control another's life through a series of rules. This causes not only rebellion, but also division. Division has led to the birth of denominations in mainstream Christianity and other religious organizations all across the world, often resulting in cults. It is human nature, I suspect, to try to find or create a church that fits our wants, needs, and preconceptions of God rather than relying on God's word. A true church helps you to build a real relationship with God.

Jesus, knowing our natures, prayed that we would find the strength to resist it. He wanted us to stay united. He wanted us to be one in spirit, mind, and purpose (John 17:20-23). God hates division. He deals with it repeatedly throughout the Old and New Testaments.

> *"I appeal to you, dear brothers and sisters, by the authority of our Lord Jesus Christ, to live in harmony with each other. Let there be no divisions in the church. Rather, be of one mind, united in thought and purpose."*
>
> — 1 Corinthians 1:10

Denominations allow for man's authority to supersede God's within a Church. Nowhere does the Bible say Jesus built a denomination, nor does the Bible teach Jesus died for any church established by man! He died for only one church, the one He bought with His own blood (Acts 20:28; Ephesians 5:25). The Bible doesn't say that a man was ever to be the head of the Church! But by its very nature, a denomination puts a man over the church.

This creates the problem of pitting one Christian against another. Nothing good can ever come of that, and, ultimately, it is the kingdom of God that suffers. Since God is not for division, who is to blame?

Satan, of course, ranks high on the list, but man's lust for power, dominance, and greed have no less contributed to the division among Christians. For the individual Christian, the effects of this division are most distressing.

The Apostle Paul writes to the Church of Corinth to fix a variety of problems that have cropped up in the church. The foremost of them, and one Paul addressed right away, is that of division (1 Corinthians 1:10). He mentions that the people had become so polarized in their loyalty to a man or an organization that Paul had to chastise them regarding where their true loyalties should lie.

> "Now this I say, that every one of you saith, I am of Paul; and I of Apollos; and I of Cephas; and I of Christ. Is Christ divided? was Paul crucified for you? or were ye baptized in the name of Paul?"

> — 1 Corinthians 1:12-13 (KJV)

Good question. Is Christ divided? The answer, of course, is no! This is great news to all of us! Paul didn't like the fighting and squabbling among the Christians. He worried that they would declare a man's opinion superior to God's (1 Corinthians 1:15). He worried that they were setting up a hierarchy based on elitism rather than the call of God (1 Corinthians 1:26-29). The last thing Paul desired was for man's ordinances to supplant God's Word—which would result in the loss of free will. Paul understood that the power of the Church wasn't in the leadership, but in the preaching of the Gospel (1 Corinthians 1:21-25).

As you can see in the Church of Corinth, division created an entire mess of problems. Each chapter in First Corinthians deals with a doctrine or issue that had arisen as a result of this division. Paul wanted to deal with them on a much more mature spiritual setting and found that he could not. Instead, he felt as if he were talking to spiritual babies, settling squabbles instead of the important issues of the Gospel.

I experienced divisions personally while in the Mormon Church because certain "worthy" members could go to the temple while others could not, and many outside family members were left wondering why I was being led into a place that they could not go. It took a thorough searching of the Scriptures and much prayer before I could see the effects and damages that these divisions had on me and my family.

God's Church versus Man's Churches

According to 1 John 5:13, belonging to the true church is as simple as claiming Christ to be your Savior. Numerous scriptures point to what it means to be a part of the True Church. I've listed a few below.

- The Lord tells us to meet often with other believers to worship our Lord in *"spirit and in truth"* (John 4:24).

- To partake of His supper and remember His body and blood that was shed for us (Matthew 26:26-29; Acts 20:7; 1Corinthians 11:23-26).

- To sing praises to God and offer prayers (Ephesians 5:19; Colossians 3:16; Hebrews 13:15).

- To be taught and edified through God's Word (Acts 2:42; 20:7; Matthew 28:20).

- To give as God prospers us (1Corinthians 16:1,2).

Denominations are man's inventions to exercise control over other Churches and, thus by extension, individual Christians. Biblically, denominations and splinter groups that use fear to control their congregation have no right to exist. These churches will be destroyed by the Lord at His coming (Matthew 15:13). Only the church established by Jesus Christ will be saved (Ephesians 5:23-27).

It can be difficult, sometimes, to recognize a true church when often it calls itself Christian and yet does not adhere to the teachings of Christ. One sure way is to see if it places heavy burdens of legalism and works on the believer in order to find salvation. Often our perception of the purpose and direction of our life becomes muddied in this type of environment. One sure way to be clear you are where Jesus wants you to be is to take notice of whether the church uses teachings made by man and gives them the same weight or a higher preference as that of God's word, the Bible. When Jesus was walking the Earth, He condemned the religious leaders of the day who were placing heavy weights on the people. He rebuked them and then he took the entire scriptures and summarized them in to <u>two commandments:</u>

> *"Love the Lord your God with all you mind, soul and strength, and love your neighbor as yourself."*
>
> — Luke 10:27

You see, <u>our sole purpose here on earth is to learn to love</u>. When we love God with all our heart first, loving others into His body will be natural for us. In addition, we don't have to fear Him or prove ourselves worthy of His love or grace. When this has been incorporated into our lives, we will care about what He cares about and, by extension, love those that He loves—which is everyone.

That is the true church.

The Church and the Cross

The highest expression of this love was the cross. Christ loved God, and because of that, He loved man enough to die for us. This is important, and it concerns me that the Mormon Church has taken away this symbol of ultimate love and sacrifice and replaced it with the Angel Moroni. Remember what it says in scripture about angels preaching a different gospel in Galatians 1:8? "But even if we or an angel from heaven should preach a gospel other than the one we preached to you, let him be eternally condemned!"

The cross is everything to us Christians. 1 Corinthians 2:2 says, "For I resolved to know nothing while I was with you except Jesus Christ crucified." This verse in itself is Freedom! You don't have to know anything but Jesus! This means you do not need to know about Joseph Smith or any of the other prophets, apostles, elders, or teachers. Only Jesus. He is the only one that saves. <u>Any other leader should only point the way to Christ and His gospel</u>, nothing more.

The Apostle Paul understood this important role and he serves as the model for all Christian leaders as he proclaims, "We preach Christ crucified." He tells us that this was a stumbling block to the Jews and foolishness to the gentiles (1 Corinthians 1:23).

In order to preach the truthfulness of the Gospel, there must be a very clear description of the person of Christ, and as Christians we preach Christ as God. Not a man made into God, nor God degraded to the level of a man, nor something in between a man and God—only the Absolute God of Heaven and Earth. If we error concerning the Deity of Christ, then we are in error of the gospel in its entirety. In preaching Christ crucified, we are proclaiming that the God of heaven came to earth to die for us so we could be reconciled to Him. This is the most important concept of the entire gospel, as we would be left to die in our sin if it were not for our Savior.

As a Christian, it worries me when Mormon President Gordon B. Hinckley states, "We do not use the cross as a symbol on our chapels, temples, or on our scriptures or in jewelry."[8] Hinckley explained the reason in a talk delivered in a general conference. He told about talking to a Protestant minister following a temple open house. The minister had asked why there were no crosses anywhere since Mormons claim to believe in Jesus Christ. President Hinckley answered, "'I do not wish to give offense to any of my Christian brethren who use the cross on the steeples of their cathedrals and at the altars of their chapels, who wear it on their vestments, and imprint it on their books and other literature. But for us, the cross is the symbol of the dying Christ, while our message is a declaration of the living Christ.'

"He then asked, 'If you do not use the cross, what is the symbol of your religion?'

"I replied that the lives of our people must become the only meaningful expression of our faith and, in fact, therefore, the symbol of our worship."[9]

---

8 Gordon B. Hinckley, *The Symbol of Christ*, (http://lds.org/ensign/1975/05/the-symbol-of-christ?lang=eng, 1975).

9 Gordon B. Hinckley, *The Symbol of Christ*, (http://lds.org/ensign/1975/05/the-symbol-of-christ?lang=eng, 1975).

As I said, this is distressing since it was the Apostle Paul that rallied us around the cross to begin with:

"But God forbid that I should glory, save in the cross of our
Lord Jesus Christ, by whom the world is crucified unto me,
and I unto the world."

— Galatians 6:14

The cross is not a symbol of death. It is a symbol of salvation and redemption. It is a rallying cry of spiritual victory. It is hope. This is why, for most Christians, the empty cross is the symbol we cling to. Jesus is not dead. He is no longer on the cross. He is risen! It begins to feel more like man's church when we strip it of the one thing that is to unite us to God: the cross.

The cross was the place of Christ's greatest victory because it was there that He submitted himself to the ultimate obedience. When He surrendered His spirit to death and then overcame it Christ showed the ultimate victory. The empty cross reminds us that all things work to our good.

In his speech, Hinckley continues, "The lives of our people must become the most meaningful expression of our faith and the symbol of our worship."[10] Does Hinckley imply that having the cross as our symbol somehow takes away from a Christian's desire to live a life that strives to reflect the holiness of Christ? If so, I must, once again, strongly object.

Listening to his speech, one might draw the conclusion that Mormons have no symbols unique to their faith. This, of course, is far from the truth. One of the most well-known symbols is that of the angel Moroni.

Ironically, this trumpet-blowing effigy stands in the same place a Christian cross would probably stand if LDS temples were Christian churches. Beehives, moonstones, sunstones, the all-seeing eye, and Masonic 'grips' are in abundance on the temple in Salt Lake City, and

---

10 Gordon B. Hinckley, *The Symbol of Christ*, (http://lds.org/ensign/1975/05/the-symbol-of-christ?lang=eng, 1975).

LOVED INTO THE LIGHT

while Mormons are quick to distance themselves from the cross, they have no problem defending the numerous five-pointed pentagrams used as decorations on both the Salt Lake City and Nauvoo temple.

I personally wish Mormons gave closer heed to the cross; in doing so, they may discover more fully why Christians see this as a symbol that reminds us of all that Jesus accomplished by suffering on the cross. It is the suffering of Christ that gives real meaning to the resurrection—and even to our own suffering. It allows us to see why the resurrection was as important as it was. But what exactly did his suffering and death on the cross accomplish? Consider this:

- **John 15:13** – Jesus pointed to His future death as an example of His great love for His people: "Greater love hath no man than this, that a man lay down his life for his friends."

- **Romans 5:9** – The shedding of His blood on the cross is what justifies us before a Holy God. We no longer must wonder if we will ever be "good enough."

- **Romans 8:34** – His death on the cross gave us an intercessor in Jesus Christ, someone who represents us before God.

- **1 Corinthians 5:7** – Jesus' sacrifice on the cross gave us the grace we needed to live a victorious Christian life.

- **Galatians 3:13** – Christ's death on the cross freed us from the curse of the law. Now, it is in Him rather than in a system, that we find salvation!

- **Colossian 1:22** – Jesus' death on the cross allowed for reconciliation of sinful man to a Holy God. No longer must we be separated.

- **Colossians 2:13** – Jesus nailed to the cross the laws that were contrary to us and thus paved the way for true forgiveness of sins.

- **Colossians 2:15** – Christ's death on the cross triumphed over Satan and death itself. Now, we need fear neither.

- **Hebrews 2:14** – By His death, Jesus freed us from the fear of death. No longer must we labor in bondage to sin and death.

- **Hebrews 9:14** – Christ's death on the cross did away with the imperfect system of animal sacrifices. His perfect blood is sufficient for all mankind for all eternity!

- **Hebrews 10:14** – Most adherents of other religions struggle to please their particular deities. However, Christ's sacrifice by itself allows His people to become perfect. The anxiety of striving to be "good enough" has been taken away, allowing us to rest completely in His finished completed work.

Christians should feel no shame when they emphasize the cross for their redemption. Paul clearly reminded the believers in Romans 5:6-8, "You see, at just the right time, when we were still powerless, Christ died for the ungodly. Very rarely will anyone die for a righteous man, though for a good man someone might possibly dare to die. But God demonstrates his own love for us in this: While we were still sinners, Christ died for us."

In his tract, titled *Calvary*, John Charles Ryle, a well-respected bishop in the Church of England during the 19th century, summed it up well when he wrote:

"Would I know the fullness and completeness of the salvation God has provided for sinners? Where shall I see it most distinctly? Shall I go to the general declarations in the Bible about God's mercy? Shall I rest in the general truth that God is a God of love? Oh, no! I will look at the crucifixion at Calvary. I find no evidence like that: I find no balm for a sore conscience and a troubled heart like the sight of Jesus dying for me on the accursed tree. There I see that a full payment has been made for all my enormous debts.

"The curse of that law which I have broken, has come down on One who there suffered in my stead; the demands of that law are all satisfied: payment has been made for me even to the uttermost farthing. It will not be required twice over. Ah, I might sometimes imagine I was too bad to be forgiven; my own heart sometimes whispers that I am too wicked to be saved. But I know in my better moments this is all my foolish unbelief; I read an answer to my doubts in the blood shed on Calvary. I feel sure that there is a way to heaven for the very vilest of men, when I look at the cross."

The True Church and the Local Church

Jesus died for only *one* church, the one He bought with His own blood. His intention, according to Scripture, was that there would be a single faith for all humanity. The church, meaning all Christians, is the body of Christ (Ephesians 1:22-23). There is one body (Ephesians 4:4). Therefore, there is only *one* church—His Church! Jesus is the Savior of His body—meaning His people (Ephesians 5:25). If we want to be saved, we must be in His body. We cannot be saved in a man-made church!

> *"And He is the head of the body, the church, who is the beginning, the firstborn from the dead, that in all things He may have the preeminence"*
>
> — Colossians 1:18

We do not read in the Bible of any human head of the church. There is no preacher, pastor, priest, pope, president, prophet, patriarch, board, or committee over God's Church. Christ is its only head! The headquarters of the one true church is in Heaven where Jesus Christ, the head, lives (Acts 2:33-36).

While there is one body, there are still many local churches. These are groups of local believers who meet together for worship, praise, and study. Paul wrote to the Christians in Rome: *"The churches of Christ greet you"* (Romans 16:16). He was not speaking of different denominations, but of the different local assemblies of Christians in each area.

These together make up the body of Christ—the one true Church.

Paul addressed the saints in Corinth as *"the church of God which is at Corinth"* (1 Corinthians 1:2). He asked the elders of the church at Ephesus to meet with him in Miletus (Acts 20:17). He spoke of *"the churches of Galatia"* meaning the assemblies of Christians in each city of Galatia (Galatians 1:2).

Though there are many local churches that make up the one true Church in Christ, God never meant for a man to form a central organization of power to wield over these churches. Except for Christ who rules from Heaven, each congregation is self-governing and independent of all the others. Each local church has its own authority as laid out in Scripture, regardless of the titles. Elders (wise-counselors), bishops (overseers), and pastors (under-shepherds) all were synonymous in the Bible, depicting different aspects of the same calling. Paul and Barnabas *"appointed elders in every church"* (Acts 14:23). Paul called the elders of the church at Ephesus (Acts 20:17). He wrote to the saints in Philippi *"with the bishops and deacons"* (Philippians 1:1). The church authority established by Jesus was meant to lead only over the local congregation of which they are members (1 Peter 5:1-2).

Finding God in Church

I know it is scary for many of you that are Mormon to think that quite possibly the church you attend is not the 'the one true church.' You might defend it, get angry and feel like these words are words of the devil trying to tear down God's true church. I understand your feelings. I too, once felt defensive when I was a Mormon. I pray that you will at least search out all things and test them according to God's Word and then pray to God about it—the very thing the Mormon Church asked you to do when you accepted their faith in the beginning. This time, however, I want you to start from God's Word, the Bible, and make your decision based on truth and God's Word alone.

God certainly wants you to have faith in Him, but He does not want you to blindly follow a religion that is less about a relationship with God and more about control over your life. My own experiences in this had a profoundly damaging effect on my family. At first, I was blind to what it was doing, and only after I came out of Mormonism did my family feel safe enough to share with me how they felt. I was then able to look at the Mormon Church from a position of spiritual health to see what it had done. I understand now the control, judgment, manipulation, separation, oppression, fear, and guilt that had been placed on me while being in the "true church."

Even before I left the Mormon Church and began attending a Bible believing church, the very laws that I was told would guarantee our eternity together were injuring my family. At the time, I couldn't see the contradiction of a family being destroyed now so that it could be together later. The only thing I knew was that my family was hurting, and I didn't know what to do about it. I fell to my knees and just cried to God, telling Him I did not want to betray Him by leaving the "true church," all the while struggling with a family that seemed to be tearing itself apart. Still, I had been forgiven of much, and I did not want to jeopardize my salvation by going to another church. It was very scary for me. As I prayed on my knees, crying to the Lord, I felt Him wrap His peace around me and tell me that everything was going to be okay. I felt directed to go to a community Christian church and just rest in God's peace.

I know I could not have left the Mormon Church without that affirmation from God. The first time I went to this other church, my own daughter became worried since attending a Christian Church was contrary to what I had not only been taught, but what I had taught her. She came to check on me, and I had to assure her that I could worship God anywhere. Just saying those words to her made the truth of them ring in my ears. God is everywhere.

Look at Paul. He preached in prison. God was there! Ministries venture into every part of the world and into every part of society. God is there, too! It is not about where you attend, what rituals you practice, what you wear or whether or not there is a pipe organ in the room. What matters is your heart and your relationship with God (Psalms 139:23).

As I continued to attend the community church and study the Bible, I felt more at peace each time. My family became more whole than I could have ever imagined! I know with a firm assurance that we are now living the way God intended. Things are natural and not forced. There is not a spirit of religion in our home—only the spirit of love, a love of God and a love for each other.

For those Mormon friends who read this, I pray that you will find the strength to push past your fears of those around you and investigate with an open heart and tender spirit the Christian faith. The "true church" should not be afraid of you seeking truth and freedom. Scripture teaches us to search, to know, and to try every spirit (1 John 4:1). You will notice a sense of freedom and love come into your home when you are living as God truly intended for you to live.

> *"I devoted myself to search for understanding and to explore*
> *by wisdom everything being done under heaven."*
>
> — Ecclesiastes 1:13

When seeking to find your church home, you will discover that there are many different styles of worship. We all need the freedom to be unique as God created us. We need to allow others the freedom to worship in their own right—even if it is different than us. Differences are not bad. God created us all unique and different. Some people like to praise and worship God to rock music, some to gospel or blues, and others to traditional music. Some people are more at ease in jeans, some in shorts, and some feel the need to dress up. Some people need or want to attend church on Saturday. God is not looking on the outward appearance of man and judging him. He looks on our hearts and wants a heart that longs to be with Him. As long as a church is teaching the Word of God and not twisting it to meet the needs of the flesh, then you can attend or have your own ministry anywhere. Paul says that in his ministry he became a Greek for the Greeks and a Jew for the Jews.

> *"Even though I am a free man with no master, I have become*
> *a slave to all people to bring many to Christ. When I was with*
> *the Jews, I lived like a Jew to bring the Jews to Christ. When*
> *I was with those who follow the Jewish law, I too lived under*
> *that law. Even though I am not subject to the law, I did this so*
> *I could bring to Christ those who are under the law."*
>
> — 1 Corinthians 9:19-20

In this way, he was able to connect with people and bring them to Christ. Paul was not, nor am I, advocating sin in order to win a soul for the Lord. God gave us commandments and we are to use our freedom wisely (Romans 6:1). God's true Gospel is a love story, a story of grace. After all, God loved the entire world by giving His only begotten Son so that we, you, me, and everyone else might have eternal life (John 3:16). As Christians, we believe and understand that Christ died for us while we were still a sinner (Romans 5:8). We didn't have to become perfect for Christ to love us.

Church is wherever we are—and it is indeed important! I am not saying that we shouldn't go to church. We are to gather with other believers to edify and encourage one another (Thessalonians 5:11). In this respect, church is vital to the spiritual health of every believer. Only don't lose sight of the fact that God's kingdom is not of this world and not bound to a segment of believers. Wherever we go, whatever we do, we represent the Kingdom of God. We take it with us!

God has given us the Bible to guide us safely through this world, to comfort us, encourage us and sustain us through this life. It is the only book we are to follow. As Jesus said in John 12:48, "He who rejects Me, and does not receive My words, has that which judges him – the word that I have spoken will judge him in the last day."

I remember attending a woman's Christian concert with a friend of mine just shortly after having left the Mormon Church. Sylvia Lange sang a song called I am Free. I just stood up with tears in my eyes, completely overcome with the Spirit, knowing I had been set free! We were the only two standing up, but I could not help it. I was so overcome with my newfound freedom of just singing about Jesus and worshipping Him alone.

A Prayer of Healing

"Lord, I thank you that You have guided me into Your truth. I thank You that you are where we as the believers are. I am so grateful, Lord, that You have placed other solid believers in my life to bring clarity to Your Word through bible study. I pray for all those in the world that do not know You personally. Help them not to fear seeking

Your truth and guide them to where you would have them fellowship. I pray for their strength to break free of the bondage that would keep them from truly knowing You. Thank You for the cross Lord, the symbol of Your love and of my salvation. Amen."

What Makes a True Prophet?

"The thoughts of the righteous are right: but the counsels of the wicked are deceit."

— Proverbs 12:5

When I first joined the Mormon Church, I was introduced to a variety of "prophets" from both the Mormon past and present day church. The concept of a modern day prophet was both interesting and encouraging. It was nice to know that God had not abandoned us, that He still spoke through men and women, that He wasn't a God afar off but a God close at hand.

What discouraged me, however, was how many times these prophets not only disagreed with each other, but also with the Scriptures—and even at times with the Mormon's own Book of Mormon. Whereas having a prophet that could speak for God was exciting and exhilarating, having one that seemed to contradict God was deflating and conflicting.

The question invariably arose: *how do we really know that a man is a true prophet of God?* Many would answer this question with a simple, "You must have faith in God," response. Having faith in God is not the issue here. What is actually being asked of us is to have faith in the man who claims he is a prophet. Having faith in God is not the same as having faith in a man.

> *"It is better to trust in the LORD than to put confidence in man."*
>
> — Psalms 118:8 (KJV)

> *"Do not put your trust in princes, in mortal men, who cannot save."*
>
> — Psalms 146:3

> *"Fear of man will prove to be a snare, but whoever trusts in the LORD is kept safe."*
>
> — Proverbs 29:25

That a prophet is undeniably human is obvious. It is also true that God uses men to further His Kingdom. These verses do not imply that all men are untrustworthy, but they do teach us that all men are capable of making mistakes. They teach us that it is *better* to trust in God than in them. Does God give us principles to teach us who and who is not a prophet? Does God give us qualifications and examples to hold those who claim to be a prophet accountable? And if so, should we not trust what God says over what man says?

I would hope so.

Prophets are to bring truth and clarity about who God is. He used Moses to not only free the Israelites from bondage, but to inform them of all His commandments. Imagine these people, wandering in the wilderness without a home. They needed someone who would stand before them and speak to God. In fact, they desperately wanted this because having someone like that brought them comfort (Exodus 20:19). When people drift away into idolatry God uses prophets to help guide His people back to the fold. Prophets are shepherds for God.

To be a prophet of God would require that this person be deeply connected to the Lord in such a way that his life would bear the fruits of a prophet. This is a position of authority, and like all authority it is subjected to a series of checks and balances to prevent the authority from exceeding itself. Much like an elder or pastor of a church is held to a higher standard in order to remain in his position, so must a prophet be guided by similar checks and balances of authority.

> *"An elder must be blameless, the husband of but one wife, a man whose children believe and are not open to the charge of being wild and disobedient."*
>
> — Titus 1:6

It is true then, that a person's life is crucial to one's ability to fill this God ordained role. There must be a measure of accountability to God's Word in how a person chooses to live his life in order to acquire and maintain the authority invested in the office of a prophet. Indeed, a person's history has an impact on how we view their words and teaching.

For example, if we were to be lectured by a burn victim on the proper means and methods to avoid being burned, we may heed the man's warning when we find out that his burns were the result of his attempt to rescue a family from a burning house. But, if we find out, instead, that he was burned because he poured gasoline all over himself and his family in a murder-suicide attempt, we would probably not give the man much credibility.

> *"Beware of false prophets, which come to you in sheep's clothing, but inwardly they are ravening wolves. Ye shall know them by their fruits. Do men gather grapes of thorns, or figs of thistles?"*
>
> — Matthew 7:15-16

We are commanded to examine a prophet's fruits to see if they have adhered to the Word of God. We aren't to take what they say as Gospel until the fruits of their commands—and of their life—has been evaluated against the Word of God and is upheld by it. No man of God should fear using the Word of God to evaluate a life. Having a proper fear of God is not about cringing from His Word, it is about having the proper respect and submission to His Word.

Was Joseph Smith a Prophet?

Mormons place all their beliefs on what one man, their prophet Joseph Smith, has said. He alone brought forth the Mormon Church and proclaimed it to be God's "true church" on earth. It would then only be fair to look at the fruits of this man's life and test out his "beliefs" to see if they line up with God's Word. Is this prophet bringing clarity or confusion about who God is? Is he teaching God's truth only from the Bible? An examination of his fruits may reveal to us the truth of his claim to be a prophet.

Galatians chapter 5 warns about falling away from grace and to be wary of new doctrines being preached. Paul warns us that a little yeast has an effect on the whole batch of dough (Galatians 5:9). This means that if you add truth with falsehood, you don't get a partially pure doctrine. You get a doctrine wholly defiled. The man who brought such confusion to God's people will be judged as described in Galatians 5:10, "The one who is throwing you into confusion will pay the penalty, whoever he may be." Since the bible warns us of false prophets, we must be prudent and investigate anyone claiming to be a prophet of God.

Many claim to know God. In order that we may discern whether this is true or not, we must investigate their actions and words. God demands truth and tells us it will set us free (John 8:32). We must put their fruits to the test (Matthew 7:15-20). We must try every spirit (1 John 4:1). Is everything this man, Joseph Smith, claiming to be truth? He claims to be a prophet of God. Should we not then examine his fruits to discover the truth of it?

Mormons laud Joseph Smith as a martyr. According to the Latter Day Saints (LDS) Church, Smith was a great prophet who translated the Book of Mormon, wrote the Doctrines and Covenants and did a great deal of work to bring these teaching to mankind, hitherto in darkness about the veracity of God's plan and will.

The Fruit of Polygamy

Joseph Smith is portrayed as an amazing prophet who has done more except Christ himself and then died a martyr. Yet one of his decrees was to declare the absolute need for the practice of polygamy. The justification for this practice, according to Smith, was the need to help women who were widowed or needed help because of lack of a husband, yet many of the women he took for wives were already married.

This sudden shift to polygamy, although convenient for Smith, was incredibly painful for Emma Smith, Joseph's first wife. Not only did she have to deal with his extramarital affair—which in itself is incredibly painful as anyone who has been through it can attest—she is now being told that it is God's will that she share her husband with another woman...or two.

Actually, in the end, Joseph Smith had somewhere around 33 wives. Apparently, Smith had compassion on a great many number of widows, although some of these 'widows' were as young as 14 years of age (Helen Kimball). It is, however, just not possible to care for that many women and give them the time and attention that is required—not to mention the attention the various children of so many marriages require. I can't imagine having thirty-three anything and doing a good job with all of them. Imagine thirty-three dogs...or thirty-three children...or thirty-three of anything!

As to his first wife Emma, she was told in essence that she would go to hell if she did not accept this doctrine (Doctrine and Covenants 132:54).

This woman loved her husband. She married him and shared vows that they would keep themselves for each other only. She expected him to be her one and only husband and she his one and only wife. Breaking of a vow, particularly a marriage vow is a betrayal in the cruelest way. Imagine being in her position. Your husband is claiming to be a prophet of God; he is giving you commandments in the name of God that forces you to accept something contrary to God's word. His new command breaks his vow to you, betrays your trust, and now you must live in a marriage that is no longer a marriage or in Smith's word "be damned to hell." Had God's Word not been discredited to her by the so called "prophet" of God, she might have had a moral ground to resist this assault on her marriage. For in the Bible, there is no place where God commanded a man to take a second wife. People did it, but not on God's command (1 Timothy 3:2).

The current LDS Church has distanced itself from this New Everlasting Covenant (polygamy) and now claims that this is no longer a teaching of the church. But how can an *Everlasting* Covenant—proclaimed to be from God by the prophet himself—be overturned? Doesn't *everlasting* mean *always*? Did God change His mind, or did He forget? Or maybe God had nothing to do with it in the first place.

Another implied danger of this type of disregard for what the Bible says is that power is transferred from what God says to what man says. Faith, therefore, must transfer until we have faith in the man more than in God. We must know God's word and search out those that claim to be prophets of God to see if their works match up with God's teachings. God said that He does not change; yet every month the current prophet and general authorities of the Mormon religion are declaring new laws through their Ensign magazine and General Conference proclamations. They claim to be the mouthpiece of God, yet they circumvent God's Word.

Joseph Smith's New and Everlasting Covenant was more than just a new doctrine delivered, supposedly, from God. It was justification for adultery. This is often the result (fruits) of new doctrine. It becomes a conscience effort for a guilt free means to sin, a way to indulge in inappropriate behavior without having to hide it or feel judged by others. No matter who you are whether you think you are guilt free or you feel a sense of conviction from God, the bottom line is God's truth will prevail and His commands are not to be altered. Terrible consequences from actions that go against His will always surface and unless you repent and turn from this sin it will be held against you.

The Fruit of Pride

According to Mormon doctrine, attaining the celestial kingdom of heaven is not just up to God and/or Jesus Christ. Joseph Smith must be consulted. "...no man or woman in this dispensation will ever enter into the celestial kingdom of God without the consent of Joseph Smith. . . . Every man and woman must have the certificate of Joseph Smith, junior, as a passport to their entrance. . . I cannot go there without his consent. . . . He reigns there as supreme a being in his sphere, capacity, and calling, as God does in heaven."[11]

Mormons place Joseph Smith on the same level as God and make it so that man no longer answers to God alone (Exodus 34:14), but to this man, Joseph Smith. In such a role, Joseph Smith steps into the position of savior. Thus this becomes another gospel. The Gospel in scripture is about Jesus Christ, and Jesus Christ alone. Adding Joseph Smith as part of that process is, in effect, creating a whole new gospel.

> *"As we said before, so say I now again, If any man preach any other gospel unto you than that ye have received, let him be accursed."*
>
> — Galatians 1:9 (KJV)

Joseph Smith believed himself to be superior to everyone else. The Doctrine and Covenants gives license to his attitude when it says in chapter 1, verse 17, "Wherefore, I the Lord, knowing the calamity which should come upon the inhabitants of the earth, called upon my servant Joseph Smith, Jun., and spake unto him from heaven, and gave him commandments."

With this license supposedly enshrined in Scripture, Joseph Smith went on to proclaim, "If they want a beardless boy to whip all the world, I will get on the top of the mountain and crow like a rooster. I shall always beat them....I have more to boast of than ever any man had. I am the only man that has ever been able to keep a whole church together since the days of Adam. A large majority of the whole have stood by me. Neither Paul, John, Peter, nor Jesus ever did it. I boast that no man ever did such a work as I. The followers of Jesus ran away from Him, but the Latter-day Saints never ran away from me yet."[12]

---

11 *Journal of Discourses*, vol. 7, 289.

12 *Joseph Smith, History of the Church, vol. 6, 408-409.*

Humility among men of God is essential. According to the Bible, pride automatically puts us in direct opposition to God. This is not a good fruit! This is not a position that any man or woman should knowingly put themselves into.

"But he gives us more grace. That is why Scripture says: "God opposes the proud but gives grace to the humble."

— James 4:6

The Fruit of Prophecies

In a publication put out in 1892, Oliver B. Huntington stated, "As far back as 1837, I know that he [Joseph Smith] said the moon was inhabited by men and women the same as this earth, and that they lived to a greater age than we do – that they live generally to near the age of 1000 years. He described the men as averaging near six feet in height, and dressing quite uniformly in something near the Quaker style."[13]

This seems fantastic to those of us who may remember Neil Armstrong's first step on the moon without being greeting by any of the moon's inhabitants. Yet at the time of Joseph Smith's claims, the moon was an exotic, impossible to reach location. His claim, at the time, was un-provable and possibly, from his perspective, would never be provable. Going to the moon in the 1800's was pure science fiction, and he could get away with his unfounded prophecy that made him larger than life.

This does not appear to be a slip of the tongue either. Another person recollects, "In my Patriarchal blessing, given by the father of Joseph the Prophet, in Kirtland, 1837, I was told that I should preach the gospel before I was 21 years of age; that I should preach the gospel to the inhabitants upon the islands of the sea, and to the inhabitants of the moon, even the planet you can now behold with your eyes."[14]

---

13 Oliver B. Huntington, *The Inhabitants of the Moon* (1892).

14 *The Young Woman's Journal*, (Young Ladies' Mutual Improvement Associations of Zion, 1892, vol. 3) 263-64.

But now we know that there are no inhabitants on the moon and there is no evidence that there ever were any inhabitants on the moon. If, as Joseph Smith claims, he got this information from God, what are we to believe about God? We are left with the undeniable problem, either God messed up or Joseph Smith made it up. Which is easier to believe?

In a more earthly bound situation, Joseph Smith, angered at being persecuted for his beliefs and actions, called upon God to destroy America and predicted, "...I prophesy in the name of the Lord God of Israel, unless the United States redress the wrongs committed upon the Saints in the state of Missouri and punish the crimes committed by her officers that in a few years the government will be utterly overthrown and wasted, and there will not be so much as a potsherd left...."[15]

If we are to examine the fruits of this man, a prophecy of this magnitude cannot be ignored. It goes without saying that as of this writing, the United States has not been destroyed and that more than a 'few years' that have elapsed since the prophecy had been proclaimed.

In another example of a prophecy falling short, Mormon Church history states that Jesus Christ would return after fifty-six years.[16] Fifty-six years after this prophecy was given would have been 1891. Jesus did not return as predicted.

The Doctrine and Covenants predicted that the American Civil War would become a global war, sucking in all nations into the conflict (Doctrine and Covenants 87:1-3). Although a few nations supplied money and arms to one or both of the sides, no other nation was pulled into the conflict.

If Joseph Smith's prophecies did not come true, can we rightly claim him to be a prophet? I think not. For me, this is one of the essential reasons why Mormons must beware. Mormons are taught to take what this man has said at face value—against all reason—and to uplift him into a place nearly equal to that of God. This is a dangerous supposition.

---

15 Joseph Smith, *History of the Church*, vol. 5, 394.

16 Joseph Smith, *History of the Church*, vol. 2, 189.

*"If what a prophet proclaims in the name of the LORD does
not take place or come true, that is a message the LORD has
not spoken. That prophet has spoken presumptuously. Do not
be afraid of him."*

— Deuteronomy 18:22

Do not be afraid of them! Sometimes those with spiritual authority will seek to control you with new doctrine or prophecy. You have God's permission to stand up to them and remove them from a spiritual authority in your life.

Joseph Smith has made other prophecies, a few that actually turned out to be true, and many that did not. But even supposing that you can prove that *all* of his prophecies have come true, that in itself does not make him a true prophet of God. The final test of a prophet is not the accuracy of his prophecies, but his adherence to the revealed Word of God.

*"If a prophet, or one who foretells by dreams, appears among
you and announces to you a miraculous sign or wonder, and if
the sign or wonder of which he has spoken takes place, and he
says, "Let us follow other gods" (gods you have not known) "and
let us worship them," you must not listen to the words of that
prophet or dreamer. The Lord your God is testing you to find out
whether you love him with all your heart and with all your soul."*

— Deuteronomy 13:1-3

Joseph Smith's doctrines were not known at the time this scripture was given and yet God knew men like him would come claiming they have all the answers. This Scripture gives us a clear warning about departing from the Word of God even if his prophecies come true.

Many of Joseph Smiths claims never occurred, but even if they had, you must be aware that his new doctrines depart so far from the Word of God that they reveal fruit that is of a different nature than the fruit spoken of in Scripture. Consider Smith's revelations of God, his teachings about the character and nature of God, heaven, hell, and Jesus Christ.

The Fruit of Joseph Smith's Life

An examination of Joseph Smith's life as given above reveals that his fruit is not in line with the Word of God or even of many of the most basic aspects of the Bible. We are forced to conclude that Joseph Smith is not a prophet.

This frightens me...not that he has failed the Fruit Test, but that so many people cling to the belief that he is a prophet. While in the Mormon Church, I stated along with many others the belief that this man was a prophet and started the true church. This is what I heard and often said, "I believe Joseph Smith was a true prophet; I believe that this is the true church." This is a sample testimony that is repeated over and over again by believers the 1st Sunday of the month on 'fasting testimony' days.

Personally, I feel it to be a type of brainwashing. To repeat over and over that Joseph Smith was a prophet and that the Mormon Church is the one true church seems only necessary if there is clear doubt. The other problem I have with this constant repetitive testimony of the church and Joseph Smith is that praise should be about God, not man. We should be praising God and what He has done and how He has helped us. We praise God to point others to Him, not to a man... never a man. My faith is strong and God's grace is sufficient for me and is for you as well. So it worries me that thousands of people are being made to accept the version of Joseph Smith as put forth by the Mormon Church instead of being free to truly evaluate the fruits of the man they so idolize.

I don't care what church a person is from; we must always evaluate the fruit of the authority claiming to speak for God.

Recognizing a True Prophet

For everyone seeking God, it helps to have people in our lives that walk beside us in our journey to know God. These people are often sent by God and are necessary to our spiritual growth.

*"It was he who gave some to be apostles, some to be prophets,
some to be evangelists, and some to be pastors and teachers,
to prepare God's people for works of service, so that the body
of Christ may be built up until we all reach unity in the faith
and in the knowledge of the Son of God and become mature,
attaining to the whole measure of the fullness of Christ."*

— Ephesians 4:11-13

At the same time, however, the Scriptures warn us of false teachers and false prophets who try to pass themselves off as men and women of God.

*"But there were also false prophets among the people, just
as there will be false teachers among you. They will secretly
introduce destructive heresies, even denying the sovereign Lord
who bought them—bringing swift destruction on themselves.
Many will follow their shameful ways and will bring the way of
truth into disrepute. In their greed these teachers will exploit
you with stories they have made up. Their condemnation has
long been hanging over them, and their destruction has not
been sleeping."*

— 2 Peter 2:1-3

How do we tell them apart? How do we discern between a true prophet of God and a false prophet sent to make clones of us? In the end, all spiritual authority must be held accountable to something. There must be a standard of truth and final authority that we can use to examine these claims. Without this spiritual microscope, or litmus test, we end up putting our faith in man instead of God.

There are several things that any spiritual authority must be held to:

1. The Fruits of Their Words and Actions (Matthew 7:15-20)

2. The Word of God (Acts 17:11)

3. Confesses to the Record of Jesus Christ (1 John 4)

A false prophet may pass one of these tests, but they will never pass all three of them. Some false prophets have not been around long enough to have their fruits examined, but you can still hold them to the other Scriptural checks. Satan once even quoted Scripture, but his fruits made his real intentions known (Matthew 4:6-7). Many devils even proclaimed that Jesus was the Christ (Luke 4:41), but neither their fruits nor their adherence to the Word of God were in line with Scriptural Authority.

So, when you look at a man or woman claiming to be a prophet, try them against all three of these checks.

The Fruit of Their Words and Actions

"Ye shall know them by their fruits."
— Matthew 7:16a (KJV)

Any spiritual authority should have the fruits of their words and actions compared to the fruits that the Scripture has already indicated are proper fruits. According to Galatians 5:22-23, these fruits are: love, joy, peace, longsuffering, gentleness, goodness, kindness, faith, meekness, and temperance.

A person's teaching and authority must embody these fruits not only in their own lives but also in the lives of their followers. By definition, a person's followers are the product (fruit) of his teachings and doctrine. If they represent the fruit of a spiritual authority, they too should embody the fruits of the Spirit. Naturally, not everyone that claims to follow someone actually does, so you need to be careful judging a man's fruits by the actions or words of one individual follower. Nevertheless, as a whole, the fruits of the followers often reflect the teachings of the leader.

True followers of God's Word will have a natural byproduct (fruit) that is unmistakable. Don't believe a person who claims to speak for God, merely because he claims he is speaking for God. We have a clear warning in Scripture to put such people to the test, to try them. Do not fall for the conservative appearance, traditional worship service, or great lesson as the signs of a true prophet of God. These things are wonderful, but it is their fruits that you must examine. Be aware that often times fruits will be hard to identify as things often look good on the outside when inward someone is dying.

There are a lot of good, sincere Mormons who are faithful to church, faithful to the teachings of Joseph Smith but who live in fear of their own beliefs. I was one of them. I feared searching Mormon Church history. I feared the leaders that would excommunicate me, the ones that taught me I would be betraying God if my family or I searched information against the Church. But God has not given us the spirit of fear (2 Timothy 1:7), and God wants us to search for the pastors and teachers that uphold His Word and will lead and guide us in truth with love. We are to be taught and edified by those that preach God's Word. When I finally turned to The Bible and developed and even deeper relationship with Jesus, I became more confident, peaceful, loving and powerful in Christ. Having a relationship with Jesus more than a relationship to the church will bring the same fruits into your life. These fruits are unmistakable to anyone who has experienced them!

The Word of God

"Now these Jews were more noble than those in Thessalonica;
they received the word with all eagerness, examining the
Scriptures daily to see if these things were so."

— Acts 17:11 (ESV)

The Bible should be the final authority for all faith and practice. There has to be something that we can point to that holds a spiritual authority accountable. If he can add, subtract, or alter the Bible, we no longer trust in God, but in this one man. This is dangerous and spiritually damning.

As a Mormon, I was told that the Bible was in error, that the Book of Mormon was more correct than the true and tried Bible. This undermined my ability to hold their prophets accountable to something that was greater than them. I had nothing to check their claims against. I had to trust them or I would be found lacking.

When a man's words and actions disagree with the Bible, we must make a choice. Who is right? Whose authority is more relevant? The Bible must be the first and final authority. It has withstood the test of time and proven itself to be blessed of God.

If the Bible is not good for instruction in righteousness, then we have a problem. If the Bible is not good for spiritual correction, the problem is even more serious. If the Bible can't be trusted to provide sound doctrine, we have a disaster (2 Timothy 3:16-17). The Bible gives us the moral authority upon which we stand. Without it, every man will do that which is right in his own eyes. That's a problem.

Use the Bible to check up on what is preached, taught, or sung in the name of Christ. There is safety within the bounds of the Bible, and when our spiritual leadership matches up with it, we are truly blessed.

Confesses to the Record of Jesus Christ

> "Beloved, do not believe every spirit, but test the spirits to see whether they are from God, for many false prophets have gone out into the world. By this you know the Spirit of God: every spirit that confesses that Jesus Christ has come in the flesh is from God,"
>
> — 1 John 4:1-3 (NAS)

There are certain universal truths to which all spiritual authority is bound by. The one found in 1 John is essential to deciding if a prophet is of God or not. A prophet, pastor, preacher, or teacher of the Gospel must submit himself or herself to the authority of Jesus Christ. This authority is on record, in the Bible, and is outlined in 1 John 4. In essence, the authority of Jesus Christ is as follows:

1. Jesus is Come in the Flesh – The Miraculous, Virgin Birth

2. Jesus is God – His Deity

3. Jesus is Love – The Power of His Authority

I discovered in the Mormon Church that the Christian Trinity, the Christian Virgin Birth, and even the concept and idea of love was totally different in the Mormon Church. I was taught that the Mormon Trinity is three separate, distinct gods (polytheism) that have authority on this earth while other gods have authority over other planets and other peoples. They do not believe in a single God who has manifested Himself in three individuals. I found out that, according to Mormon Doctrine, there is no Virgin birth. That Elohim, the Mormon god, physically impregnated Mary. Even my understanding of love changed. Although many individual Mormons demonstrated love for their families, the church itself practiced judgmental oversight, control, and bred fear in me of anything non-Mormon. But because I didn't understand the nature of the record of Jesus Christ, I was unable to truly see it for what it was.

The truest sign of a true prophet is one who is submissive to the authority of Christ. When the love of God and of Christ dwells in a person, then we know that God dwells in them (1 John 4:12, 15-16). Love and submission are two sides of the same thing. What you love, you are submissive to, and what you are submissive to you love. So when someone is submissive to Jesus Christ, they demonstrate that by the way they love, and when someone loves Christ, they are submissive to His will. This will extend beyond the boundaries of family and friends. It will be shown to enemies, brothers and sisters in Christ, neighbors—everyone!

How well does the spiritual authority love? Love doesn't seek to control another person's love. Love isn't bound by constraints. When only a few select people get your love, it is not Biblical love. Biblical love (1 Corinthians 13) is far-reaching and all encompassing.

More than even how the proclaimed prophet loves, a better question is how well do you and I love? It is hard to recognize love when we do not have it ourselves (1 John 4:7-8). Trying to determine if someone is a counterfeit or not is counterproductive. However, when you know the real thing, that which is counterfeit is automatically made known to you. In this case, it is not about judging the spiritual authority; it is about being submissive to His authority so that the love of Christ is revealed in you. At that point, you will know the spirit of truth and the spirit of error automatically!

> *"If a man say, I love God, and hateth his brother, he is a liar:*
> *for he that loveth not his brother whom he hath seen, how can*
> *he love God whom he hath not seen?"*
>
> — 1 John 4:20 (KJV)

Prayer of Healing

"Lord, I thank You for giving me the spiritual authority and discernment through the Bible to help guide me to Your perfect will. Help me to search and know those I allow to speak into my life. Give me wisdom through the Bible to know if they are teaching Your Word. Help my own fruits to reflect Your love and grace, so that I may know You and Your love. Lord, help those that have been beguiled by false prophets that have fallen prey to man's word. Deliver them and show them Your truth. Help them to see the false prophets in their lives. Amen."

The Dangers of Polygamy

*"The heart is deceitful above all things and beyond cure.
Who can understand it?"*

— Jeremiah 17:9

J oseph Smith, the founder of the Mormon Church, was a man and only a man. Being human, we all have thoughts and desires that are not always lined up with God's will. Even if you think it is the right thing to do, you cannot always trust what you think or believe. We must test it against God's Word to see if it lines up. God also tells us that iron sharpens iron, so it is important to have others hold you accountable to God's Word. It is foolish to trust your own intuitions and feelings without seeking sound accountability.

One of the more hurtful and damaging additions that Joseph Smith implemented into his church doctrine was that of polygamy—the practice of having more than one spouse, more properly known as *polygyny*. Technically, Polygamy can work both ways. A man can have more than one wife and a woman can have more than one husband. Historically, however, and in the Mormon Church, polygamy was allowed only for the man. He could have more than one wife while any one of his wives was allowed only to have him as her husband.

Mormons no longer practice polygamy outwardly—except for some of the more fundamental offshoots such as the Fundamental Mormon Church which splintered off as a direct result of the mainstream Mormon move to stop polygamy practices. Despite this, the belief and concept is still practiced within Temple rituals. Marriages sealing more than one wife within the temple are practiced today in the mainstream Mormon faith. In the Celestial Kingdom—their highest kingdom, multiple wives will exist. It is very much still a part of the Mormon Church culture. This is why they will not condemn the practice. Their best effort is to claim that God changed His mind for the present circumstances.[17] This means that if opportunity and societal inhibitions are relaxed—and God changes His mind *again*—it could be reinstituted.

Remember, Joseph Smith claimed this to be a New and Everlasting Covenant (D&C 132), so by definition, it can't be abolished. Mormons also believe that in the Celestial Kingdom, a man having been married to multiple women on earth will have those same women bound to him in the Kingdom—this is believed to be true if you were married to these women at the same time or if you married one and then another after the first one died. This is completely contrary to Scripture. When the Sadducees brought this problem to Jesus regarding the woman who had married, consecutively, seven different men, Jesus said:

> *"Jesus answered and said unto them, Ye do err, not knowing the scriptures, nor the power of God. For in the resurrection they neither marry, nor are given in marriage, but are as the angels of God in heaven."*
>
> — Matthew 22:29-30 (KJV)

Mormons would argue that the practice of Polygamy was biblical and allowed by God. By taking certain scriptural stories from the Bible

---

17 President Wilford Woodruff, *Official Declaration 1*, (LDS Church, 1890)

out of context, Mormons emulate them instead of learning from them. A solid understanding of God's word will prove that polygamy is not of Him. Let us take a closer look at God's design for marriage and discover the ways earlier men in the Bible failed at His original plan.

We must first understand that God created Adam and Eve, not Adam, Eve and Denise. That being said, polygamy was *never* God's plan. It has always been man's plan. God says in Genesis 2:24, "Therefore shall a man leave his father and his mother and shall cleave unto his wife: and they shall be one flesh." This command is again repeated in Matthew 19:5 and again in Ephesians 5:31. In 1 Timothy 3:2, it says a bishop then must be blameless, the husband of *one* wife. True Scripture and correct interpretation confirms that a man is to have one wife.

You say, "Wait! David and Solomon had multiple wives! So did Abraham." To begin with, Scripture expressly forbade a King from marrying more than one wife (Deuteronomy 17:15-17). So David and Solomon broke God's law and instead followed the patterns of other monarchs around them. Solomon, after having his heart turned from God because of his polygamy warned us about this practice when he said in Proverbs 5:18, "Rejoice with the wife of thy youth!" Meaning the first wife—if you truly loved her the way God intended, you will not want or need another wife.

And what of Abraham? God never meant for him to take another wife. The incident with Hagar was only a result of Sarah and Abraham's impatience for a child. They never consulted God about their decision, since God would have expressly forbade it. Nowhere did God command it or condone it. Indeed, it did lead to many, many problems culminating in Hagar and her son, Ishmael, being banished from Abraham's household. Not exactly the ideal picture of a polygamous relationship.

Personally, I think one woman is more than most men can handle already! Realistically, how can a man have more than one woman and sincerely connect and have the marriage that God intended? The word 'cleave' means just what you would think it to mean: to cling to, to adhere to, and to live united, never to be separated. How can a man do that with more than one wife? The Bible says that a double minded man is unstable—his household certainly will be. Even from the Biblical examples, polygamy is very damaging and confusing to everyone involved.

I always felt polygamy was wrong, but I was confused because of the explanations given to me by the Mormons. It seemed like either the Mormons did not understand their own religion or I was directly being lied to. I did not know true Scripture well enough to counter what I was being taught. I was told that the Mormons took more wives during times of great persecution when many of the men were killed and that the widows and their children needed to be taken care of. Here are some things I did not know and was never told:

1. That Polygamy was illegal.

2. That Joseph Smith kept polygamy hidden and denied it when asked.

3. That missionaries were sent overseas to bring back young women for the older men to marry.

4. That Joseph Smith had somewhere around 33 wives or that Brigham Young had 53 wives.

5. That some of the wives they took were mere children that could have had a bright future being married to a man they truly loved.

6. That Joseph Smith married other men's wives. In several cases, he sent their husbands on missions and then married these women while the husbands were gone. Mormons generally are not aware he married girls as young as 14 (Helen Mar Kimball). These relationships were all conjugal.

7. That Emma Smith was brokenhearted and did not approve.

8. I did not know that polygamy was not of God.

I learned many of these things after I left the church and became brave enough to really study the other side of the Mormon faith. Polygamy, in fact, started with Joseph Smith having an affair and basically writing a new commandment to suit his needs. His poor wife Emma was extremely distraught over this and constantly fought against it. Smith needed to find an easy way to avoid facing the consequences of his sexual scandals. Thus, he wrote scripture that would justify his indiscretions, conveniently claiming to have had a revelation from God (D&C 132). In this new chapter, he claims that God told him that if his wife, Emma, would not accept his actions in marrying another wife, she would be destroyed—condemned to hell. The way he wrote scripture in order to control and manipulate his wife to go against God's original plan for their marriage cannot be overlooked! You must ask yourself if a kind, just, loving, moral God would have such blatant disregard for the sanctity of marriage. God is love and love always protects (1 Corinthians 13:7).

In the Mormon faith you are taught not to read anything against the prophet Joseph Smith, that you would be apostatizing and disrespecting him if you did. The Bible commands us to put every prophet to the test (1 John 4:1-2). While I was a Mormon I did not know that this was even in the Bible. I was caught up in distortion, not knowing what was right. It seemed everyone I asked did not know how to answer me, because they themselves did not know.

I became more confused and started to question whether or not I would be in a relationship in the "Celestial Kingdom" where men could have more than one wife. They explained this to me by saying that this would be the case if there were not enough *worthy* men in the "Celestial Kingdom." At the time, I didn't think to ask what would happen if there wasn't enough worthy women. Little by little, I was accepting these lies as part of God's plan and teaching them to others to help them become *worthy enough* for the Celestial Kingdom.

I didn't know that salvation was only by our faith and His grace (Ephesians 2:8-9), that no matter how many works I did, I would never, never be *worthy enough*. Neither did I realize that a man's actions in the Bible were not permission for anyone to do the same. Many of these stories are to teach us *not* to follow in their footsteps. Just because some men in the Bible were involved in polygamy, doesn't give us permission to indulge in it. If anything, it teaches us what a total disaster it is.

Can't Polygamy Be Love?

The short answer is, no. Polygamy is not a Biblical expression of love. It is important to make a distinction here regarding the concept and idea of Biblical love. Polygamy is not an expression of love. It is unholy and condemned by God. Love is a fruit of the Spirit as described in Galatians 5:22-23 and 1 Corinthians 13. A fruit of the *Spirit* can never indulge in a fruit of the *flesh* such as lust, adultery, covetousness, fornication, or envy. If love brings forth these fruits of the flesh, is it love? Absolutely not!

If a man loves one woman properly as described in the Scripture (Ephesians 5:25-27) and will cling to his one wife (Ephesians 5:31), then he will not have—or he will control—these desires for other woman. He would not excuse his fleshly desires by marrying another woman and disgracing or demeaning his original wife! To pretend that he loves both equally is a ridiculous suggestion. Jacob didn't love his wives equally (Genesis 29:30) and Hanna found herself belittled and attacked by her husband's second wife (1 Samuel 1:1-6). Where is the love in that?

So what is Biblical love? Many people have construed love to be many things. But Jesus said this:

> *"If ye love me, keep my commandments."*
>
> — John 14:15 (KJV)

It is interesting that Jesus' view of love was not an appetite. It wasn't about a fleshly feeling, a lust, or the fulfillment of a desire, but about obedience to His commands. We see a similar concept in 1 John 5:3, where the love of God is expressed by our keeping of his commandments. 2 John 1:6 even *defines* love as obedience to His commandments:

> *"And this is love, that we walk after his commandments."*
>
> — 2 John 1:6 (KJV)

This is love, because by following the commandments that Jesus laid down, we are demonstrating that we have bought into what He has said. In other words, keeping His commandments is how we demonstrate that we are on His side, that we agree with Him, that we are on board with who He is and what He has said. Love is never about the command, but about the totality of the person who gave the command.

Every parent that has experienced a child who willfully disobeys their commandments has experienced pain and disappointment. Whereas, when a child deliberately obeys without being prompted or coerced, there is little that can be more thrilling to a parent than that. When a father or mother hears, "I want to be just like you," it thrills the heart. It is one of the greatest expressions of love that can be given.

When we decide to follow Jesus, we do so by following His commands. If we change them, alter them, add to them, or subtract from them, we are, in effect, saying that we don't love Him enough to do them. A husband or wife doesn't always have to agree with the desires of his or her spouse, but a loving spouse will try to fulfill those desires...not because the desire is right or wrong, but because someone he loves has them—and his love compels him to want to fulfill them. God's desires are always right, yet when we choose not to obey, we are in effect saying we don't love Him. That's scary.

But take it to the level of marriage. If a couple makes a vow to never leave nor forsake each other, if they promise to keep themselves only for the other, then what does it say when one or the other deliberately breaks that vow? How can such a person say they really, truly loved their first spouse? What an insult to her.

One of the problems that polygamy creates is the clash of fulfilling the conflicting desires of two people. A husband, or wife, will constantly struggle to properly love his or her spouse if there is another spouse in the mix. Notice the following verse:

"No man can serve two masters: for either he will hate the one, and love the other; or else he will hold to the one, and despise the other. Ye cannot serve God and mammon."

— Matthew 6:24 (KJV)

If this is true for who we choose to serve, how is this not true when a man has two wives and he is commanded to *love* them (Ephesians 5:25)? Each woman's desires, goals, and needs are bound to conflict with each other at some point. Which one does he give in to? Which one gets preferential treatment? How can he make the right choice in this case? Too often, his actions show that he hates the one and loves the other.

A man with two wives is like a man having two minds. This creates instability (James 1:8). This hinders love. A man, if he truly loves his wife, will prove that he believes in her, has accepted who she is and what she is, and is willing to submit his own desires to hers. Yes, you heard me. Submission and love is the same thing. When you love someone, you submit to them and when you submit to someone, you love them. God loved us so much that He submitted His son to a cruel death on the cross (John 3:16). Great love is embodied when a man will lay down (submit) his life for his friend (John 15:13).

How can a man with more than one wife do this? How can he follow the Biblical command to love his wife, if he has more than one? He can't. He won't. He doesn't.

Dangers of Polygamy

Polygamy opens the doors to many more dangers than the fact that it does not allow for true Biblical love. Here are some of the more obvious dangers with polygamy.

1. It is a horrible precedent. History has shown us that precedent is used as a justification for current action. Some of the splinter groups of the Mormon Church have used this precedent to justify a continuation of the practice. And as long as the man who started it is treated with veneration, there will always be those who will follow his precedent as justification of their own lustful passions.

2. It could be reinstated. It is impossible to ignore the fact that it is a simple claim for a prophet to say that God 'spoke' to him, and therefore you must listen and do as 'God' commanded.

With the precedent already in place, the possibility of it being reinstated is very valid. Think about it, already we are legalizing marriages between the same sexes, two consenting adults... where will it end? What about between a child and an adult? Why not between three people, or four, or five? When society and the laws of the land change and accept polygamy, will the Mormon Church get a new 'revelation' and revert back to practicing their "new and everlasting" covenant?

3. It has a negative impact on all aspects of marriages. God in His great wisdom gave Adam a single helpmate, a single partner that was to travel with him in his life, to love him, to support him, to be there for him, to walk side by side in life. When you add another woman (or man) to that element, you dilute the whole mix and thus its importance and effectiveness. A woman will never have her husband's total love and dedication. A man will never achieve the full potential of his marriage to a woman because he has demeaned that woman and diluted her effectiveness in his life. It is exactly the same result as an affair. The two women (or more) often compete and barter for their husband's time and affection. This leads to all sorts of problems and difficulties. Emma Smith was unable, in the end, to make the sacrifice that the doctrine of plural marriage required. She struggled between her faith in her husband's prophetic role and her aversion to a principle that he, as a Prophet, had been instructed to institute.[18]

4. Children suffer from such unions. Mothers obviously favor their own children over the children of her husband's other wives. The children are immediately thrust into a level of competition with each other and for their father's attention and affection. Spread that out over many, many wives and there is simply no way one man, one father, could raise every child in a Biblical and nurturing way. Studies from current polygamous societies (specifically Islamic Malaysia) show that children, especially

---

18 Linda King Newell & Valeen Tippets Avery, *Mormon Enigma: Emma Hale Smith*, 2nd ed., (University of Illinois Press, 1994)

from first wives, have a strong negative outlook on the other wives and children. Fathers choose favorites—often based on his current favorite wife. Especially when there were more than two wives and ten children, a common complaint among the children is that their father no longer recognized them. He would often ask, "Which mother are you from?" Many children suffer feelings of isolation, abandonment, and neglect.[19]

5. It becomes a cover for sinful and lustful desires. Polygamy is nothing more than an excuse, a justification, to indulge in sin. When we institute doctrine for the sole purpose of excusing sin, it becomes a danger in the worst way. Once you go down this road, you begin to create other doctrines to fulfill fleshly desires. How would you justify theft? Would you decree that God told you to take it for the greater good? How do you justify murder? Maybe you felt God told you to punish wickedness. How do you justify sexual lust? By decreeing that God told you to form polygamy.

6. By accepting polygamy as a valid Scriptural doctrine, a couple invites this spirit into their home on an unconscious level. Her husband may never actually take another wife in this life, but the implied permission is ever present. When Abraham got permission from Sarah to sleep with Hagar, did you ever hear him arguing against it? No! Once his wife accepted it, he jumped right in bed with the other woman (Genesis 16:1-6). So a man may feel that if his wife can accept this behavior from a prophet that was supposedly caring for other women, then maybe she will not be too upset if he cares for another woman. This opens the door to the enemy.

These dangers represent only a small fraction of the issues that polygamy creates. Joseph Smith started polygamy for the purpose of justifying his sexual sin. The fact that the Mormon Church has sought all along to justify the practice, makes it culpable in his sin. At least

---

19 Sisters in Islam (SIS), www.sistersinislam.org.my

11 of the women Joseph Smith married had a husband that was still alive when Joseph Smith took her. For these women, it was not that they had two husbands. No, Smith effectively had them divorce their former husbands. After all, Joseph Smith wrote in the Doctrine and Covenants 132:57 regarding his role in polygamy, "And again, I say, let not my servant Joseph put his property out of his hands...." He regarded his wives as his property, and he wasn't about to share them with other men.

What is a True Marriage?

God meant a true marriage to be between one woman and one man—for life. The Bible presents monogamy as the plan, which conforms to God's ideal for marriage. The Bible says that God's original intention was for one man to be married to only one woman:

> *"For this reason a man will leave his father and mother and be united to his wife, and they will become one flesh"*
>
> — Genesis 2:24

Not *wives* and not *fleshes.* It is singular, not plural.

While Genesis 2:24 describes what a marriage is rather than how many people are involved, the consistent use of the singular should be noted. In Deuteronomy 17:14-20, God expressly forbids kings from multiplying wives to themselves. Having more than one wife is a violation of this command. Solomon's life is a perfect example of the dangers that defying this command brings (1 Kings 11:3-4).

In the New Testament, 1 Timothy 3:2, 12 and Titus 1:6 express again the importance of having only one wife. In fact, this became a qualification for spiritual leadership! If spiritual leadership must adhere to having only a single wife, then why would this not be true for everyone? Ephesians 5:22-33 speaks of marriage. It speaks of it in the singular and only uses the plural to include *all* marriages throughout all ages. This was never a momentary command. This was meant for all people everywhere for all time.

More than just conforming to God's plan, marriage is a picture of the union between the church and Jesus Christ. Polygamy infers that the church could unite with many different gods, which is blasphemy and idolatry! God's ideal design for marriage is monogamy. That is what He designed in the Garden of Eden. He gave Adam one wife, which was Eve. Polygamy does not honor God and is not His design for marriage.

A Prayer of Healing

"Lord, I thank You for your plan for marriage. I thank You that you have a heart for women, and that You would never desire to see her brokenhearted from betrayal. You desire to see her loved as You loved Your church. You are faithful, Lord, and You are our healer. I pray for anyone that has ever been betrayed by a husband or wife. I pray they come to know You in the most intimate way that brings healing and clarity to the loving God that You are. I pray that all marriages will be a triple cord with You as the strongest cord holding them together. Lord, I pray for any religion that takes Scripture out of context and distorts Your truth, and I pray they repent and renounce any of the evil practices that they have participated in. I pray that You will bring order to the chaos of polygamy happening today. Place the woman and children where they will be able to honor Your Word with biblical marriages, being blessed with peace and love. Thank You, Lord, for Your example and love, in Jesus name, Amen."

Testimony of Helen Mar Kimball

The following testimony is taken from Helen's diary when polygamy was first introduced to her at fifteen years of age. Later, under the pressure of Mormonism, she accepted polygamy as good. However, her first reaction and the emotional turmoil the entire doctrine inflicted upon her family cannot be dismissed.[20]

---

20 www.wivesofjosephsmith.org/26-HelenMarKimball.htm (Reprinted with Permission)

In 1843 Apostle Heber C. Kimball had an important talk with his only daughter, fourteen-year-old Helen Mar. She wrote: *"Without any preliminaries [my Father] asked me if I would believe him if he told me that it was right for married men to take other wives...The first impulse was anger...my sensibilities were painfully touched. I felt such a sense of personal injury and displeasure; for to mention such a thing to me I thought altogether unworthy of my father, and as quick as he spoke, I replied to him, short and emphatically, 'No I wouldn't!'...This was the first time that I ever openly manifested anger towards him...Then he commenced talking seriously and reasoned and explained the principle, and why it was again to be established upon the earth. [This] had a similar effect to a sudden shock of a small earthquake."*

Then father *"asked me if I would be sealed to Joseph...[and] left me to reflect upon it for the next twenty-four hours...I was skeptical-one minute believed, then doubted. I thought of the love and tenderness that he felt for his only daughter, and I knew that he would not cast her off, and this was the only convincing proof that I had of its being right. I knew that he loved me too well to teach me anything that was not strictly pure, virtuous and exalting in its tendencies; and no one else could have influenced me at that time or brought me to accept of a doctrine so utterly repugnant and so contrary to all of our former ideas and traditions."* Unknown to Helen Mar, Heber and Joseph had already discussed the prospect of Helen Mar becoming one of Joseph's wives. Heber now sought her agreement. Helen recalls, *"Having a great desire to be connected with the Prophet Joseph, he offered me to him; this I afterwards learned from the Prophet's own mouth. My father had but one Ewe Lamb, but willingly laid her upon the alter."*

The next morning Joseph visited the Kimball home. *"[He explained] the principle of Celestial marriage...After which he said to me, 'If you will take this step, it will ensure your eternal*

salvation & exaltation and that of your father's household &
all of your kindred.['] This promise was so great that I willingly
gave myself to purchase so glorious a reward. None but God &
his angels could see my mother's bleeding heart-when Joseph
asked her if she was willing...She had witnessed the sufferings of
others, who were older & who better understood the step they
were taking, & to see her child, who had scarcely seen her fif-
teenth summer, following in the same thorny path, in her mind
she saw the misery which was as sure to come...; but it was all
hidden from me." Helen's mother reluctantly agreed and in
May of 1843, Helen married Joseph Smith.

After one year of marriage Helen was widowed when Joseph
Smith was killed in Carthage.

What Happened to My Sexy Wife? – Garments

"I delight greatly in the LORD; my soul rejoices in my God. For he has clothed me with garments of salvation and arrayed me in a robe of righteousness, as a bridegroom adorns his head like a priest, and as a bride adorns herself with her jewels."

— Isaiah 61:10

I f you don't happen to be a Mormon, the subject matter of this chapter may set you to scratching your head in confusion or out-right incredulity. If you are a Mormon or someone who is testing the LDS waters, this chapter may enlighten you in ways you never before thought of, assuming you can conquer your anxiety and fear regarding a perspective that is not strictly Mormon. Either way set aside your initial reaction before continuing on, bathe this issue in prayer to Almighty God and Jesus Christ, and read this with your Bible handy.

The issue of Mormon Garments—special, spiritually blessed underwear that helps to ward off evil from the wearer—is more than a subject matter for either ridicule or amusement. It is a microcosm of the entire Mormon Religion. The concepts, doctrine, and beliefs that surround the issue of Mormon Garments are a description of the totality of the full Mormon faith. To understand the reasoning behind the Garments is to understand the reasoning behind Mormon doctrine.

With that, this issue is more than a poke at something apparently ridiculous from an outsider's perspective and more than an attempt to bash a doctrine of faith from an insider's perspective. This issue is revealing regarding the nature of Mormonism as a whole. It is an unmasking of the whole, not just a part.

Mormon Garments

Mormons believe that the latter day restoration of Temple ordinances included instructions concerning the wearing of a garment of what they believe to be essential to the priesthood. Members of the Church who receive their endowments in the House of the Lord (their Mormon Temple) will covenant to wear their sacred priestly undergarments throughout the rest of their lives. The undergarments have symbolic marks of spiritual significance to the wearer. These garments are manufactured and distributed by an agency of the Church.

The following quote reflects the Mormon view and belief regarding these undergarments.

"Church members who have been clothed with the garment in the temple have made a covenant to wear it throughout their lives. This means they are worn as underclothing both day and night. The promise of protection and blessings is conditioned upon worthiness and faithfulness in keeping the covenant. The fundamental principal ought to be to wear the garment and not to find occasion to remove it. Thus, members should not remove either all or part of the garment to work in the yard or to lounge around the home in swimwear or immodest clothing. Nor should they remove it to participate in recreational activities that can reasonably be done with the garment worn properly beneath regular clothing. When the garment must be removed, such as for swimming, it should be restored as soon as possible. The principles of modesty and keeping the body appropriately covered are implicit in the covenant and should govern the nature of all clothing worn. Endowed members of the Church wear the garment as a reminder of the sacred covenants they have made with the Lord and also as a protection against temptation and evil. How it is worn is an outward expression of an inward commitment to follow the Savior."[21]

General authority, Carlos E. Asay, adds that the garment "strengthens the wearer to resist temptation, fend off evil influences, and stand firmly for the right."[22]

The Book of Mormon also instigates fear into the Church member by casting a shadow of fear on their salvation regarding these Garments. Alma 5:21-22 reads, "There can no man be saved except his garments are washed white; yea, his garments must be purified until they are cleansed from all stain....How will any of you feel, if ye shall stand before the bar of God, having your garments stained with blood and all manner of filthiness?" And a little later in 5:27 we read this, "Have ye walked, keeping yourselves blameless before God? Could ye say, if ye were called to die at this time...that your garments have been cleansed and made white through the blood of Christ?"

During my time as a Mormon, I had a desire to wear my Garments as I was taught so that I could live in the highest kingdom with Christ. Day by day, I tried to wear them perfectly. But despite my desire, the Garments were very uncomfortable and would often cause me to become irritable either because I was too hot and they were sticking to me or my clothing choices were limiting me from ever truly being comfortable. I lived in fear of judgment and worried whether I was wearing them often enough to grant the permission necessary to enter the temple. This became one of the first areas that began to slowly taint my relationship with God. It became a fear-based relationship with the need to be perfect. I had no idea of the righteousness that God wanted to clothe me in.

---

21 Carlos E. Asay, *The Temple Garment –An Outward Expression of an Inward Commitment*, (Ensign magazine Aug. 1997).

22 Ibid.

Joseph Smith and Garments

Joseph Smith was hypocritical in his garment practices. He instructed the members of his Church on how to wear the Garments, yet he himself did not follow his own rules. Of the four men who were in Carthage Jail at the time that Joseph and Hyrum Smith were killed, three of them had removed their Garments—one of which was Joseph prior to leaving Nauvoo. Willard Richards was the only one of the four who was wearing his Garments at the time of Smith's death.

What were the reasons for removing their Garments? The answer seems rather contradictory. The commonly believed reason for the removal of their Garments was to hide their identities lest they fall into the hands of their enemies. Heber C. Kimball reported in his journal that Joseph instructed those of the Quorum who were going to accompany him to Carthage to remove their temple Garments prior to leaving.[23] Their motivations for removing the Garments were to protect them from 'evil' men. Does this mean that Smith did not have faith in the Garments to protect him? Does this mean he lacked faith in his own commandments and in the supposed commands given by a God he purportedly served? This contradiction in action is not so shocking when held up against the fickle nature of the human spirit. We are contradictory beings. But Mormons believe that Smith was so much more than just a man. They hold him up nearly equal to God Himself.

Elder John Taylor confirmed the saying that Joseph, Hyrum and himself were without their robes in the jail at Carthage while Willard Richards had worn his. The others had taken their Garments off, though, due to fear.

W. W. Phelps said Joseph told him about that time, that he had laid aside his Garment on account of the hot weather.[24] The hypocrisy in this is profound. He took it off because it was too hot? That makes sense, except Mormons aren't allowed to remove their garments simply because they are uncomfortable.

---

23 http://en.fairmormon.org/Joseph_Smith/Martyrdom/Removed_garments

24 Linda King Newell and Valeen Tippetts Avery, *Mormon Enigma: Emma Hale Smith*, (Doubleday, Second Edition), p. 189.y

The fact that Willard Richards was the only one who escaped the 'martyrdom' unscathed appears to have led to the belief that he had been protected because he was the only one of the four wearing his Garments at the time. Elder Kimball Spoke of Elder Richards being protected at Carthage Jail[25]—having on the robe, while Joseph, Hyrum, and Elder Taylor were shot to pieces. John Taylor survived but was badly wounded.

This idea that the Garments would have physically protected Joseph and Hyrum was further elaborated on by Hubert Howe Bancroft in his History of Utah. Bancroft notes the following regarding the temple Garment: "This garment protects from disease, and even death, for the bullet of an enemy will not penetrate it. The Prophet Joseph carelessly left off this garment on the day of his death, and had he not done so, he would have escaped unharmed."[26]

This still begs the question: Why didn't the great Prophet have faith in his own rules and laws? Joseph's hypocrisy points to something greater than a mere lack of faith. Since he was the founder, so to speak, of the Mormon Church, it touches upon every aspect of the Church. If the foundation is flawed, how can the structure be sound?

Legalism of the Garment

Mormon Garments are an extension of the Mormon philosophy. Garments are a requirement to attain the highest kingdom, one of the works that is deemed necessary to achieve salvation outside of or in addition to Jesus Christ. Called legalism, this philosophy or doctrine is like a cancer. Once you introduce it into your life it begins to attach itself to every other area as well. Your walk with the Lord becomes tainted causing you to feel that somehow you are in control of the relationship, that your actions and deeds will somehow win the love of God and make you worthy to enter Heaven or some spiritual kingdom. Whatever happened to God being love (1 John 4:8)? I thought we loved Him because He first loved us (1 John 4:19).

---

25 George D. Smith, *An Intimate Chronicle: The Journals of William* Clayton, (Signature Books, Salt Lake City 1995) p. 223.

26 Hubert Howe Bancroft, *History of Utah*, (1889) p.257.

Garments are legalistic. They say that they draw you closer to God, but here are the rules:

1. You cannot roll them or pin them to hide them under long shorts or sleeveless shirts.

2. You cannot try them on before you buy them.

3. You may not remove the tags.

4. You may not throw them away (there is a specific way to dispose of them).

5. Women must wear them under their bra (so they're sliding around all day).

This may sound amusing to those who have never lived within the Mormon culture, but for those that have and do, it is very oppressive. Mormons tie righteous protection, godly benevolence, and salvation to these Garments. For those that truly believe in it, Garments are more than just an expression of your affection—they are mandatory for your protection and salvation. This rule plays with the mind and emotions in unexplained and unforeseen ways.

On the one hand, you are trying to do all the right things in order to please God as you are taught. On the other hand, you would just like to not worry about them; you feel envious of those that still have their freedom—and then you feel guilty for even thinking that way! You feel trapped between the need to be 'righteous' according to Mormons and the desire to be free of these Garments that interfere with life and intimate relationships with your spouse.

To add to your already conflicting feelings, you are continually bombarded by teachings such as the one found in this excerpt from a letter by Elder Kofford to a young lady who has not yet been to the temple:[27]

---

27 Elder Cree-L-Kofford, Quorum of the Seventy, *Marriage In The Lord's Way, Part Two*, (Ensign, July 1998)

Excerpt of Elder Crawford's Letter

Kerstyn, having never been to the temple, you're going to have questions about how to wear the temple garment. You'll have the basis for answering most of those questions if you will listen to the counsel given to you in the temple. Always remember that one of the covenants we make is to wear the garment properly. Though it would be inappropriate to discuss some items about the garment in this letter. Here are some thoughts I hope will be useful.

My counsel is that you wear the temple garment at all times. Never cut or fold the garment in order to make it fit the clothing you may desire to wear. Wear the garment as it was designed to be worn and then find outer clothing, which appropriately covers it. If you find yourself in circumstances where the clothing styles are not consistent with wearing the garment, then change clothing styles. That may mean you don't wear shorts, tank tops or other articles of clothing that are not consistent with properly wearing the garments. The length of dresses, shorts, and other articles of clothing should be consistent with that guideline.

Frequently people will want to know if it's all right to take off the garment to mow the lawn, to wash the car, or participate in other household or business activities. The answer in one word is no. What if you're participating in athletics? Is it possible to wear the temple garment properly while participating in a large number of athletic activities? In those situations where this is not possible, then as we've been instructed, it will be permissible to remove the garment during the period of time you're engaging in that activity.

I would not, however, remove my garment a long time prior to participating, and I would replace it as soon as I could appropriately do so, after I had completed the participation. Activities such as swimming, competitive basketball and tennis may fall in this category.

I will add, strictly, as a personal opinion because of what the garment means to me, that if I had a hobby that did not

allow me to wear my garment properly, I would rather change
hobbies than to go without the garment.

Regarding Garments, Elder Russell Nelson went so far as to say, "…it is worn as underclothing both day and night. The promise of protection and blessings is conditioned upon worthiness and faithfulness in keeping the covenant. … Endowed members of the Church wear the garment as a reminder of the sacred covenants they have made with the Lord and also as a protection against temptation and evil. How it is worn is an outward expression of an inward commitment to follow the Savior."[28]

When it's necessary, they explain, the Garment may be temporarily removed, but members are told that after the activity, they should put it back on as soon as possible. Swimming is given as an example of an activity that would justify removing the Garment.

Those who walk with the Lord naturally desire to be closer to Him. The Mormon Prophets and elders are always willing to counsel on this, but rather than helping you to learn how to spend time with God, they point you to a series of actions, rituals, and rules that you must adhere to in order to be close to God. Instead of bringing you closer to the Lord, they point enthusiastically to a legalistic system of control.

How do you know if you're caught up in a legalistic system that decorates itself with religious trappings? Legalism can be defined as any attempt to gain acceptance or forgiveness from God through your own works or merits. It is another attempt at achieving salvation outside of the wondrous gift of Jesus' death on the cross (Ephesians 2:8-9, Romans 6:23). It's not something to be taken lightly. Legalism says that Jesus' sacrifice wasn't quite good enough, and that you need to tack on a few of your good works to ensure your right standing with God. God hates legalism because it belittles His great work on the cross (Galatians 2:21). He came to save us from the law and yet we keep going back to the law.

---

28 Elder Russell M. Nelson, *Of the Quorum of the Twelve Apostles*

"I do not treat the grace of God as meaningless. For if keeping the law could make us right with God, then there was no need for Christ to die."

— Galatians 2:21 (NLT)

As one who has experienced the problems of legalism, let me sketch out for you the well-known symptoms:

1. *You lack joy.* It's impossible to be legalistic and joyful at the same time. Joy comes from knowing that your sins are forgiven. Misery comes from trying to earn forgiveness from God—a task that anyone will find impossible, if honestly evaluated. You always have this vague, nagging guilt that comes from feeling like you have not quite done everything possible. After all, how can you know exactly what is enough when you are dealing with a perfect, holy, sinless, all righteous God? You can't.

2. *Criticism is the native language of the legalist.* Because spiritual awareness for a legalist is viewed from a works perspective, a legalist will see everyone in that light. You become like a shark that can smell the slightest drop of blood in the water, sniffing out sin and failure. When you see someone thrashing and struggling with sin, the criticism frenzy begins.

3. *Legalism retards your freedom to think.* In some ways, this is attractive to people. Some find security in being told what to do and when to do it. In this way, they don't have to take charge of their own walk with God. It becomes mindlessness. Garments are but one example of this. You do it because you are told to, without question, without thought. The exercise itself replaces any meaningful desire to form a true, dynamic relationship with the Lord. It's like paint-by-numbers: it requires no artistry, imagination, or discipline, just numb methodical obedience.

4. *Legalism replaces spirituality.* Jesus told the woman at the well that God is seeking those who will worship Him in spirit and in truth (John 4:23-24). But legalism replaces that worship with

a system of works and rewards. I would hate to base my relationship with my children in such a way, but I myself have been treated in such a manner by authority. This system may work for an employer and employee, but not for my children or my husband. And certainly not with my loving Father in Heaven!

5. *Legalism gives you the power of self-judgment.* I suppose another attraction to a legalistic religious system is that it allows you or your human superiors to judge your own spiritual state. You get to put a stamp of approval or failure on yourself. You get to judge when you are worthy and when you are not. Some may like that. But once again, such a concept dilutes any true relationship. In the end, when the dust settles, your relationship with Jesus is what will matter the most.

I went through this very mind game. I wanted to constantly feel close to God. I tried to do this by obeying every rule. If a prophet or elder released new rules through the Ensign magazine (a Mormon magazine that is considered doctrine) or General Conference (this is where all the important leaders give a speech that is also considered doctrine), I would adhere to them as perfectly as I could. I felt that in order to be forgiven for all the bad things I'd done; I needed to live my life exactly as I was instructed. I thought if this elder said I shouldn't go swimming and I should keep my Garments on as much as possible, then that is what I would do. I started by not swimming with my family anymore on Sundays. I even started to question having sex with my husband on Sundays since I would need to remove my garments to do so. It was a horrible mind game and kept me in spiritual bondage.

I had a friend of mine who was having marital difficulties, and surprisingly, her bishop counseled her to stop wearing the Garments. It seemed the message here was that in order to salvage and secure her marriage, she needed to stop wearing spiritually protective Garments. Why not avoid the difficulty in the first place by not wearing the garments ever in your marriage? Take preventive measures and live, as a married couple should—free to see each other's bodies as God intended, avoiding the problem of disconnect in the first place!

I say, if a married woman needs to wear a garment at all, let it be a sexy thong! It'll do more to protect the marriage and sanctity of the home than the Mormon Garments.

Bondage of the Garment

Mormons will tell you that wearing the garments and attending the temple is sacred, but the truth is, it is all very secretive. This is what is so manipulating about the whole thing. They set you up so that leaving would make you feel as if you are not only disobedient to God but also turning away from your family. The requirement for being together with your family in eternity is that you maintain your Temple membership, attend regularly, and comply with all the rules of wearing your Garments constantly day and night.

You are held in bondage.

I tried to adhere to the rules perfectly. One time when my husband and I came to southern California just to get away by ourselves, we were in an elevator and he was playing with me wanting to see an inch of skin. Mind you, we were *alone* on the elevator. I was in such bondage about how I was to wear my Garments that I could not relax enough to have fun and enjoy the moment.

Frustrated with my fear, he asked, "Why are you so paranoid to show an inch of skin? Honey, you're not being immodest. Nothing's wrong. It's an inch of skin; you're not doing anything wrong."

"You know this is how I'm supposed to wear them," I countered as I tucked my Garment back in place.

I felt like he was causing me to be disobedient to the Lord. Can you imagine? I felt like my husband, who was literally trying to calm me down, was causing me to be disobedient to God. I accepted this Mormon teaching prior to getting married, and my goal was to go through the Temple and obey the rules perfectly in order to be accepted by the Lord. This is what I thought was required in order to gain my salvation.

Even prior to wearing Garments, I was still in bondage. I felt uncomfortable when I had a sleeveless top or dress because Garments wouldn't work well with these articles of clothing. My mind was so tormented with all the pressure of how I was required to act, wear and even be.

Garments control you and dictate what you can and cannot wear—all the time! Even in the privacy of your own home when you are alone with your spouse. The Garments hold you psychologically captive. Before you go to the Temple, you're this young, playful person who has met the person that you want to marry. You're in love and looking forward to married life. But once you are introduced to Garments, everything changes.

I saw a woman with her daughter and her daughter's fiancé prior to the young couple's marriage in the Temple. The daughter was 22, and her excitement about marriage was obvious in her playfulness with her soon to be husband. It was sad, for that would all change for her. She didn't know it, because her mother was forbidden to tell anyone what happens at the Temple. Even if the mother could, this young woman would never grasp how hard her life would be with Garments controlling everything she wears and does. She will go through with it because of the tremendous pressure from family and friends. She will live in bondage during a time she should be exploring the wonderful world of marriage. She will go in free and emerge a woman in bondage.

All this torment and bondage has resulted from one man's desire to impose a belief system that would allow him to dominate those around him, a man by the name of Joseph Smith. The rule of Garments is a perfect small-scale replica of the greater bondage that Mormonism imposes on those who try to be good Mormons.

Symbols of the Garment

As stated already, the doctrine and almost mystical, magical aura Mormons place upon these Garments is a microcosm of the entire Mormon faith. Part of this near mysticism is that of the many and varied symbols Mormons use—not only in general practice but sewn directly on the Garments worn as underclothing.

When I was a Mormon, I did not understand the symbolism sewn into my Garments. I just accepted them with blind obedience. I was naïve, and so because my Garments were white, I came to believe I was pure in my life. But taking a closer look at what symbols sewn into the Garment really mean has changed my point of view completely on this. If we are wearing symbols at all, they should be a reminder as to how we have been set free in Christ. I now wear a cross when I choose to wear something that reminds me of Christ. It is through the cross we as Christians have been set free. True freedom and purity comes only through Jesus Christ and a repentant heart.

Symbols have meaning, however, and the ones attached to Garments do too. The cross, unfortunately, is not one of these symbols since Mormonism does not recognize the cross as a good symbol of Christianity; rather they have chosen the symbols of Free Masonry (Joseph Smith was a Free Mason).

Symbols have been used by religious groups, cults, in pagan rituals, and in witchcraft for the purpose of spiritual invitation. Each symbol represents something by its meaning and thus invites spiritual influences to affect those wielding the symbols.

Most new converts to Mormonism are unaware of these facts. In fact, before you can even enter the Temple, you must attend church and take classes for at least one year. Thus, there must be an emotional, physical, and financial investment before you ever really know what it is that you are investing in. You are not permitted to wear or try on your Garments until you go through the Temple service. Once you have already invested the time and made an emotional commitment with family and friends surrounding you, it is that much harder to back out. It is much harder to express your incredulity over the entire matter.

Let's take a closer look at some of the symbols that are represented on the Garments:[29]

1. The Compasses – is a V-shaped symbol on the left breast and represents the North Star.

2. The Square – is a reverse L shaped symbol on the right breast. According to 1883 LDS Church President John Taylor, the

---

29 David John Buerger, *The Mysteries of Godliness: A History of Mormon Temple Worship*, (Salt Lake City: Signature Books, 2nd ed., 2002).

Square represents the justice and fairness of our Heavenly Father.

3. The Collar – Represents that the Lord's "yoke is easy and his burden is light," or the "crown of the Priesthood."

4. The Double Knotted Strings – Represent the Trinity and the Marriage Covenant.

5. The Navel Mark – Represents "strength in the navel and marrow in the bones."

6. The Knee Mark – Represents "that every knee shall bow and every tongue confess that Jesus is the Christ."

These meanings are what the Mormons claim to be attached to these symbols. However, in Free Masonry, the Compass and Square have completely different meanings. Worse, some historians claim that these symbols are sexual in nature and entirely unrelated to biblical or scriptural truths.[30]

For several decades, the original 19th-century garment pattern, which had become standardized in the 1840s, was understood within Mormon doctrine as being *unalterable*. In 1906, LDS Church President Joseph F. Smith characterized as a "grievous sin" any attempt, in the name of changing fashion trends, independently to modify the 1840s garment pattern—which he described as "sacred, unchanged, and unaltered from the very pattern in which God gave them." However, while the original pattern of the garment is still in use by some Mormon fundamentalists, over the years, the LDS Church has modernized the original pattern.

Sorcery of the Garments

Garments are a form of sorcery. Sorcery operates through objects. Anything that would be considered lucky, or a charm to ward off evil, or something to bring you power is a form of sorcery. Garments

30 James Shaw & Tom McKenney, *The Deadly Deception* (La Fayette, LA, Huntington House Inc., 1988), Appendix B, 142-144.

fit this definition, because it is practically a charm to ward off evil, something people hold superstitiously to instead of relying upon God (**Deuteronomy 18:14**).

In addition, Mormons believe that Garments are a symbol of purity—a direct contradiction to the truth of how God operates. He does not judge man by his outward appearance, but by his heart. "But the LORD said to Samuel, 'Do not look on his appearance or on the height of his stature, because I have rejected him. For the LORD sees not as man sees: man looks on the outward appearance, but the LORD looks on the heart'" (1 Samuel 16:7). There are many men and women within the church that are wearing the Garments and are anything but pure. But because they wear them, they think they are pure.

God rebukes those that try to establish their own salvation.

Anything we do of our own initiative—outside of God's direction through the Holy Spirit—will be an idol or an act of witchcraft or sorcery. Jesus never did anything by His own initiative. He said, "The Son can do nothing of Himself, but what He sees the Father do" (John 5:19). Jesus did not wear Garments or participate in legalistic ceremonial practices in the temple. The moment we try to start something that isn't initiated by God, we are acting in the flesh and this is a sin.

The most important message we can give anyone is the message that Jesus Christ came here to set us free. He paid for this freedom with His own blood on the cross. Paul said he came to preach Christ crucified. 1 Corinthians 2:1-2 says, "If we are preaching anything else we have been bewitched."

> *"O foolish Galatians, who hath bewitched you, that ye should not obey the truth, before whose eyes Jesus Christ hath been evidently set forth, crucified among you?"*

> — Galatians 3:1

Satan's tactic is to keep the church from advancing by obscuring what happened on the cross. The Bible calls any force that obscures the work of the cross witchcraft.

"What is the big deal, why wear the Garments at all?" you might ask. This all may seem very trivial, even funny, that someone would be so committed to essentially wearing long-johns covered in pagan symbols all the time. However, when a LDS member is controlled by their desire to please God, having never been taught true authentic Christianity, they believe as I did that this act of obedience would keep them close to God. They also believe that wearing the Garments is a protection to them. With more and more reminders as to how often to wear the Garments, Mormons are practicing more sorcery than they are true worship and submission to God's will. This is the danger.

Sorcery tries to access power through an enchantment, an object of power. This is no different than the Mormon Garments.

I have friends who are happy to be Mormons and genuinely believe that they are doing the right thing, but most are still annoyed by wearing the Garments. It is difficult to find the right fit and still they are not very comfortable. When I was Mormon, I had to order special Garments to fit since the elastic was too tight on my thighs. The tags also bothered me and scratched my skin, but I was told I could not remove them. It was as if desecrating the object would invalidate the power and presence of God in my life. This is the very definition of sorcery!

Garments, a Relationship Killer

Beyond the oppression I felt with wearing the Garments, and beyond the physical discomfort of wearing them on hot days, they also drove a wedge deep into my marriage.

God purposely created men to be turned on sexually by visual stimulation. He also created women to be very attractive and sexy to a man's eyes. Why should man take what God has made so beautiful and cover her up from the eyes of her husband? A husband ought to enjoy his wife's body and a wife ought to enjoy her husband's body (1 Corinthians 7:4-5). It is already hard enough for a married couple to keep things exciting while trying to take care of children, jobs, and the general household. Now, the Mormon religion has made it that much harder by placing married people in unsexy garments day and night.

Imagine trying to turn your husband on by exposing the very unsexy long-johns that you have been wearing all day. Even if you are the kind of woman who tries to keep things exciting by running to get your sexy undies, you must first undress all your layers and then dress into your sexies, do the wild thing only to quickly dress again in your long-johns to be protected spiritually once more.

Trust me, this is *not* very romantic.

It takes all the fun out of being sexy for one another and is very time consuming, often causing one or both to lose interest. Eventually you fall into an even more puritanical, boring marriage.

My whole attitude, personality, and demeanor changed radically because of the Garments. I put what I thought was my relationship with God at odds with my relationship with my husband. God calls us to be a three-fold cord, but I was no longer the woman my husband had married. The oppression these Garments created in me spiritually and emotionally replaced my flirty, playful nature with a rigid rules oriented nature.

The Garments forced me to change the way I dressed, changing everything about me. Now, let me be clear. I'm speaking of the God ordained relationship we call marriage. Naturally there needs to be personal discipline least we inadvertently cause another to fall into lusting. My husband needed me to be sexy at least under my modest clothing. I ignored those needs completely out of a false sense of religious obedience. The oppression of the Garments went beyond legalism and began to have a domineering effect on who I was as a person and as a wife.

And Satan is all too ready to step in to the void. You get a Victoria Secret catalog in the mail and Satan sees to it that your husband gets his hands on it first. He sees these sexy women and can't help but compare that to what he has seen on you. He wishes you would dress like that for him, but he knows that to ask you to would put you at odds with your religious convictions—no doubt starting a fight. So he stays quiet, but his mind lingers on those pictures. Do you not see where this is going? Soon he feels his wife is not his, but merely on loan to him from the church. He is playing second fiddle to get her attention. Disaster awaits.

My own husband told me after we had left the Mormon Church that he had become jealous of God, because he felt like I did not belong to him. His needs were not being met, and he felt powerless to address it. It created such a mess in my marriage—all in the name of getting close to God. Now that my husband and I have been set free in Christ, he has been able to reveal to me what he felt when I wore the Garments. He mentioned that he understood what the Catholic clergy must go through to stay celibate so that they can, according to Catholicism, enjoy the presence of God and God only. History has taught us how well that has worked out.

My husband has said that Garments are childish in nature. They are something that you have to do in order to 'prove' that you are worthy of something that God gives freely. The Garments make the choice for you instead of your own internal discernment.

The regimen of wearing Garments is difficult from a practical point of view.

There are many undergarments available to a 'normal' conservative Christian in order that their clothing looks presentable and nice. These wonderful options are not available to a Mormon. As a Mormon, you have the controlling choice of wearing either the long-john type of undergarment that goes to your ankles or the one that goes to your knees. The short garments cut off at the lower thigh. Those are available in either a horrible nylon or a cotton mix that after a few washings have balls all over them. Garments are hot, uncomfortable and unattractive to look at. God never said you had to be uncomfortable while you are being modest.

Another problem that I know to occur is either the woman or the man becomes so 'righteous' in their Garment duties that they become the Garment police for his or her spouse. This adds a judgmental spirit into the marriage that forces separation—physical, yes, but also emotional. I distinctly remember how judgmental I would get when my husband would remove his Garment because it was too hot. I didn't, and my spirit towards him distanced us from each other.

Aside from the negative impact these Garments have on the marriage, they add conflicting aspects to your other relationships within the church. Another Mormon can spot if you are wearing your Garments. The Garment lines under your clothing are difficult to conceal completely. At times, you will be required to do a Temple interview to reveal if you are wearing your Garments 24 hours a day, both day and night. You will either:

1. Feel guilty and confess the truth that you are not wearing them constantly (few do).

2. Feel self-righteous because you are wearing them exactly like you are supposed to.

3. Or you will lie, as I know many do. They tell the bishop that they are wearing the garment exactly as they should be. This is usually the choice most members make if they have an upcoming wedding to attend or they choose to attend the Temple regularly.

When you allow yourself to be controlled by manmade rules, the end result will be death, death to fun, romance, and possibly your marriage. Satan desires to put a wedge in between you and your spouse. He will do it with fear, guilt, control, manipulation, and more. His plan is to rob you of the joy the Lord has given to you.

The Armor of God

Ephesians 6:13-17 teaches us what it is that we *should* put on everyday and keep on. The Bible does not instruct us to wear a garment that is manmade. Instead, we are instructed to wear spiritual armor that actually has power against spiritual forces (Ephesians 6:12).

"Therefore put on the full armor of God, so that when the day of evil comes, you may be able to stand your ground, and after you have done everything, to stand. Stand firm then, with the belt of truth buckled around your waist, with the breastplate

*of righteousness in place, and with your feet fitted with the
readiness that comes from the gospel of peace. In addition
to all this, take up the shield of faith, with which you can
extinguish all the flaming arrows of the evil one. Take the
helmet of salvation and the sword of the Spirit, which is the
word of God. And pray in the Spirit on all occasions with all
kinds of prayers and requests. With this in mind, be alert and
always keep on praying for all the saints."*

— Ephesians 6:13-17

Ephesians 6:12 clearly indicates that the conflict with Satan is spiritual, and therefore no tangible weapons can be effectively employed against him and his minions—such as a Garment made by man. Satan uses many tactics to misguide us, get us to fail, and encourage us to step outside the will of God. Our loving Father has given us instructions through His word of what we are to do in order to ward off the enemy.

1. *The Belt of Truth* – The first element of our armor is the belt of truth, verse 14. This is easy to understand since Satan is said to be the "father of lies" (John 8:44). Deception is high on the list of things God considers to be an abomination. A "lying tongue" is detestable to Him (Proverbs 6:16-17). We are therefore exhorted to put on the belt of truth for our own sanctification and deliverance, as well as for the benefit of those to whom we witness. The truth spoken of here is not our own truth, but the truth found in Jesus. Jesus is the truth (John 14:6). Protection against deception is best done through the truth found in Christ—not a piece of cloth.

2. *The Breastplate of Righteousness* – Also in verse 14, we are told to put on the breastplate of righteousness. A breastplate shielded a warrior's vital organs from blows that would otherwise be fatal. This righteousness is not works of righteousness done by men. Rather, this is the righteousness of Christ, imputed by God and received by faith. Only this can guard our hearts against the

accusations and charges of Satan. Only His righteousness can secure our innermost being from the Devil's attacks.

3. *The Gospel of Peace* – Verse 15 speaks of the preparation of the feet for spiritual conflict. The idea of the preparation of the gospel of peace as footwear suggests that we must be ready to advance into Satan's territory, spreading the Gospel as we go (Isaiah 52:7). However, we must be aware of the traps so that the message of the Gospel is not hindered. Winning souls to Christ is the job of every Christian—something Satan is all too aware of. He has placed many obstacles in our path to halt the propagation of the Gospel. But hell cannot prevail against it! If we go armed with the Gospel, we will knock down all of hell's barriers (Matthew 16:18).

4. *The Shield of Faith* – The shield of faith spoken of in verse 16 armors us against Satan's attacks of doubt and fear. With faith, we stay strong in God's Word, His love, and His grace. But without faith, we fall prey to the Devil's many traps of doubt and fear—all the things that remove us from God's protection. Peter doubted and feared even with Jesus standing before him and began to sink in the storm (Matthew 14:31). But with faith, all things are possible. Our faith—of which Christ is "the author and perfector" (Hebrews 12:2)— is like a golden shield, precious, solid, and substantial.

5. *The Helmet of Salvation* – The helmet of salvation in verse 17 is protection for the head and mind. Knowing we are safe in Jesus' love, grace, and salvation is the greatest protection against self-doubts. If the Devil can twist your thinking in the wrong way, then he can get you to do wrong that much easier. With the assurance that comes with knowing you have eternal life, we will not be as susceptible to false doctrine or temptations. The unsaved person has no hope of warding off the blows of false doctrine because he is without the helmet of salvation and his mind is incapable of discerning between spiritual truth and spiritual deception (1 Corinthians 2:14).

6. *The Sword of the Spirit* – Verse 17 gives us its own interpretation of what the sword of the Spirit is—it is the Word of God. While all the other pieces of spiritual armor are defensive in nature, the sword of the Spirit is the only offensive weapon in the armor of God. It speaks of the holiness and power of the Word of God. A greater spiritual weapon is not conceivable. In Jesus' temptations in the desert, the Word of God was always His overpowering response to Satan. What a blessing that the same Word is available to us! Satan will seek to challenge this. He will want you to believe that you don't have it, or that it is in error, or that it is insufficient. But Jesus fended off Satan's temptations by merely quoting Scripture (Matthew 4:1-10)!

7. *Praying in the Spirit* – In verse 18, we are told to pray in the Spirit (that is, with the mind of Christ, with His heart and His priorities) in addition to wearing the full armor of God. We cannot neglect prayer. Prayer is part of the armor. Call it the straps, buckles, and fasteners to keep the entire armor of God firmly in place. Prayer is the means by which we draw spiritual strength from God. Without prayer, without reliance upon God, our efforts at spiritual warfare are empty and futile. The full spiritual armor of God is our true shield and protection.[31]

Mormonism has replaced the Armor of God with their Garments. But when it comes to fighting a spiritual battle, would you rather arm yourself with The Armor of God or the underwear of Mormonism? The armor designed by man will fail, but the armor of the Lord will endure forever.

God's Armor Provides Protection Against Satan

The Armor of God is the only thing that can protect you from Satan...not a manmade Garment that touches your skin. The impli-

---

31 Points 1-7 are used with permission by GotQuestions.org

cations here are much larger than mere clothing. It is about a way of life. Satan will do anything he can to get us outside the will of God, and control is how he does this. One of the more telling differences between God and Satan is that Satan will try to control you against your will while God only acts when you have chosen to freely surrender your will to Him.

Satan seeks to control us, and he will use our fallen natures against us. This type of control is better known as witchcraft. Witchcraft is the work of the flesh. It has three key elements:

1. To dominate

2. To manipulate

3. To intimidate

Satan also uses our innate desire to be like everyone else against us. This is generally how cults manipulate and intimidate you into obedience in order to dominate you. Witchcraft operates in the flesh by instilling rituals and manmade rules to control your mind.

With the control that comes from wearing Garments, you eliminate choice from the individual and you remove freedom, relying only on the law. This is in contrast to the Armor of God. It is faith that protects you from Satan.

> *"Above all, taking the shield of faith, wherewith ye shall be able to quench all the fiery darts of the wicked."*
>
> — Ephesians 6:16 (KJV)

Jesus, in Luke 22:31-32, warned Peter that Satan wanted to destroy him. Jesus then said that He would pray for Peter that his "faith fail not." This is the key. If Peter's faith remains strong, he can resist the Devil. It has nothing to do with a Garment. Protection against evil is about donning the Armor of God, faith being one of the things we are to armor ourselves with every day.

God's Armor Protects Your Joy

Joy is not something that God asks you to sacrifice for Him. In fact, it is one of the fruits of the Spirit (Galatians 5:22). If you are commanded to do something that is supposedly spiritual, but it begins robbing you of the joy that God would bless you with, then something is very, very wrong. The Armor of God is designed to help you enjoy all that God has for you. After all, God *commanded* us to rejoice in the Lord always (Philippians 4:4). God would not command something that would cause you to be uncomfortable and irritable, causing disconnect in your marriage. The Armor of God is one of the many ways God has provided for us to preserve our joy.

The solution here is not to follow a list of dogmatic manmade rules that serve no Biblical purpose, but to don the Armor of God and let it renew your mind. When we begin to think differently, we will live differently. Let the Holy Spirit give you a different way of thinking and evaluating things. Let Him convict you on how you should be dressing modestly.

> *"You turned my wailing into dancing; you removed my*
> *sackcloth and clothed me with joy,"*
>
> — Psalm 30:11

When our minds are renewed, we will discover the good, acceptable, and perfect will of God (Romans 12:1-2). But we cannot do this by force, manipulation or guilt. This will not promote real change. This will only cause rebellion.

Romans 6:14 tells us, "For sin shall not have dominion over you, for you are not under law but under grace." We are either under law or grace. We can't have them both. If we are under law, we are not under grace. And if we are under grace, we are not under law. With law it will be impossible to please God—which robs us of our joy. In this area of Garments, you will ultimately have to be the one deciding if you will conform to law and wear them, but as a Mormon, you will constantly be subjected to guilt for not wearing them. They bring nothing but a controlling, oppressive and brainwashing spirit that breeds guilt. Joy is robbed from you.

Garments are nonsense, and they do not bring you to a closer walk with God. Learning to live by the power of the Holy Spirit and the joy of the Lord has been very rewarding and has brought me the closeness with God I'd always longed for. Only in this way have I found the joy spoken of in the Bible.

It is interesting that in Bible days, both men and women wore long garments that extended below their knees. In order to do anything active, the first thing a person had to do was get those long garments up above the knees for free movement of the legs. In order to accomplish this, the person put a belt on, pulled the long garment up, and tucked it into the belt. This enabled the person to become free and ready for action. Unless this was done, the long garment would have impeded him, frustrated him. When we encumber ourselves with religious dogma it causes us to forgo our freedom. This leads to frustration, not joy. Christ says, put on the belt of truth and the truth will set you free!

God conquered death so we would have life—and joy in this life. Anything with life has movement. When we start dying inside, we stop moving, we become paralyzed in some form. We lose our joy. We are supposed to have life and movement in some form. Mormons tell us that the Garments are able to come off for sports and sex. It is interesting that the very things that bring joy and life require us *not* to wear the Garments.

The lesson is simple. For us to have life, to come to the Lord, we must remove anything that is blocking ourselves from Him. Only by shedding manmade trappings and donning the Armor of God will we find the spiritual strength to resist the Devil's attacks and walk in His grace. Then we have joy. It brings life to a marriage, rejuvenation to your sex life, and joy in it all.

Only by removing the Garment do we bring forth life.

God's Armor Preserves True Righteousness

God has removed all fear of punishment for those who are His children. We must trust God and allow Him to be our shield and protection. If we are walking with the Lord He will give us discernment and will help us to make proper clothing choices. We have to let God be God and stop trying to gain our righteousness through external rituals and rules. We must walk in our freedom. When we continue to put on our fig leaves and hide from God, we try to do it on our own instead of walking in His grace.

> *"Is the law, therefore, opposed to the promises of God?*
> *Absolutely not! For if a law had been given that could impart*
> *life, then righteousness would certainly have come by the law.*
> *But the Scripture declares that the whole world is a prisoner*
> *of sin, so that what was promised, being given through faith in*
> *Jesus Christ, might be given to those who believe."*
>
> — Galatians 3:21-22

The law *cannot* bring us righteousness. But when we put on His armor, we have His righteousness (Ephesians 6:13-18, Romans 3:21-22). Trust Him who really is in control. When we try to take control, we end up imprisoning ourselves.

When we put on the armor of God, we have access to all the things that help to make us good Christians. We have His grace, His mercy, His love, and His righteousness. This is the key to staying righteous. It isn't in a physical Garment blessed much like the Catholics bless their holy water. We don't need to wear a charm to ward off evil. We just need to walk with God. We need to bathe everything in prayer. By walking in the Spirit, we have armored ourselves against all the wicked darts of the enemy.

Righteousness cannot come from what you do. An act of good can never erase an act of sin. You can't murder someone, rescue a child from drowning all in the space of ten minutes and expect the courts to drop the murder charge. It just doesn't work that way. Sin must be paid for. So, the only way to get righteousness is from one who is already completely righteous and who is willing to pay for your sin.

In this case, Jesus Christ!

We are to be a clear representation of who God is. We are to allow our faith, not our clothing, to distinguish us from others. Jesus told us that His burden is easy and His yoke is light (Matthew 11:30). He warns us about the Pharisees who put heavy burdens on others (1 John 5:3). In Luke 11:46, Jesus replied, "And you experts in the law, woe to you, because you load people down with burdens they can hardly carry, and you yourselves will not lift one finger to help them."

Joseph Smith placed heavy burdens on the members of the Mormon Church with the law of the Garment, and yet he removed his Garment despite telling his followers that they must wear them day and night.

If righteousness is your goal, then wrapping yourself within the righteousness of Jesus Christ is the only way to achieve it. The Bible tells us that on our own, there is no one who is righteous—not a single person (Romans 3:10).

A Prayer of Healing

"Lord, I thank You that you are my covering and protection. I am so grateful to you for allowing me to come to You just as I am with nothing to hide. Thank You for loving me with all my flaws and imperfections. You are my shield and my strength, my deliverer and my redeemer. I ask for Your discernment, Lord. Help me to dress modestly in a way that pleases You. I ask You, Lord, to help me feel comfortable with my body around my spouse so that we can stay intimately connected as You have designed us. Thank You for setting me free, Lord Jesus. With the freedom You have given me, I will honor You. In Your mighty name, amen."

Rules, Rules, Rules – Losing the Connection

"But now, by dying to what once bound us, we have been released from the law so that we serve in the new way of the spirit, and not in the old way of the written code."

— Romans 7:6

I s the law bad? No. Romans 7:12 tells us that the law is holy, good, and just. Can the law get us to Heaven? No. Romans 3:20 tells us that no person can ever be justified in God's eyes by keeping the law. So then, is it okay for a Christian to sin? No. Romans 6:1-2 teaches us that grace is not a license to sin.

For many people, this presents a rather sticky paradox. On one hand, you have those that use the law to entrap and control people's lives even going so far as to say that if you do not do all you are told to do, you can't go to Heaven. On the other are those who use grace as a license to sin and believe that it doesn't matter to God how we live or what we do.

Both are wrong.

During the time the fledgling Hebrew nation spent wandering in the wilderness, God laid out a list of commandments for the Hebrews to follow and obey. These commandments were given to protect the people and to help them learn of God's ways. By the time Jesus was born on the earth, man had transformed the commandments given by God into a set of religious rules that were impossible to follow—but more insidiously, gave a group of religious elite power and control over the lives of their fellow man. The very things created to help people develop an understanding and relationship with God was now preventing His people from allowing Him to direct their path.

That hasn't changed in the last 2,000 years. Man is still looking for a means by which they can achieve worthiness in God's eyes. The idea of surrendering to His will and seeking grace for our insufficiencies are often thought to be, ironically, either too hard or too easy. Some balk at surrendering to God, because that would involve faith and trust. Others find simple faith too simple, too easy, or not fair. Satan would have us believe anything that would pull us away from being able to receive the grace of God. He would either have us cast it away as simplistic, or feel we need to somehow earn it.

There are many problems with the systematic structure of religious rules made by man. One of those problems is that we begin mistaking the rules for a relationship. We interpret religious righteousness as a set of rules instead of surrendering our lives to a loving, omnipotent God. We become loyal to the rules created by man rather than trust the plans of the Lord.

Jesus is calling us into submission to Him, not to a set of rules. He does not want man to dictate rules to you. His desire is that you stay connected to Him through His Word and the Holy Spirit so that you will be powerful and free to pursue Him. The Holy Spirit is a divine comforter and guide. In God's Word, the Bible, Psalm 119:105 tells us, "Your word is a lamp unto my feet and a light unto my path." This means that by His Spirit and through His Word—the Bible—God will show us exactly what we are to do in any given situation.

The Bible is not a set of rules; it is a love letter from a Creator to His creation. The reason you or I follow any commandment is because we *get* to, not because we *have* to. If you take away the relationship, the 'rules' are meaningless. The Bible is the wisdom of a caring Father given to guide all who will listen. It shares different stories of those that walked with God and those that thought they did not need God, deciding to try life on their own and so failed.

Time after time the Bible shows us that rules created by man cause damage to the emotional and spiritual condition of the human heart. In Proverbs 4:23, God has warned us to guard our heart above all else.

"Above all else, guard your heart, for it is the wellspring of life."

— Proverbs 4:23

God wants us to learn how to receive His love. We will then naturally be able to share this love with others and bring the wellspring of life into all of our lives.

Manmade rules separate us from that very relationship God seeks to have with us.

When rules become the character of a relationship instead of a byproduct of love in the relationship (John 14:15), judgment and criticism naturally follow. Suddenly, perfection is expected and failure is punishable, even by those outside of the relationship. What you eat, drink or wear becomes the focal point of 'religious living' for those that have made rules the character of their belief and faith. The most obvious result of such a position is that they will criticize and judge the lives of others in an effort to justify their own living and 'religious righteousness.' This judgment begins to wear away upon others so that all involved begin to live a hypocritical life to seem good outwardly, but inwardly are filthy (Matthew 23:27). In the New Testament this very way of living gave birth to the Pharisees—a term once revered but now synonymous with the hypocrite.

Perhaps the worst result of such a lifestyle is the development of guilt in a person's life. The inability to live up to a list of expectations—essentially what rules end up being—mires a person in a perpetual feeling of failure and ultimately guilt of those failures. It is an unhealthy lifestyle, filled with guilt and fear.

As is the nature of a rule dominated relationship, new ones continue to develop, because the relationship is not really a relationship but a system of control. Soon even the tiniest decisions are made for you. It is not that your way is wrong, but in their eyes you must do certain things in certain ways or you are not of God. Examples of such pharisaical living may include Sundays are meant only for reading scriptures, going for a walk on Sunday becomes forbidden as they see this as breaking the Sabbath (even though technically, the Sabbath is Saturday), wearing a white shirt and tie as a sign of purity, getting married and having children right away to supposedly honor God, and so on. There are many ways to honor God. When we place rules on others and dictate how they must worship, praise, pray, or serve Him, we are not emulating Christ but rather the New Testament Pharisees. Christ did not come to judge.

> *"And if any man hear my words, and believe not, I judge him not: for I came not to judge the world, but to save the world."*
>
> — John 12:47 (KJV)

You see, when a relationship is defined by rules instead of love, it brings bondage into our life. Satan's greatest desire is to see us oppressed. He knows that if we live under the law as the means to reach God, then we will become oppressed and depressed as we fail, and fail, and fail. This will deplete our energy and bring sickness into our life. He also knows if we are living under the law we will not be submitting to the Holy Spirit, but instead will be looking to the law to define our spiritual health—truly, an exercise in frustration! This is Satan's greatest desire because he knows that we can do nothing without the Holy Spirit.

In Romans 7:18, the Apostle Paul said that he had the desire to do what was good, but he could not carry it out in his own flesh. It's just not possible. He tells us that sin, seizing the *opportunity afforded by the commandment*, produced in him every kind of covetous desire. For apart from law, sin is dead.

That is powerful, but he continues by saying that he had been alive apart from law, but when the commandment came, sin sprang to life and he died. Meditate on that a moment. The very commandment that was intended to bring life in reality only brought death.

So when laws become the essence of our spirituality, this religious spirit brings forth nothing but death.

Doing something out of mandate and routine breeds monotony, boredom, and death to the spirit, not a relationship. Thousands of people are struggling because they've been taught that this is the exact 'relationship' they need to have with God. They are taught that it is a set of rules that will hopefully guarantee eternity.

With so many written and unwritten inconsequential rules in the Mormon Church, there is a culture that breeds judgment from one member upon another. It also causes you to become a hypocrite because you can never obey all the rules, but feel you must look like you do. Even if you have the best intentions, you will have an untenable weight placed on your shoulders by human preferences that have nothing to do with a godly relationship.

Because you are hungry for a relationship with God and you feel the only way to get that relationship is through rules, you will naturally try to dictate these rules upon others that you have influence over—such as your family. Instead of teaching them to rely on God's direction and allowing them to make choices based on their own walk with God, you judge and condemn them by these same rules.

The pressure is tremendous, particularly for a Mormon woman, and it is through these impossible rules that the enemy gains a foothold into her life.

Keeping Up Appearances

Manmade rules create an atmosphere where appearances are more important than spirituality. The effort to keep up the appearance of being perfect causes the believer to become more of an actor instead of being authentic. The fear of what other Mormons may think will cause many to exaggerate, lie, and project false enthusiasm and zeal— all in an effort to keep up appearances. No one wants to be an outcast. No one wants to be told he or she is going to hell because they failed to live up to some manmade rules. Jesus did not die on a cross so that you could be further bound and enslaved! He wanted your spiritual pursuit to be that of having a relationship with Him, not one of fear of rejection by others.

Worse, keeping up appearances means you must compare yourself with those around you. This is necessary when your religion is about rules instead of relationships. The only way to feel worthy is to be at least equally as worthy as those around you. After all, this is all we have in the way of measuring ourselves. So if we want to feel good, we must compare ourselves to others.

However, this is expressly forbidden!

> *"We do not dare to classify or compare ourselves with some who commend themselves. When they measure themselves by themselves and compare themselves with themselves, they are not wise."*
>
> — 2 Corinthians 10:12

Another danger is that of actually preferring the rules to the relationship. For some, the rules give them a sense of superiority and thus comfort and security. They find it easier to follow a set of man-made rules than to actually develop a dynamic relationship with God. Indeed, for these, they will seem ultra-spiritual from one angle and supremely arrogant and condescending from another.

No matter which one you are, I invite you to open your eyes to others around you. Discover how this bondage is hurting them. Many appear to be fine outwardly, but inwardly they are suffering. This is not God's plan.

In my own life, I have experienced this on many different levels. My husband's father, Carl, was a non-Mormon married to a Mormon woman. After asking my husband if I could share a little bit about his father in my book, I was astonished at his answer. He told me that he was glad that finally his father would have a voice, that finally someone could see things from his perspective and have a little acceptance of him. It almost brought me to tears. I was very touched how much this meant to him.

Although his father never vocalized these words, my husband grew up reading his dad's body language and now, as a man, understands his father better than he ever did.

According to noted psychologist Abraham Maslow, after survival and having our biological needs met, the need to belong is our highest priority.[32] This is true whether you are a spiritual seeker who wants to feel at one with everything or an inner city gang member who will do almost anything to be accepted by his homies. This connection with others is one of the most important sources of joy we have!

This is why the Mormon Rules cause members to do everything they can to fit in and be accepted—even if they have to lie and pretend. The constant need to be perfect causes people to never feel good enough.

Carl simply wanted to come home after working long hours and relax and have a beer. Whether you are a drinker or not, you can understand the need to unwind. Maybe you'd like a cup of coffee, or to watch a football game on a Sunday. Whatever it is that helps you relax, you don't want to come home after a long day to experience ridicule. Unfortunately, he was mocked and treated like an outcast in his own home. He was labeled as someone who was grumpy and then demonized for not wanting to adhere to a set of rules he neither understood nor agreed with.

Poor guy, no wonder he wanted to work so much.

My husband tells me that this is one of the reasons His father did not want to hang out with Mormons. The non-Mormons didn't give him any grief. They treated him with love and were willing to include him in their activities.

The next generation often follows the example of the previous one, and when my husband started his own family, he also suffered silently. He didn't want to "rock the boat." He hated being a Mormon, but he'd been raised to believe that it was the "true church." He didn't want to fail his family and live an eternity apart from them—according to Mormon doctrine. His guilt kept him in bondage, unable to break free. Eventually he would come to know the real Jesus who would set him free and now he is *free* in Christ!

Too often, people implement manmade rules in an effort to judge people around them. It is an effort to evaluate someone's heart. But only God knows the heart. People see what you do; God sees why

32 www.psychology.about.com/od/theoriesofpersonality/a/hierarchyneeds.htm

you do it. When taking action comes from your heart rather than from the rules others set, you have the means to move forward in life, unshackled by things that would, in the end, separate you from God and the joy He means for you to have in this life.

There are many written and unwritten rules in the Mormon religion. There are many questions to ponder about being a Mormon. Who told you that these rules were from God? Are they in the Bible? The black and white mentality on inconsequential rules causes you to feel bitter because you might be missing something that you feel is beneficial to you or your family.

Take for example, R-rated movies like *Schindler's List*. It is an R rated movie, and yet it is very educational. The Mormon Church doesn't allow its members to watch this because of a label. Instead of giving each member the choice, by way of rules it is made for him or her. Another example would be a friend or family member's birthday party on a Sunday. We're not permitted to go as Mormons, but sometimes there is more to these decisions than a simple black and white choice. Sometimes our *love* for that person—or even the desire to maintain family relations—means attending a party like this.

Jesus cared enough about a wedding celebration to break a Mormon rule by turning water into wine. Weddings were weeklong festivals with banquets with many distinguished guests and prominent teachers. This required careful planning. The host was to provide enough wine to last for seven days. To run out of wine at a wedding feast would have been a social blunder that would have been a source of embarrassment to the family for years. Jesus acted out of love. In Mark 3:4 Jesus asks, "Which is better, to do good or evil on the Sabbath?" You see, Jesus is all about relationship and people, not rules.

When there are so many rules, there is no way you can avoid breaking them, and this leads to guilt and resentment. I have also seen many members go into complete rebellion. But when we know that the Lord loves us despite our imperfections, despite our failures, despite our inability to be perfect, it brings freedom and purpose back to our lives (Romans 3:10, 5:8). Christ came to set us free from guilt and the oppression that holds us down.

Rules and law can diminish and interfere with your love and relationship with the Lord. Imagine, ladies, being handed the following list just after exchanging your wedding vows:

- Kiss your husband on the cheek in the morning to prove your love to him.

- Every evening put on a dress and kneel in front of him and massage his feet to prove your submission to him.

- Change your bed sheets daily to prove your care of your husband.

- At night, face east and give your husband another kiss to demonstrate your obedience to him.

- Etc…

All of these rules would cause you to resent your husband instead of love him. You wouldn't be open to his love, because your own love is no longer an expression of you, but an expression of something you are not. It isn't real, so how can you recognize that which you've never given? You are not serving out of the love of your heart, but you're being told what love looks like and then commanded to perform. That is not love. A love relationship is the true relationship with Christ. He loves us so much that while we were still sinning, He died for us (Romans 5:8).

Please let that sink in! He did not require us to get our act together before Jesus would die for us. He loved us first, so He acted first. He wanted to do whatever it took to save us.

Love heals and transforms, but rules cause resentment, bitterness, oppression and guilt.

Manmade rules are not of God. He gave us commandments because He knows our nature, knows we need guidelines. At the same time, however, He gives us freedom to use our minds to choose and to allow the Holy Spirit to convict us in the areas that we need improvement in. When Jesus met with the woman caught in adultery, He did not tell her, "Well you shouldn't have been wearing that outfit. If you would have obeyed this rule and that rule, this would not have happened."

No! God does not judge. He shows the way. He says, "Go and sin no more." He doesn't hand her a book of rules. He trusts that the Holy Spirit alone will convict her heart and the grace and love that was shown to her will be enough to transform her. Mormons do not trust God and His ability to love a believer into choosing the good life He has for them. Instead, rules are the things they use to force you into their own concept of what you should be and what you should do.

For example, the rules of 'Garments' dictated what I could and could not wear. I never had the freedom to determine if a particular outfit was appropriate. I never got to choose. So, by definition, I never chose to do right because it was the right thing to do. I had to do what was required of me. It robbed me of doing right because of my love for my Savior, and opportunities that were appropriate.

Once your eyes have become opened to this, do not fear. God will be with you. Perfect love casts out all fear (1 John 4:18). He will comfort you and bring people into your life to walk beside you. He will fill you with His Holy Spirit, and you will feel free and at peace—freedom and peace that neither man nor this world could *ever* give to you. He will give you a merry heart (Proverbs 15:3). He will cause you to become a new creation.

"Neither circumcision nor uncircumcision means anything; what counts is the new creation. Peace and mercy to all who follow this rule even to the Israel of God."

— Galatians 6:15-16

Freedom in Christ

Did you know that Jesus came to set us free? His desire is that you live an abundant, happy and healthy life. Are you aware that this rigid, perfect lifestyle required of a Mormon is extremely bad for your health?

I've seen some evidence that suggests that Mormons have among the highest antidepressant use among other statistical groups. It makes me wonder if participation in Mormonism is adding undo pressure on individuals—bondage and depression. The reason for this is because works are not flowing from being loved by the Lord alone. The desire for works and perfection comes out of fear and worry about whether or not you are doing everything right to *deserve* God's love. You will never deserve it. God says there is no one righteous, not even one (Romans 3:10).

Having been a Mormon who truly wanted to serve God and raise my family the same way, I'd have to agree. This is not God's plan for your life! This is the enemy's plan. The pressure to have the appearance of everything being perfect is overwhelming. A good Mormon is taught to spot other Mormons through their behavior and style of dress. You see, if we really trust God and His ability to love a believer into the good life we will not need rules to tell us what is right and wrong. The Holy Spirit alone will bring conviction into the life of the believer and they will have the desire—because of their love for Him—to serve the Lord and be connected to Him. This is the desire of our Lord: to have a relationship with you. This is just like the love relationship you develop with anyone else you care about. You want to give them things, see them happy, and communicate with them simply because you care about them. You seek not to hurt them or disappoint them—not because you fear it will destroy your relationship, but because you love them.

> *"So Christ has truly set us free. Now make sure that you stay free, and don't get tied up again in slavery to the law."*
>
> — Galatians 5:1 (NLT)

When I was a Mormon I felt so much pressure. As a woman in the church, I had many responsibilities and rules to live up to that weighed me down. Now, as a Christian, I can see the reasons why I felt hopelessness, depression, gloom, oppression, confusion, negativity and so on. I can now clearly see how the enemy got a foothold into my life through demonic oppression. Oppression leads to a sense of heaviness or obstruction in the body or mind; it weighs you down and causes depression. Emotional and mental oppression are big business for the Devil. His strategy is to steal everything God wants us to have. It is sad for me to still see this in Mormons I know and meet.

Oppression causes illness; it also paralyzes you emotionally so that you cannot do the work the Lord has designed for you. Oppression is from the enemy and rules only for the sake of appearances and control cause oppression. There are so many rules in the Mormon Church and more added constantly through the prophets and quorum of seventy—their appointed leaders, the ones that feel they are in authority to dictate rules for you to live by.

Some may respond, "All of us have rules. Even the Christian churches have their own rules." That is true, but when bringing the gentiles in to the fold, James said in Acts 15:19, "It is my judgment, therefore, that we should not make it difficult for the Gentiles who are turning to God."

See, the Jews were trying to pile rules on to the backs of those seeking salvation in the newly risen Savior. The early church stopped and said, "No." Jesus promised that His burden is light and His commandments will not be grievous (Matthew 11:30, 1 John 5:3).

Please note that you are not always aware that you are oppressed and for many that do, the oppression becomes all they know. It becomes familiar and thus hard to get rid of. It is when you get your freedom that you begin to realize how stifled and oppressed your life has been with legalism and man's rules. With your newfound freedom, you will soar to new heights, enjoying a real relationship with Christ! Just as a bird held in a cage for many years will not recognize it is captive, neither do those in oppressive religions realize they are in bondage. It is only when the bird is free to fly outside of the cage that he discovers the bondage he was in. Soon he takes flight and discovers the many places he was meant to fly.

The core purpose of both God and the Devil are expressed quite well in this verse: "The thief comes only to steal and kill and destroy; I came that they may have life, and have it abundantly" (John 10:10). Full life is found in the comfort and guidance of our Savior alone. Only He is able to sweetly convict our hearts and draw us near to Him. He will break our chains and set us free.

Jesus is there to deliver you and set you free (Psalm 50:15). The Bible speaks of a woman who had been crippled for eighteen years. When Jesus healed her, there were those who criticized it simply because Jesus had done so on the Sabbath day (Luke 13:10-16). Jesus responded, "...ought not this woman, being a daughter of Abraham, whom Satan hath bound, lo, these eighteen years, be loosed from this bond on the Sabbath day?" Jesus wants to free you from not only the bonds of Satan, but also manmade chains that would keep you enslaved!

This is exactly what Jesus criticized the religious elite about in Matthew 23:4. He said, "They [the teachers of the law and Pharisees] crush people with unbearable religious demands and never lift a finger to ease the burden."

Jesus broke the spirit of infirmity not only in this woman, but He has broken the spirit of infirmity for all who will love and accept Him as Savior (Hebrews 7:28). The woman had a spirit of infirmity. Do you know what that means? It means no strength, frail, tired, overcome with trouble. This sounds a lot like depression, something that the members of the Mormon Church struggle with greatly. Open your eyes. Search the Bible. Find out if what I am telling you is true.

You can have freedom!

Breaking Free

The good news is oppression can always be broken no matter how serious the sin that caused it or how long it has gone on. The first step is to get rid of the cause for oppression. If you are feeling oppressed or have any symptoms that make you feel distant or cut off from God, call on Jesus immediately. Just say His name and ask Him to come into your life and guide you.

"If you confess with your mouth Jesus is Lord and
believe in your heart that God raised Him from the dead,
you will be saved."

— Romans 10:9 (KJV)

Jesus does not want you to be white washed tombs full of dead men's bones. "What sorrow awaits you teachers of religious law and you Pharisees. Hypocrites! For you are like white washed tombs-beautiful on the outside but filled on the inside with dead people's bones and all sorts of impurity" (Matthew 23:27-28).

When Jesus spoke of impurity on the inside, He was speaking of the greater spiritual laws like lying, un-forgiveness, being judgmental, hypocritical, boastful, deceitful, distrustful, envious, lustful, pretentious, idolizing, fearful, and the list goes on. Read the Matthew 23; it starts with pointing out the sin of religion and ends with Jesus crying out God's love for all people who don't really know Him. This is His love for you.

You break free by making the relationship with Jesus Christ paramount. You focus on your walk with Him. You desire to know Him. The greatest commandment in the entire Bible is to simply love God with everything you do. You do that, and you won't ever worry about breaking some obscure law. Think about it. If you love someone, will you steal from them? Will you kill them? Will you be covetous of what they have? No!

So if you focus on the relationship you will never have to worry about rules and laws. Your own conscious will smite you when you do something that is not out of love. This is true freedom. This is how you break free.

A Prayer of Healing

"Thank You, Lord, that You came to set me free. I want to trust You, Jesus, and hear Your voice. I will submit to You and You alone. Please forgive me for allowing rules to take the place of Your voice that convicts me in my life. Thank You for healing me from the oppression of the law. Thank You for delivering me from my infirmity. Thank You for Your Word that guides me along my path in life. I love You, Lord, and no one will get in the way of our relationship ever again."

Baptism, a Necessary Ordinance?

"For you are all children of God through faith in Christ Jesus. And all who have been united with Christ in baptism have put on Christ, like putting on new clothes. There is no longer Jew or Gentile, slave or free, male and female. For you are all one in Christ Jesus. And now that you belong to Christ, you are the true children of Abraham. You are his heirs, and God's promise to Abraham belongs to you."

— Galatians 3:26-28

Is Baptism a necessary ordinance for salvation? The Bible tells us that all you need to do to immediately enter into His kingdom as His child is to confess with your mouth that Jesus is the Christ and that you are personally trusting Jesus as your Savior (Romans 10:9-10). As Christians we believe that Jesus is the living water (John 7:38), that what He did on the cross is sufficient for all of our sins—that nothing needs to be added to it. Being Born Again is being born into Jesus' family and accepting His living water. Baptism is a symbol of that act, like putting on a wedding ring to show all who see it that you are part of something greater than yourself.

However, unlike Christians, Mormons believe that you must physically be baptized in order to gain salvation. According to Mormon doctrine, baptism is one of the essential parts to attaining access to the Celestial Kingdom. In the Mormon faith acceptance by God is conditional on what you do for Him instead of what Jesus did for you (2 Nephi 31:17-18, Book of Mormon).

Brigham Young is quoted as saying, "However much we may profess attachment to God and his cause we are not entitled to the blessings and privileges of his Kingdom until we become citizens therein. How can we do this? By repenting of our sins, and obeying the requirements of the Gospel of the Son of God which has been delivered to us. Hundreds and thousands of people have believed on the Lord Jesus Christ and repented of their sins, and have had the Holy Spirit to witness unto them that God is love, that they loved him and that he loved them, and yet they are not in his Kingdom. They have not complied with the necessary requirements. They have not entered in at the door. You have not the power to baptize yourselves, neither have you power to resurrect yourselves; and you could not legally baptize a second person for the remission of sins until some person first baptized you and ordained you to this authority."[33]

According to Young, many people who have trusted Jesus Christ are not in the Kingdom because they did not get baptized.

These two beliefs are diametrically opposing to each other and cannot be lightly dismissed. They are so contradictory in nature that if either of them is correct, then the other, by default, means you have not attained salvation. Both views repudiate the other. You can't have both.

If the Christian viewpoint is correct, then salvation is wrapped up solely in Jesus Christ and in nothing else. But from a Mormon viewpoint salvation is attainable only after certain other requirements are completed—such as baptism. From the Christian perspective, it does not appear that the Mormon has faith in Jesus Christ at all...or not enough for salvation. Mormons don't believe that faith is sufficient and so the Christian wonders if there is faith at all. Without faith how

---

33 *Brigham Young,* Teachings of the Presidents of the Church (The Church of Jesus Christ of Latter-day Saints, Salt Lake City, Utah), 152-153, 160.

could the Mormon really be saved? The Mormons, on the other hand, don't think the Christian has gone far enough to actually achieve salvation and is still lost and outside the Kingdom.

It is impossible for them both to be right. There can be no marriage between the two viewpoints since they automatically invalidate the other. Which one is right? Which belief is true? Ultimately, what you or I think matters little in the face of what God knows. It is not about defending my position or your position, but about aligning ourselves with God's position. It is important here to know what God thinks of this very sensitive subject of baptism.

Mormon's baptize children as young as eight years of age, and even though I believe eight-year-olds can definitely come to a saving knowledge of Jesus Christ and then follow the Lord in a believer's baptism, it seems from my experience that most of these children get baptized because it is a family or religious requirement. It is the expectation and legalism involved that is not based on God's truth. These children watch their peers all getting baptized when they turn eight and so feel they must too—even if they have no true concept of why. They do it because it is expected. Children have a hard time standing up against that type of pressure.

A clear understanding of what baptism is will make a lot of difference in how we view the importance of baptism in our lives. To be clear, baptism is important, just not to attain salvation. For example, I think it important that my children learn to love me, as they grow older. But their love is not a requirement for my love. Their love is important, but whether they love me or not, they are still my children. Baptism is important in the development of your relationship with God, but whether you are or aren't, your faith in Jesus is what makes you a child of God.

What is Baptism?

The word 'Baptism' means a burial. Notice the following verses:

> "Know ye not, that so many of us as were baptized into Jesus Christ were baptized into his death? Therefore we are buried

with him by baptism into death: that like as Christ was raised
up from the dead by the glory of the Father, even so we also
should walk in newness of life. For if we have been planted
together in the likeness of his death, we shall be also in the
likeness of his resurrection:"

— Romans 6:5 (KJV)

Baptism is much like a wedding ring. A wedding ring in and of itself does not make a person married—or the lack thereof, unmarried. But it is a statement, a symbol of the vows, unity, and sacredness of a marriage. What's more, the wedding ring is the first thing that a newly married man or woman does for his or her spouse. They put on the ring, proclaiming to everyone who sees it that he or she is taken, that they are not ashamed of their marriage. It is a wonderful thing.

Baptism is much like that. Although baptism does not give a person salvation—or the lack of being baptized make a person unsaved—it does tell everyone that knows you that you have been baptized that you belong to Christ and that you aren't ashamed of that relationship. This is what baptism is. It would be similar to pledging allegiance to a flag, or putting on a wedding ring.

It is a symbol of the death, burial, and resurrection of Jesus Christ. It is also a symbol of the death of your old life, the burial of that old life, and your resurrection as a Christian (2 Corinthians 5:17). It is something that we do for God—not to attain salvation, but because we choose to identify with him. It is a statement of love. The baptism waters do not wash away sin—only the blood of Jesus Christ can do that (1 John 1:7). Baptism is how God asks us to identify ourselves with Him. But it does not save you. It does not take you to Heaven.

Here are some things to consider:

1. The thief on the cross never got baptized, and Jesus said that this same thief would be with *Him* in paradise (Heaven) (Luke 23:43). Jesus went to Heaven and so did the thief on the cross next to Him. Thus, the thief without ever having been baptized, went to Heaven! Clearly, faith and trust in Jesus is sufficient for salvation without being baptized.

2. Jesus Himself wasn't baptized until He was thirty years of age. Would Jesus have gone to Heaven if He had died before His baptism? Of course He would! And why would the perfect Son of God need to be baptized anyway? Clearly, baptism didn't save Jesus. But it did *identify* Him to what John the Baptist was preaching!

3. John didn't want to baptize Jesus. Instead, he wanted Jesus to baptize him (Matthew 3:14-15). Clearly, John understood the purpose of baptism. He wanted to be identified with the Lamb of God! That is why he wanted to be baptized, but Jesus refused and required John to baptize Him instead! This was important, as stated in the last point, because God had sent John. Jesus needed to be identified with the message of John the Baptist to fulfill all righteousness.

4. Jesus rarely, if ever, baptized anyone (John 4:2). If baptism is so important to our salvation, why wasn't the Son of God doing it? Wasn't He to be our Savior? It seems that baptism wasn't about salvation. It was about identifying themselves with Christ. This would explain why He did little of it and gave it over to His disciples to do.

5. Joseph of Arimathaea was said to be a secret follower of Christ (John 19:38). How could this be? Baptism was never a private ceremony. It was always a very public matter since it was a profession of faith—a means to identify oneself with Christ. So, if Joseph was a disciple, why was it not important that he be baptized and make this public proclamation? It does not say or even hint that the man was going to Hell because of this.

6. Paul actually expressed gratitude that he hadn't been the one to baptize people in Corinth (1 Corinthians 1:14). He was lamenting the fact that people were divided over who they identified themselves with ("I am of Paul, and I am of Apollos, and I of Cephas" 1 Corinthians 1:12). He states, "Is Christ divided?" in verse 13 of 1 Corinthians. He wants people to identify themselves with Christ—not with Paul. Baptism, done correctly, is about identifying yourself with Jesus Christ.

7. Many people use Acts 2:38 to prove that baptism is necessary for salvation. But the question asked of Peter that led to his answer in that verse wasn't a question of salvation; it was a question of how to handle guilt and regret. Peter accused this crowd of rejecting Christ and condemning the Son of God to death. Worried and convicted about their actions, they asked, "What do we do?" Peter then went on and said that they needed to repent of their former beliefs, trust Christ for salvation and then identify with Christ (baptism). But because he wrapped it all up in a single answer to their question, many take it to mean that salvation is necessary for the remission of sins. This is not so. Peter, during a speech in the very next chapter, proves this when he leaves out baptism as a means to have sins blotted out (Acts 3:19)! Clearly Peter never believed that baptism was important for salvation. He thought it was important for the purpose of identifying with Christ—as a public expression of their faith.

Baptism is a means for the Christian to publically identify him or herself with Christ. In America, we have such freedoms and liberties that we often misunderstand the significance that the act of baptism shows to the rest of the world. To openly admit your identity as a Christian in many countries often means you can't get a job or you may even lose your job, making it difficult to provide for your family. In many cases, it means imprisonment or death, all because they have identified themselves as followers of Christ. For them to be publically baptized is a true test of their faith.

Baptism has many different connotations in scripture—water baptism is but one of them. For example, there is something called the baptism of the Holy Ghost (Acts 11:16), and Jesus spoke of a baptism of suffering to his disciples:

"But Jesus said to them, 'You don't know what you are asking! Are you able to drink from the bitter cup of suffering I am about to drink? Are you able to be baptized with the baptism of suffering I must be baptized with?'"

— Mark 10:38 (NLT)

Baptism, as stated, means a burial—to be completely immersed in. You would be surprised at how many people have experienced a baptism unrelated to their water baptism. God baptizes us in various different ways according to His will. Notice the following verse:

"Then remembered I the word of the Lord, how that he said, John indeed baptized with water; but ye shall be baptized with the Holy Ghost."

— Acts 11:16 (KJV)

Mormons, laudably, want to do everything Jesus did. But while they place emphasis on water baptism, they seem to ignore these other two forms of baptism. Perhaps it is better to try to *be* like Jesus instead of trying to *do* like Jesus. When you *are* like Jesus, the doings come naturally and wonderfully. But when all you '*are*' is about what He *did* and not who He '*was*,' you become like the Pharisees who were outwardly wonderful, but inwardly dirty (Matthew 23:27). Back in the Old Testament, Pharaoh's magicians were able to *do* some of the miracles that God *did* through Moses (Exodus 7:22). But just because they were able to *do* some of what God '*did*' doesn't meant that they *were* like God, not at all.

More than that, it is just impossible to do everything that Jesus did. Only Jesus was perfect. Only Jesus could die on the cross and atone for our sins. John, in utter awe of Christ, said that if everything that Jesus did was written down, the world would not be able to contain it (John 21:25). Thankfully, the Christian is asked to conform to His image, not to be another Christ. God is so good to us and treats us like a loving Father. It is this love that allows us to beseech His mercy, find forgiveness, and grow close to Him. Then, what we do is not something we *have* to do; it is something we *get* to do. That makes all the difference in the world.

Qualifications to be Baptized

Since baptism is a way we identify with Christ, every Christian ought to want to get baptized. In fact, it is something that pleases

God. Just as a bride would feel strange if her new husband refused to wear the wedding ring, so to, I suspect, that God feels disappointed when His own people refuse to get baptized and identify with Him.

But what exactly are the qualifications? You find them in the wonderful story of Philip and the Eunuch (Acts 8:26-40). The Eunuch asked why, after listening to Philip talk of Jesus Christ, he couldn't get baptized. Clearly this black Ethiopian man wanted to identify himself with Christ. But before he could get baptized, Philip had to make sure of something.

> *"And as they went on their way, they came unto a certain water: and the eunuch said, See, here is water; what doth hinder me to be baptized? And Philip said, If thou believest with all thine heart, thou mayest. And he answered and said, I believe that Jesus Christ is the Son of God. And he commanded the chariot to stand still: and they went down both into the water, both Philip and the eunuch; and he baptized him."*
>
> — Acts 8:36-38 (KJV)

Here are *all* of the qualifications that a person must meet in order to be baptized:

1. You must believe that Jesus is the Son of God (the Messiah).

That's it. There are no other qualifications or requirements for a person to be baptized.

Baptism is an outward sign of the declaration that you believe in Jesus. It is a powerful symbol to yourself and others of the commitment that you have already made. For example, if you go on a diet and lose a bunch of weight, you have already lost the weight; the size of your new jeans is just a symbol that confirms what has already happened.

Baptism doesn't have to be how we traditionally think of it with formalities and specific prayers. An example of this happened when my daughter was a missionary in India. While riding on a train in Mumbai, she spoke to a Muslim man next to her on the train about the Lord, and he decided to accept Jesus into his life and turn from the Muslim religion. She felt the Lord telling her to ask him if he wanted to be baptized, and he said 'yes.' Since they were on a train, it was not possible to have a traditional water baptism. Instead, she poured her water bottle over his head as he shouted for joy at his conversion!

In that example, the qualifications were met. Here is a former Muslim who now, through baptism, has identified himself with Christ. His salvation was assured the moment he trusted Jesus as his Savior. But he wanted more than that. He wanted people to *know!* He wanted to be identified with Christ, so he got baptized.

Baptism for the Dead?

Mormons participate in a non-biblical practice known as 'baptizing for the dead.' In essence, this practice is the result of a misunderstanding of 1 Corinthians 15:29 (KJV) which states, "Else what shall they do which are baptized for the dead, if the dead rise not at all? Why are they then baptized for the dead?" To simplify, in the Mormon faith a person can be baptized on the behalf of a dead person in order to help them into the Celestial Kingdom. Supposedly, the act allows the departed another chance to accept the Mormon gospel and get saved. This also makes it possible to seal that person into other ordinances such as marriage.

This is one of the reasons why Mormons are so devoted to genealogies. They are determined to find their ancestors so they can be baptized on their behalf.

The passage of 1 Corinthians 15 is not talking about baptism. It is talking about the resurrection. Nowhere does it teach that being baptized for someone else will help that person attain a higher level of heaven or even get the opportunity because of this practice. There is no doubt that the verse is confusing. No less than thirty or more distinct efforts have been made through the years to explain it. The simple meaning of the verse—not the passage—does indicate that a group of people was being baptized on the behalf of someone else. But whether these people were Jews, pagans, or heathens is not indicated.

However, we do have a hint. Paul references these people as 'they' instead of 'we.' Up until that time, he was using 'we,' 'our,' 'me' or 'your' (1 Corinthians 15:14, 17, 19). He switches to 'they' in verse 29 when he talks about this practice and immediately back to 'we' in the very next verse to conclude his thoughts on the entire passage. Clearly, the practice of baptizing for the dead was something that someone else was doing, not something that he or the Christians did. It appears as if Paul was using it as an illustration to drive home the point of the resurrection. He was stating how very real the resurrection is, that even those that are not of the Christian faith practice it. If taken away, it invalidates many, many different beliefs.

For the Christian, taking away the resurrection invalidates *all* of what Christ did on the cross (1 Corinthians 15:16-21). It is a very serious issue. But in regards to the baptism for the dead, it is a practice that most likely pagans believed—not Christians. It is amazing how the Mormons have built an entire doctrine and practice filled with rules, regulations, and requirements all around a verse that contains less than 30 words! Remember, as we have discovered, baptism isn't about salvation. It is about identification. It is expressing our desire to stand with Christ, to be counted on His team, to prove that we are not ashamed of Him. Thus, baptism for the dead in this capacity makes absolutely no sense.

The practice is popular, however, among Mormons because it brings a bit of hope to people unsure of their loved one's salvation. When someone you know and care about dies outside of God, there is a natural fear of that person ending up, God forbid, in Hell. If, however, you had a way to get that person out and into Heaven, you would no doubt jump upon it.

As much as I can sympathize with that hope, it is not Biblical. Everyone must make up his or her own mind while on this earth. It is our choice to accept or reject salvation through Jesus Christ. The Bible is clear:

> *"So then every one of us shall give account of himself to God."*
>
> — Romans 14:12 (KJV)

"And as it is appointed unto men once to die, but after this the judgment:"

— Hebrews 9:27 (KJV)

What is comforting is the knowledge that God gives everyone a chance. No one will go through this life without a chance of turning to Christ. We can't judge someone's heart. We don't know if there was a time when they turned to Christ and trusted Him. That is the wonderful thing about God. Where we need works to see someone's faith (James 2:18), God only needs to see someone's heart to know if they have faith (1 Samuel 16:7, Ephesians 2:8-9). We know that God loves the entire world. We know that He isn't willing for a single soul to die and go to Hell. We know that He sent His Son to die for us.

Because we can't see someone's heart, we cannot judge his or her faith. We can only trust that God kept His Word and that somehow, someway, they had a chance. For the Scriptures say in Romans 14:11 (NLV), "'As surely as I live,' says the LORD, 'every knee will bend to me, and every tongue will confess and give praise to God.'"

Baptism and Salvation

"For you are all children of God through faith in Christ Jesus. And all who have been united with Christ in baptism have put on Christ, like putting on new clothes. There is no longer Jew or Gentile, slave or free, male and female. For you are all one in Christ Jesus. And now that you belong to Christ, you are the true children of Abraham. You are his heirs, and God's promise to Abraham belongs to you."

— Galatians 3:26-28

Jesus said you must be born again. He even tells us in scripture that no one will see the kingdom of God unless he is born again (John 3:7). How then are we to interpret this and do what Jesus desires? Here Jesus is speaking to Nicodemus—a man who was a member of the Jewish ruling council, who knew the law inside and out and was among the religious elite of his day—did not understand baptism. But then many people get it wrong, because they become very legalistic about it and try to capture into a physical action something intangible as the spirit. This is what Jesus was speaking of when he spoke of the wind. Like the wind you may hear its sound, but you cannot tell where it comes from or where it is going (John 3:8).

We cannot judge even those that are baptized! We do not know where they come from or where they are going. We do not know their heart! There are certainly a lot of people that have been baptized that do not even have God in their heart. There are many reasons people get baptized, some get baptized to be accepted in a family, some to receive their inheritance, some do it believing it to be the only way for God to love them, some do it just to look good in front of men like the Pharisees that pray and give alms on the street corners to be seen by men.

> *"Take heed that you do not do your alms before men, to be seen of them: otherwise you have no reward of your Father which is in heaven. Therefore when thou doest thine alms, do not sound a trumpet before thee, as the hypocrites do in the synagogues and in the streets, that they may have glory of men. Verily I say unto you, they have their reward. But when thou doest alms, let not thy left hand know what thy right hand doeth: That thine alms may be in secret: and thy Father which seeth in secret himself shall reward thee openly."*

> — Matthew 6:1-4 (KJV)

Unlike alms, baptism is an outward declaration to tell people that you are following Jesus and allowing them to witness the change in your life. Nevertheless, it is still between you and the Lord. God is asking for a clean heart with the right motives. Remember, God looks on the heart.

If you keep the Bible in context and interpret it correctly (not just by a single verse), you will understand what is meant by being born of water in John 3:5. When you compare it with the very next verse, he explains it: "That which is born of the flesh is flesh; and that which is born of the Spirit is spirit." So, the 'born of water' is the flesh, or physical birth—not a water baptism performed outside of the womb. Any mother knows that when she carried her unborn child, her child was surrounded on the inside by water; in the same way, it is what is happening on the inside that matters.

Baptism is a symbol to the outside world that you are following Jesus, but God cares about so much more than just your outward show. He wants to see changes on the inside.

> *"Yet a time is coming and has now come when the true worshippers will worship the Father in spirit and truth for they are the kind of worshippers the Father seeks. God is spirit and his worshipers must worship in spirit and truth."*
>
> — John 4:23

Christians believe you can be saved without baptism. The Bible tells us that all you need to do is confess with your mouth that Jesus is the Christ and you immediately enter his kingdom (Romans 10:9). Jesus is the living water. Being born again is being born into Jesus' family and accepting his living water. Baptism is a symbol.

When the Bible teaches about salvation, rarely is physical water baptism ever mentioned. Instead, emphasis is given to faith, belief and trust in Jesus Christ and what God did for us so that we can have eternal life. His love for us alone saved us! It is the greatest love story ever told. To deny this is to say that what He did for us in dying on the cross was not "enough," that we must do something more in order to save ourselves. Salvation is by faith alone apart from the works of human righteousness.

- **John 3:16** - *"For God so loved the world, that He gave His only begotten Son, that whoever believes in Him shall not perish, but have eternal life."*

- **Ephesians 2:8-9** - *"For it is by grace you have been saved, through faith and this is not from yourselves, it is the gift of God, not by works, so that no one can boast."*

- **Romans 5:1** - *"Therefore, having been justified by faith, we have peace with God through our Lord Jesus Christ."*

- **Acts 16:30-31** - *"And after he brought them out, he said, 'Sirs, what must I do to be saved?' They said, 'Believe in the Lord Jesus, and you will be saved, you and your household.'"*

- **John 6:28-29** - *"Therefore they said to Him, 'What must we do to do the work God requires?' Jesus answered, "The work of God is this: to believe in the one he has sent."* If you add physical baptism to the salvation process as something that "must be done" in order to be saved, you twist scripture so that the emphasis upon salvation by faith alone is removed and you have fallen from grace.

- **Galatians 5:4** - *"You who are trying to be justified by law have been alienated from Christ: you have fallen away from grace."*

- **Titus 3:5** - *"When the kindness and love of God our Savior appeared, he saved us, not because of righteous things we had done, but because of his mercy."* Christians are baptized purely as an act of love as a true follower of Christ, but it is not a necessary part of our salvation.

- **Romans 6:4** - *"Therefore if anyone is in Christ, he is a new creature; the old things passed away; behold, new things have come."* Baptism by the Holy Spirit renews a person so that they can have a "clear conscience" through Christ before God. "So that we too may live a new life."

- In **Acts 10:44-47**, we read that the gift of the Holy Spirit was given before physical water baptism took place: *"While Peter was still speaking these words, the Holy Spirit fell upon all those who heard the message. The circumcised believers who had come with Peter were astonished that the gift of the Holy Spirit had been poured out even on the gentiles. For they heard them speaking in tongues and praising God. Then Peter said 'Can anyone keep these people from being baptized with water? They have received the Holy Spirit just as we have.'"* Thus scripture demonstrates that salvation occurs by faith in Christ alone, prior to water baptism.

- In **Corinthians 1:17,** Paul tells us that Christ did not send him to baptize, but to preach the Gospel. Apparently, there is more saving power in the Gospel than in the baptismal waters!

- **Acts 22:16** tells us not to delay getting baptized. What do we make of that? *"Now why do you delay? Get up and be baptized, and wash away your sins, calling on His name."* This passage describes the washing "away" of sins. The way to wash away our sins is by "calling on His name." This washing away of sins occurs the moment a person calls upon the name of Christ for salvation, not at the moment of physical, water baptism.

- **1 Peter 3:21** - *"Corresponding to that, baptism now saves you—not the removal of dirt from the flesh, but an appeal to God for a good conscience—through the resurrection of Jesus Christ."*

A Prayer of Healing

"Lord Jesus, we thank You for taking upon You the baptism of suffering that we could not do for ourselves. We thank You that You save us the moment we ask. Please help us to rest in Your grace which produces the fruits of a righteous baptism, Amen."

Temple Ordinances, a Roadblock to God

*"And when Jesus had cried out again in a loud voice,
he gave up his spirit. At that moment the curtain
of the temple was torn in two from top to bottom.
The earth shook, the rocks split..."*

— Matthew 27:50-51

*"Therefore, brothers and sisters, since we have confidence
to enter the Most Holy Place by the blood of Jesus, by a new
and living way opened for us through the curtain, that is, his
body, and since we have a great priest over the house of God,
let us draw near to God with a sincere heart and with the
full assurance that faith brings, having our hearts sprinkled
to cleanse us from a guilty conscience and having our bodies
washed with pure water."*

— Hebrews 10:19-22

Perhaps one of the worst feelings in the world is being unable to approach someone you need or love. To be cut off from them is like being held hostage to loneliness with no ability to hear from them or feel their love. This is exactly what it is like to be apart from God. Placing a temple veil in between God and us perpetuates this feeling by keeping us apart from Him. We were created to be in constant relationship with God. Unfortunately, sin has separated us. But would a loving God let sin permanently separate us?

Is the temple the answer to gaining a relationship with God or is there another way? I have great news, it is for this very purpose that God sent His son to bridge the gap and reconcile us to Him! God's own Son, the sinless, spotless Lamb became sin for us so that we could have full access to God (2 Corinthians 5:21). This was God's ultimate act of love to reconcile us to Him. God hated the veil and the separation from His people. He provided a way so that we would no longer have anything between Him and us. After Jesus Christ came and died on the cross the veil was split! There would no longer be a need for a temple. This is a profound truth that should make every Christian shout for joy! What an opportunity we now have! There is nothing to stop our prayers from reaching God's ears except our decision not to pray. There is nothing stopping us from claiming God's grace except our own desire to ask for it. Nothing can prevent us from walking and interacting with God except our own negligence. Christ's death ripped the veil in the temple! It gave us full access to Him anytime, anywhere!

And yet, among many different religious groups there seems to be an effort to bring back the veil and create a barrier between man and God. This is a tragedy and divides more than just man from a loving God, but also creates division in nearly every other aspect of the many lives it affects. While I was a Mormon I saw the effects of the temple not only on my family and myself, but also in other families in many different ways. Mormonism, unfortunately, creates a barrier between God and man that divides us from Him. Religion has made it so that only through another human man ordained in a place they profess to be holy (the Mormon Temple) can we finally have access to God.

The Mormon Temple is central to the Mormon culture. It is steeped in mysticism and secrecy. It is a dominating influence and, according to their doctrine, a necessary part of salvation.

Not knowing authentic Christianity I was deceived into believing I needed the temple to get to God. This would have many adverse affects on my life. Having now gained an understanding of the Bible and God's will for my life, my family and I have been completely restored, enjoying a fruitful relationship with God. Much of what goes on in the Mormon Temples are wrong and anti-biblical. I would have liked for a Christian to have at least tried to open my eyes on the temple while I was a Mormon—even if I wouldn't have listened. I wish someone had cared enough to say, "Hey! That is not Biblical! Christ isn't like that!" Because I wished someone had done it for me, I am doing it for you.

This is my way of saying, "I care," because I really do.

The Mormon Temple and Endowments

Mormons believe that their Temple is a key component to getting to Heaven. The Mormon Eternal Progression believes that eventually all good Mormon males will get their own planet, and will need to choose their own Jesus to be the savior of that world. They get to be a god. This belief is predicated, however, on a Mormon's participation in their Temple Ordinances. These Ordinances are necessary for salvation according to the Mormon faith.

Elder Boyd K. Packer said, "Ordinances and covenants become our credentials for admission into His presence. To worthily receive them is the quest of a lifetime; to keep them thereafter is the challenge of mortality. Once we have received them for ourselves and for our families, we are obligated to provide these ordinances vicariously for our kindred dead, indeed for the whole human family."[34]

President Howard W. Hunter explained his opinion of the importance of temple ordinances, "All of our efforts in proclaiming the gospel, perfecting the Saints, and redeeming the dead lead to the holy temple. This is because the temple ordinances are absolutely crucial; we cannot return to God's presence without them. I encourage every-

---

34 Conference Report, (April 1987, 27; or Ensign, May 1987, 24), www.lds.org

one to worthily attend the temple or to work toward the day when you can enter that holy house to receive your ordinances and covenants."[35]

Notice the emphasis on the word 'worthy.' Not every Mormon is introduced to the Temple Ordinances until they are deemed worthy and only after they have been faithful to the church for at least a year. Because the entire matter is held secret, those about to go through their 'endowment ceremony' have no idea what it means or what it entails until they actually go through it. Again, we see the concept of worthiness in President Gordon B. Hinckley's remarks, "These ordinances become the most profound expressions of our theology. I urge our people everywhere, with all of the persuasiveness of which I am capable, to live worthy to hold a temple recommend, to secure one and regard it as a precious asset, and to make a greater effort to go to the house of the Lord and partake of the spirit and the blessings to be had therein."[36]

Why not regard Jesus Christ and the Holy Spirit as our most precious asset? It would seem logical to just rely on Christ unless you had an eternal progressive view of your own godhood. With that being the case, Jesus is merely a small stepping-stone to something larger. For the Christian, there is nothing more. Jesus is the Beginning and the End. He is everything. He is the Truth. He is the Way. He is the Life (John 14:6).

Being found worthy is the first step to being admitted into the Temple. Once there you are 'endowed' which, according to Brigham Young, is a series of covenants that you make with God to live a good life. He said, "Let me give you a definition in brief. Your endowment is, to receive all those ordinances in the house of the Lord, which are necessary for you, after you have departed this life, to enable you to walk back to the presence of the Father, passing the angels who stand as sentinels."[37]

The endowment is supposedly how the Mormon receives power to resist Satan here on earth. It leaves me to wonder why only worthy

35 Conference Report, (Oct. 1994, 118; or Ensign, Nov. 1994, 88), www.lds.org

36 Conference Report, (Oct. 1995, 72; or Ensign, Nov. 1995, 53), www.lds.org

37 Discourses of Brigham Young, selected by John A. Widtsoe, (Salt Lake City: Deseret Book Co., 1941), page 416

saints need the power to resist the evils of this earth, and why you must be worthy to receive this power? Are not those who are 'unworthy' in more need of this power of resistance? And, if you are worthy, have you not already resisted the evils? Why then do you need this endowment?

These questions aside, the Mormon view is that the Temple Endowment is a very, very special ceremony given only to the worthy. Here is a short list of worthy requirements:

1. Being morally clean

2. Sustaining the Prophet as the only one on earth authorized to exercise all priesthood keys

3. Living according to the standards of the Church

4. Having no unresolved sins

5. Being completely honest

6. Being an active member in good standing for at least one year

7. Paying a full tithe

8. Having a righteous relationship within the family

9. Sustaining local and general Church leaders

10. Keeping the Word of Wisdom

11. Having no apostate affiliations

12. Wearing the Mormon Garment both day and night as commanded

Despite the improbability of many of these requirements, the list is more about binding you to Mormon ideology than about righteous living which only further separates you from a relationship with God. It removes your faith and trust in Him as you must get worthy before you can even come to God.

Holding this recommend interview causes your worthiness to be determined by the local Church leaders. Your fate is now in their power as you rely on them to receive your temple recommend. This 'recommend' must be presented at the temple in order to gain entrance. Notice the following quote by Spencer Kimball:

"It is true that many Latter-day Saints, having been baptized and confirmed members of the Church, and some even having received their endowments and having been married and sealed in the holy temple, have felt that they were thus guaranteed the blessings of exaltation and eternal life. But this is not so. There are two basic requirements every soul must fulfill or he cannot attain to the great blessings offered. He must receive the ordinances and he must be faithful, overcoming his weaknesses. Hence, not all who claim to be Latter-day Saints will be exalted. But for those Latter-day Saints who are valiant, who fulfill the requirements faithfully and fully, the promises are glorious beyond description: "Then shall they be gods, because they have no end; therefore shall they be from everlasting to everlasting, because they continue; then shall they be above all, because all things are subject unto them. Then shall they be gods, because they have all power, and the angels are subject unto them (D&C 132:20)."[38]

Many things are involved in the Endowments. My own experience is not unique. As a Mormon, trying to do the right thing, I wanted to go—felt I *had* to go to the Temple. At the time, my husband who grew up a Mormon was not deemed 'worthy' by his Church and honestly didn't really want me to go anyway. He was afraid of the changes the temple would have on the family and me. He had seen division, judgment and other self-righteous attitudes in other families, so he naturally feared it. But I felt I had to go to secure my salvation and help my family. My husband, who decided it was easier to say nothing to me, lest he get me and the rest of his family upset, waited outside in the car while I went into the temple alone since he was not allowed to go in without a temple recommend.

There are many, many rituals, secret handshakes, oaths (that even once carried the death penalty prior to 1990), and words that must be memorized and recited. You are not informed prior to going what will happen. But here are some things that I had to go through:

38 Spencer W. Kimball, *The Miracle of Forgiveness*, p. 9.

1. I was asked to strip naked and to put nothing on except a sheet or poncho for the washings and anointing. I felt uncomfortable and questioned why this was necessary in order to be washed clean by God. My clothing was placed in a locker with a lock on it. I questioned this because I thought I was in a holy place with honest people being guarded by angels.

2. Then I was required to put on the garments, something I would do 24/7 for the rest of my life. I then dressed in identical white clothing as everyone else participating in the ceremony. It was hard for me, because it seemed as if my identity didn't matter.

3. For the ceremony, I wasn't given any real information as to what to expect. After I was seated with the doors shut, I was given the option to leave, however doing so would have been a huge interruption and very embarrassing to me, not to mention the end of my progression to live in Heaven with Jesus. So I continued. When it was finished I would make oaths never to speak of what happens in the temple. These oaths went way beyond a simple promise (see the section on Temple Mysticism below).

4. There was a lot of pressure from family and friends—not my husband, but certainly his family—who would be very disappointed in my "unfaithfulness," "rebellion," and "unworthiness" if I didn't attend the temple. My husband's family had been greatly concerned about us because we had not yet been through the process and been 'sealed' to each other and to them.

5. During the ceremony, I was told to repeat the words that force you to swear before god, angels, and witnesses under the threat of eternal punishment not to reveal what I learned during the ceremonies. I took many secret oaths and vows that day, each one a surprise to me since I was not led to know what these vows would be until I was asked to speak them. We raised our hands and swore never to reveal the oaths and covenants made in the temple. For a long time I was afraid. God does not operate in fear or threaten people! Yet I feared. Ironically, the Church's own recorded history is now the 'enemy' that members are

warned against studying or looking into. Searching out Mormon history is considered apostasy.

6. I received a new name, Naomi. I was required to perform many secret handshakes, and quote ritualistic phrases. This included wearing a strange temple robe and a faux fig leaf apron and a strange hat for the men and veil for the women. Forgetting any of it was looked down upon. These key phrases would allow me to enter into God's Kingdom. It was like a secret society with passwords and everything.

7. I was surprised by the fact that my family and friends in attendance had participated in these bizarre ceremonies repeatedly in the past and had been pressuring my own participation. While trying to do the right thing, I felt a sense of unrealism—like "you must be kidding"—during the entire proceedings.

8. I was separated from the men, which would eventually bother me when my husband began attending the temple. I wanted to be near him and share the experience together, but this is something we were not given a choice in.

9. Going through the Temple is required in order to participate in things such as a wedding or a mission's trip. This is very important as it pertains to not only your own marriage and mission trips, but also those of your children and other family members. Many would *suffer* through the ceremonies just to receive their prospective "blessings."

Some of the other Temple practices include Baptisms for the Dead, Temple weddings, and being sealed to your family. Many of these rites have similar aspects and components from the secret handshakes to the division of men and women.

Temple goers act like the only way to receive a gift of endowment is to go to the temple. How ridiculous! God's gifts are freely given to each Christian. They are not dispensed through the church or a person. It is between you and God! You do not need a Temple worker, a new name, robes, handshakes to remember, or special words to say to enter God's kingdom. Just ask! God says He prepares a place for you (John 14:2). He never says in the Bible that you need to go to the Temple to receive your new name and all the other rituals to enter His Kingdom. Just ask! He will give you a new name; you shall no longer be called wounded, outcast, broken, lonely or afraid. Instead, your new name shall be confident, joyfulness, overcoming one, faithfulness, friend of mine, one who seeks My face.

Temple Marriages

Being married within the Temple is essential in the Mormon faith. Marriage and being sealed within the Temple are necessary, they believe, to attaining the highest level of Heaven. To be married outside the Temple is not to have a marriage that is bound eternally in Heaven. If a spouse should die and a man remarries, his new wife may also be sealed to him in the temple furthering the polygamy practice in Heaven. So much of the power is given to the husband, as he is the one that knows the wife's new name and must call it to resurrect her at the appointed time.

Worse, the actual ceremony is more about Mormon control than it is about the marriage. It is done in secret, of course, and only those with a Temple Recommend are actually allowed to attend the ceremony. Everyone else must wait outside. This is incredibly hurtful and divisive to families. Yet the Mormon Church insists that this is the way it must be done. Only in this manner, through them, can a marriage be sealed for all eternity!

This is a different gospel than the one Jesus preached. He said in Matthew 22:30, "For in the resurrection they neither marry, nor are they given in marriage, but are as the angels of God in heaven." And again, we find the same thing in Mark 12:25, "For when they shall rise from the dead, they neither marry, nor are given in marriage, but are as the angels which are in heaven." In case that isn't clear enough, you'll find it repeated again in Luke 20:35.

Some get around this by doing a two-step process of marrying first in the temple and then holding a public, civil ceremony. Even still it is hurtful to those that cannot see their family member being married and enjoying the looks on their faces, as they are married for the first time. The civil service feels more like an appeasement to them as the bride and groom have already experienced the "true wedding."

For most young Mormon girls, they have no, absolutely no clue what to expect. Since their families are forbidden to tell them and they are discouraged from reading anything negative about the Mormon Church, they go with eagerness and youthful ignorance to the greatest day of their life, not comprehending how this will adversely affect their life.

1. As a young couple they are not offered or given premarital counseling so they are not prepared for marriage itself. Every marriage whether viewed earthly or eternally requires preparation for success. Meaning not just success of staying together, but staying passionately in love together.

2. They will both be required to wear Garments—holy underwear that strips mostly the young woman of the ability to be sexy for her husband. The playfulness of youth now gone, teasing each other with a hint of skin will be over. The garment itself will change the choice of their outerwear as new rules have begun.

3. Some or many of their own family will be unable to attend the wedding causing years of bitterness to follow, simply because they were deemed "unworthy."

4. The ceremony itself will not be individualized and personal, but will be geared to marry many on that day.

5. The division between the two will begin that day as they sit on opposite sides of the room, not sharing their experience or their thoughts about what is happening. This will proceed for years as they have taken secret oaths not to discuss it.

6. During the ceremony, they will hear threats, warnings, and dire secrets never to be repeated outside the Temple, this being an example will set them up for future secrets between the two.

She will be told that she is bound to her husband for all eternity and that only by his grace and ability to call her name can she attain to the highest Kingdom. This sets the wife up to feel very much under his control.

Imagine marriage as God intended it to be, with the husband and wife sharing in every experience along their journey in life. Imagine it where they are free to share with the world their beautiful ceremony and where there are no secrets or threats. Think of a marriage where the only symbol they wear is the cross to help them remember all that Christ has done for them so they can do the same for each other. Wouldn't it be great to have a marriage where, as helpmates, they practice the true ordinances of Christ' Gospel of praying for one another, forgiving and loving one another? Imagine a union where the only temple they attend is the temple of their bodies, which God gave them, and where they are free to come together openly with one another without the need to hide anything. That is the beauty of a true marriage.

Satan or God's Priesthood?

The Temple Ordinances are filled with symbols of the occult and borrowed rites and symbols from masonry. Joseph Smith was a Mason and brought many of the rituals, secret handshakes, and mystery with him when he started the Mormon religion. Mormon teaching explains the secrecy away by claiming that it is sacred. But that is not what the word 'sacred' means! Sacred means 'special,' not secret! It is like a marriage covenant, everyone knows about it and it is a special covenant, but certainly not a secret one.

The secret oaths, vows and covenants are part of Satan's plan; remember He is the god of this world (2 Corinthians 4:4). One should pay special attention to whose priesthood robe they are placing on themselves. When you place the fig leaf apron on, ask yourself whom is it that is asking you to do so. You will be surprised to find out you are actually doing as Satan commanded. He says in the temple "See, you are naked. Take some fig leaves and make you aprons. Father will see your nakedness. Quick! Hide!" It is Satan that encourages the separation between you and God. As a believer in Christ, you have a new God, the true life giving God, and are no longer bound to do as Satan commands. Because Jesus is the new and everlasting Melchizedek Priesthood, the source of eternal salvation, we are to go to Him, and Him only (Romans 5:6-10). There is no longer a separation requiring anyone to intervene as a priest! He alone is our High Priest (Hebrews 9:11)!

Take notice of the prominent symbols in temple, they will also give you a clue as to whose priesthood the Mormons are patterned after. The Sunstone symbol of Baal (a Biblical false god or demon), the moonstone of the witch goddess Dana (Artemis), and the satanic pentagram symbol are all very evident. Nowhere is there a single cross or even a picture of the cross, a symbol of our High Priest Jesus Christ.

> *"And he put down the <u>idolatrous priests</u>, whom the kings of Judah had ordained to burn incense in the high places in the cities of Judah, and in the places round about Jerusalem; them also that burned incense unto <u>Baal, to the sun</u>, and to the <u>moon</u>, and to the <u>planets</u>, and to <u>all the host of heaven</u>. And he took away the horses that the kings of Judah had given to the <u>sun</u>, at the entering in of the house of the LORD, by the chamber of Nathanmelech the chamberlain, which [was] in the suburbs, and burned the chariots of the sun with fire."*
>
> — 2 Kings 23:5, 11

I know it is very scary, but the Mormon Temple has little to do with Jesus Christ. It has more to do with pagan rituals and idolatrous traditions than anything else. To me, the greatest tragedy in all of this is how deceptive they have been about it all. This takes away from a person's ability to search these things out before they begin to walk into the power of Satan's priesthood. This is one of the reasons it is very difficult to get a Mormon to see; Satan has a very strong hold on them. I remember going through the temple ordinances wondering about it all, being very confused. I asked many questions, but every time I did, the question would be passed off to someone else.

This was very time consuming as I continued to be directed in circles, never really getting a clear answer. I felt that I possibly needed to study more. Not finding my clarity, and being further consumed in this unknown demonic power, I finally embraced the teachings—until I was set free by Jesus Christ!! I have found my True Priest, my clarity, and received my answers. Now it is important for me to share them with you!

Jesus is so open and clear about everything! Learning the truth through His word brings clarity. He never organized a secret society, secret handshakes, or even used a symbol at all to differentiate His followers from others. In fact, the followers of Christ were first called Christians—by nonbelievers (Acts 11:26). The Christians were so open and clearly practiced their belief in Jesus that even those who did not believe could see the relationship between the Christians in Antioch and Jesus Christ.

Jesus never practiced vows of secrecy or held a secret society where others could not go. There were no threats of death for revealing what they knew. Instead, the disciples were encouraged to share what they knew!

Jesus warned about this sort of thing to the Pharisees:

> *"And Jesus went into the temple of God, and cast out all them*
> *that sold and bought in the temple, and overthrew the tables*
> *of the moneychangers, and the seats of them that sold doves.*
> *And said unto them, It is written, My house shall be called*
> *the house of prayer; but ye have made it a den of thieves. And*
> *the blind and the lame came to him in the temple; and he*
> *healed them. And when the chief priests and scribes saw the*
> *wonderful things that he did, and the children crying in the*
> *temple, and saying, Hosanna to the Son of David;*
> *they were sore displeased,"*
>
> — Matthew 21:12-15 (KJV)

It is interesting that as soon as Jesus ran out of the Temple those that were using it for their own gain, those that normally would not be deemed as 'worthy' came to Jesus in the Temple. The Pharisees were very angry over the fact that their Temple, the structure that set them above the rest of the people…that proclaimed them as better than the rest of the people, was being taken over by the blind and defective along with a bunch of children singing praises to Jesus. These religious elite didn't want these people in the Temple. They wanted it to be only for a select group of people. This is a form of idolatry when the person is set up to be greater than someone else. The Bible tells us in Romans 12:16, "Live in harmony with one another. Do not be proud, but be willing to associate with people of low position. Do not be conceited."

What is more, Mormon doctrine teaches that you will eventually become a god yourself; if you do everything that you are supposed to. The Bible teaches that there is only one God and that there are no others—ever! So going to the Mormon Temple is more than just exposing yourself to pagan symbols and demonic rituals. It is declaring your candidacy for godhood—the ultimate in idolatry.

There is no greater act of idolatry than to claim that you are a god. Jesus was being attacked for claiming He was the Son of God—that He was equal to God. Jesus used a passage in Psalms 82 to illustrate their ridiculous charge of blasphemy. He never claimed that the prophets and judges of old (whom where called gods) were deity, were able to become deity, or could ever lay claim to such a thing. He was showing them that if the word of God came to these men (the judges) whom they revered, why were they charging Jesus with blasphemy?

No, when you think you can become a god, equal to God, this is idolatry. Satan tried it in Isaiah 14 and was cast down as a result. What result do you think you will have?

The Temple—The Great Divider

In 2 Corinthians 10:2 Paul writes that it is not wise to compare and measure ourselves against each other. He knew the effects that such comparisons can produce in the lives of both the one doing the comparing and the one being compared to. It is an exceptionally dangerous thing to do. Notice the following verses:

"Two men went up into the temple to pray; the one a Pharisee, and the other a publican. The Pharisee stood and prayed thus with himself, God, I thank thee, that I am not as the rest of men, extortioners, unjust, adulterers, or even as this publican. I fast twice in the week; I give tithes of all that I get. But the publican, standing afar off, would not lift up so much as his eyes unto heaven, but smote his breast, saying, God, be thou merciful to me a sinner. I say unto you, this man went down to his house justified rather than the other: for every one that exalteth himself shall be humbled; but he that humbleth himself shall be exalted."

— Luke 18:10-14 (KJV)

Here we have one man comparing himself to another man and feeling justified because he wasn't *as bad as* the other guy. This is divisive in so many ways. Consider this: comparing yourself to those who are 'worse' than you makes you feel that you don't have to grow, don't have to improve, don't have to get better yourself. You justify your own wrongs by saying, "Well, I'm not as bad as so and so!" Comparing yourself to those who are 'better' than you can be discouraging and ultimately depressing. It may prevent you from moving forward like the Children of Israel did when comparing their military might to that of the inhabitants of the Promised Land. They thought themselves so inferior that they turned back and defied the Lord out of fear (Numbers 13:31-33).

Ultimately, this is what the Mormon Temple is doing. It places physical, mental, emotional, and spiritual divisions among people, families, friends, and neighbors. It is not a means to connect with God, as much as it is a means of division. But this is not what God wants. God does not want division among the brethren. God wants unity!

"Behold, how good and how pleasant it is for brethren to dwell together in unity!"

— Psalms 133:1 (KJV)

Nevertheless, the Mormon Temple is a place of division. For example:

1. When entering the Temple, families are divided. Men and women are required to sit on opposite sides from each other even if both are deemed to be 'worthy.' There is no unity as a family as children are not allowed to attend the endowment session.

2. For family members that are not deemed 'worthy,' they must wait outside the Temple completely. They aren't even allowed in! As already mentioned, the first time I went to the Temple, my husband wasn't allowed to attend. He sat out in the car and waited. The vows I took even forbade me to tell him what happened...my own husband!

3. It divides your faith from God. In effect, the Temple encourages you to work out your own salvation and ignore what Jesus did on the cross. You are suddenly, even if you don't realize it, in competition with Jesus over who saves your soul. The Temple determines who is saved, who will be married, what Kingdom you will go to and who your wife or husband will be in the Kingdom.

4. If you hold a Temple Recommend (a certificate stating that you are worthy), you are being told that you are better than someone else who does not. This has become an object of pride and arrogance.

Jesus ran into similar problems with the Temple in His day. Upon entering the Temple He saw the money changers (venders) that sold animal sacrifices to those without. Jesus became so enraged (yes, angry) at what they were doing to people that He drove them all out of the Temple! These venders had made a deal with the priests. The priests would find some flaw in the sacrifice that a poor person would bring to offer at the Temple, thereby invalidating it. The poor person would have no choice but to buy a new sacrifice from the venders. The vender and the priest would split the profits.

But more than just the money making scheme, these venders and priests were selling grace and forgiveness. Suddenly, a beggar was not worthy enough until *they* (the priests) said they were worthy. Suddenly, this person had to go through the vender and the priest in order to make an offering to God. This is so contrary to what God wants!

Salvation and God's grace is His free gift! It is freely given to all!

> *"Therefore as by the offence of one judgment came upon all men to condemnation; even so by the righteousness of <u>one the free gift came upon all men</u> unto justification of life."*
>
> — Romans 5:18 (KJV)

God is not looking for more division. He is looking for reconciliation. Satan is the great accuser. Satan is the one who seeks to divide us from God. How can something create so much division and bring union? It can't.

The Temple—Chained to the Dead

The Mormon belief of Baptism for the Dead (see last chapter) creates an environment that suggests to their faithful that the dead are more important than the living. The emphasis is placed on genealogies in order to find as many ancestors as possible so they can be baptized by proxy creates two issues of note:

1. It binds people more firmly to the Temple since only at the Temple can they get baptized for dead ancestors and thereby give these people, wherever they may be at, a chance to accept the Mormon gospel. Which means, unless you are found worthy enough, your dead ancestors cannot get a second chance at salvation.

2. It trivializes the living by placing the focus on those that are gone from this life. You can see this in the tremendous effort Mormons have placed on determining their genealogies. It keeps you busy doing work for the dead.

Notice what Christ said:

"But as touching the resurrection of the dead, have ye not read that which was spoken unto you by God, saying, I am the God of Abraham, and the God of Isaac, and the God of Jacob? God is not the God of the dead, but of the living."

— Matthew 22:31-14 (KJV)

There is an important teaching here that Jesus makes. First of all, those that have passed on are not truly dead. God does not rule over the dead, but of the living. The implication here is that those that have passed on have made their decision already. They are now either enjoying the benefits of their decision to trust Christ or are suffering the consequences of rejecting Christ. Nowhere, and I mean nowhere, does the Bible even hint that we that are left here on this earth can do something that they cannot not do for themselves. The Mormon fascination with this is distressing.

I remember a time when I drove an hour one way just to get to the Temple. I went there, of course, because it was expected of me. I would watch the same video, do the same handshakes, say the same secret words and leave the same as I arrived. But when I got there, the Temple was closed for cleaning. Frustrated, I turned around and began the drive home. On the way, I saw a woman on the side of the road that was obviously homeless and in need. Feeling like I needed to do *something* since I was robbed of the opportunity to attend a Temple Ceremony, I pulled over and helped this woman. I gave her some money and told her about Christ's love. I left there different than when I stopped to help. That homeless woman touched my life in a way the Temple never had. I had made a difference for someone!

I was reminded of the following verses:

"Pure religion and undefiled before God and the Father is this, To visit the fatherless and widows in their affliction, and to keep himself unspotted from the world."

— James 1:27 (KJV)

This is what true religion busies itself doing! The Sadducees in Matthew 22 were asking Jesus questions about what happens to dead people in Heaven. Jesus rebuked them by saying, first of all it was none of their concern, and secondly that they really didn't understand what happens to people after they die. Good point. Perhaps we should spend more time on making a difference to those that are living.

> *"And he said unto another, Follow me. But he said, Lord, suffer me first to go and bury my father. Jesus said unto him, Let the dead bury their dead: but go thou and preach the kingdom of God."*
>
> — Luke 9:59-60 (KJV)

Here Jesus emphasized this truth even more powerfully. Here He warns a young man to let the dead care for itself, but instead to preach the Gospel to the living. This is what I did for that poor lady. This is how I made a difference, and in making a difference, a difference was made in my own life.

Many people walk around carrying a 'Temple Recommend' who are cheating on their wives, practicing idolatry, do not honor their parents, steal, lie, and cheat. Because man can only see the outward, and not the inward, many people are still being baptized for their dead ancestors who technically should not be worthy to even be in the Temple. Yet they are. So here is the dilemma presented with this situation:

1. Since God knows their heart, does He then invalidate the baptism for the dead or temple sealing, even if a "priesthood holder" did it in the Temple according to all correct rituals?

2. If so, then why does the Church worry about anyone's worthiness since God will take care of that anyway? Just let people get baptized and sealed for their ancestors and let God sort it out.

3. If the ordinance is legitimate because it is done in the Temple, then why worry about any one's worthiness? Just baptize for as

many dead people as you can! Isn't it important to get the gospel to all these people who have passed on?

4. And if it is merely about a person's worthiness, which man cannot accurately judge, then what is the point of the actual physical baptism for dead people? Is not their worthiness in God's eyes enough to give their ancestor's a second chance? What happens if someone does not have access to a Temple? And is it not possible that Mormon Bishops have made mistakes and yet denied a Temple Recommend to someone who is truly worthy? What about them?

No matter how you look at it, it seems a rather irrelevant practice. Let's just focus on the living and let the dead care for the dead!

Where is God's True Temple?

To begin with, it is important to know what the Temple of God really is. It is not a physical building...not anymore. Now that Jesus has died on the cross and paid for our sins, the Temple of God is within every Christian. The Christians *are* the Temple of God!

"Don't you know that you yourselves are God's temple and that God's spirit lives in you? If anyone destroys God's temple God will destroy him, for God's temple is sacred, and you are that temple."

— 1 Corinthians 3:17

God's spirit lives inside of us! We don't need to go to the Temple to find God. We already have God with us. For the Christian, this is truly a wonderful thing! We have constant access to God, anytime, anywhere. Our Great God loves you! He is your provider, your comforter, protector and so much more! Most importantly He is always available!

This reminds me so much of the woman at the well in John 4. Once she realized that the man she was talking to was much more than a man, she became curious. Clearly Jesus was a Jew and Jews never thought of the Samaritans as 'worthy.' In fact, most Jews would go out of their way to avoid Samaria altogether if they could help it, and they considered the half Jew, half Gentile Samaritan as no better than dogs. But here Jesus was, a Jew, talking to her. So she bluntly said in verse 20, "Ye say, that in Jerusalem is the place where men ought to worship." She was referencing the Temple. For centuries, when a Jew wanted to worship God, he had to go to the Temple, and this worried her because she was not only a Samaritan (a dog to the Jews) but she was a rather notorious sinner as well. There was no way she would be deemed 'worthy' in anyone's eyes!

Yet she wasn't talking to just anyone. She was talking to Jesus Christ, the Son of God. Let's find out His reaction to having to go to the Temple to find God. He said:

> *"But the hour cometh, and now is, when the true worshippers shall worship the Father in spirit and in truth: for the Father seeketh such to worship him. God is a Spirit: and they that worship him must worship him in spirit and in truth."*
>
> — John 4:23-24 (KJV)

Just before making this statement, Jesus directly told her that she would not have to go to Jerusalem (the Temple) in order to worship God! If this were true for this 'unworthy' woman, then why would it not be true for each and every one of us? Do you see the freedom here? Do you see how worshiping God is now an act of the spirit instead an act of the flesh? Don't let someone dictate to you how to worship God! Don't believe for an instant that you must go through ordinances set up by man, run by man, and invented by man just to get to God.

God does not need to hide behind man. He does not need secrecy to be found. In fact, Jesus wants it to be easy to get to Him!

> *"But Jesus said, Suffer little children, and forbid them not, to come unto me: for of such is the kingdom of heaven."*
>
> — Matthew 19:14 (KJV)

155

Some children wanted to see Jesus, but because they were noisy, immature, or a bit irreverent, the disciples didn't want to let them get too near Jesus. In other words, the children were not yet worthy of approaching Jesus according to the disciples. Jesus, however, had a completely different opinion. He wanted the children to have full access to Him at any time! Jesus even pronounced one of his harshest warnings to the disciples regarding this issue. In another passage, Luke 9, he took a child and set him in his lap. Then he warned that if anyone caused a child to sin that believes on Him, it would be better if a milestone were hung around his neck and cast in the sea! Refusing a child to come to Jesus, causing a child to feel that he can't come to Jesus, can't get his sins forgiven, can't walk with the Savior is something that Jesus did not tolerate (Mark 10:14)!

Finding Jesus is simple. If you have accepted Jesus as your Savior by faith, you have full access to Him at any time and any place. If you have not trusted Jesus as your Savior, you can do that any time and any place. There is nothing, nothing that can prevent you! There is no secret formula for salvation, no place that God hides from you, no ritual or ordinance that can prevent you from entering into His presence any time or anyplace you choose. I would not dare to say otherwise! And neither should any other man or woman.

"For I am persuaded, that neither death, nor life, nor angels, nor principalities, nor powers, nor things present, nor things to come, Nor height, nor depth, nor any other creature, shall be able to separate us from the love of God, which is in Christ Jesus our Lord."

— Romans 8:38-39 (KJV)

A Prayer of Healing

"Thank You, Lord Jesus that You are our High Priest, and that it is only through You that salvation comes. I thank You that nothing can separate us from Your love! I thank You Lord that You love all people the same, and You call them unto You, anytime, anywhere. I thank You that You are a God of unity, and that You desire to walk with us constantly in our marriages and our families. That it is by trusting You and placing You in our marriage that we become a triple cord that cannot be broken. Thank You for your grace, for splitting the veil and giving us full access to the one and only God of the Universe. I love You, Lord. Amen."

Who Can Be Forgiven?

"If one of you should wander from the truth and someone should bring him back, remember this: Whoever turns a sinner from the error of his way will save him from death and cover over a multitude of sins."

— James 5:19

Forgiveness and Murder

Forgiveness is a necessary part of faith. If there is no forgiveness, there is no need for faith. For what does it all matter if we cannot find redemption? No one who has ever sought forgiveness has ever felt that it was an unnecessary part of his or her redemption and walk with God. But some believe that forgiveness is not granted to all. Some feel that there is a line you cross that God will actually *refuse* to grant you forgiveness no matter how strongly you seek it.

In the Mormon faith, they believe that if you have committed murder, you cannot be forgiven. In their book, the Doctrine and Covenants, written by Joseph Smith, it declares in D&C 42:18, "And now, behold, I speak unto the church. Thou shalt not kill; and he that kills shall not have forgiveness in this world, nor in the world to come." Bruce R. McConkie, who is one of the Quorum of the twelve disciples, said, "...a sin for which there is 'no forgiveness' meaning that a murderer can never gain salvation. He cannot join the Church by baptism; he is outside the pale of redeeming grace."[39]

As Christians, we believe there is no sin that Christ's blood cannot wash away (1 John 1:9). Christ turns away none who are willing to come to Him in an attitude of trust and repentance, no matter what they have done—murder included (John 6:37). It is interesting that the three men God used to pen most of the Bible were all murders: Moses, David, and the Apostle Paul. Yet each managed to find forgiveness and purpose afterwards.

A very serious and dangerous belief that the Mormon Church has, which most Mormons are not aware of, is the belief in blood atonement. Joseph Fielding Smith tells us in the Doctrines of Salvation, "But men may commit certain grievous sin—according to his light and knowledge—that will place him beyond the reach of the atoning blood of Christ. If then he would be saved he must make sacrifice of his own life to atone—so far as in his power lies—for that sin, for the blood of Christ alone under certain circumstances will not avail. ATONEMENT AND SINS UNTO DEATH. Joseph Smith taught that there were certain sins so grievous that man may commit, that they will place the transgressors beyond the power of the atonement of Christ. If these offences are committed, then the blood of Christ will not cleanse them from their sins even though they repent. Therefore their only hope is to have their own blood shed to atone, as far as possible, in their behalf. This is scriptural doctrine, and is taught in all the standard works of the Church."[40]

They are talking of suicide, which makes little sense. Suicide is self-murder. Murder is a sin Mormons believe that the blood of Christ will not atone for. So how can committing suicide and shedding your own blood atone for it? Only the blood of Jesus Christ was perfect. No one else is. How can the shedding of anyone else's blood atone

---

39 Bruce R. McConkie, *Mormon Doctrine*, pp. 520.

40 Joseph Fielding Smith, *Doctrines of Salvation*, vol. 1, pp. 134-135.

for anything? According to the Bible, it can't. According to Mormon Doctrine, it can.

Although Mormon Apostle Bruce McConkie begins to talk about the doctrine of blood atonement in a dismissive way, he then goes on to admit that some sins (such as murder) cannot be cleansed by Christ's blood and that the sinners own blood needs to be spilt to atone. He writes, "But under certain circumstances there are some serious sins for which the cleansing of Christ does not operate, and the law of God is that men must then have their own blood shed to atone for their sins. Murder, for instance, is one of these sins; hence we find the Lord commanding capital punishment."[41]

It is a total distortion of truth to teach that Christ's blood is insufficient to cleanse sinners from the sin of murder but then teach that the sinners own blood can provide atonement. As was noted earlier, Christ's blood atones for all sin even the serious sin of murder.

I never knew of this belief while I was a Mormon! After I left the church and began to look into Mormon Church doctrine on my own, I discovered this belief. I cannot relate properly how betrayed I felt knowing that I was once in a belief system I really knew nothing about. This belief in the blood atonement saddened me terribly since I personally know people that have transgressed so terribly that they often feel there is no hope. But there is hope! Hope in a living God that can save and forgive anyone! Had I known about this belief earlier, I would have certainly left the church immediately. I can see why they do not teach this belief to new converts, being of sound mind, they would leave immediately. Instead, they hope you will never find out about their history, at least not until you are already caught up in their web of confusion and integrated doctrine. If you *believe* that you are involved in the 'true church,' you will fear losing your salvation and thus be held hostage.

I bet that most Mormons do not even know of this belief. Please, if you are a Mormon and reading this, search this out! Study it! It will astound you. If you are not a Mormon and knowledgeable about this belief, please have compassion and know that most Mormons do not know of this belief system. Challenge them in love to find out. This is a

---

41 Bruce R. McConkie, *Mormon Doctrine*, pp. 92.

very scary and sick belief that is obviously very dangerous. I've already mentioned the Apostle Paul. He was murdering Christians and yet found forgiveness. David murdered Uriah and found forgiveness. Moses murdered the Egyptian and found forgiveness. They all found purpose. Murder is a vile, horrendous sin that should never be condoned, allowed, or promoted. But to say that the murderer is beyond the saving grace of Jesus Christ is even worse. It is a pronouncement of eternal damnation on a soul...we don't have a right to do that.

Let's discuss 1 John 3:15, "Anyone who hates his brother is a murderer, and you know that no murderer has eternal life in him". Most people ignore the first part of the verse that says even if you *hate* someone (particularly a brother in Christ) you are a murderer in God's eyes. I wonder how many people could be considered a murderer according to that verse? Another verse must be considered, 1 John 3:9 says, "No one who is born of God will continue to sin, because God's seed remains in him; he cannot go on sinning, because he has been born of God. Wow! If you are born of God you can't sin...and yet every Mormon and Christian continues to sin now and then. So what does it mean?

It means that there are two natures inside of us once we trust Jesus Christ as our Savior. One nature is the flesh and the other is born of God (born again). These two natures, according to Paul, are always in conflict (Romans 7). The nature that is born of God cannot sin. The flesh nature, however, most certainly can sin. The key is love. Love or the lack of love is how we shift from focusing on one nature or the other. If you love correctly, you will not sin for in love hangs all the law (Matthew 22:38-40). But when you don't love, you will allow the sin nature to dominate in your life again—and we know that in the sin nature there is *no* eternal life! No one can get to heaven through their sin nature or the deeds of the flesh. We need the new nature that is born of God—born through faith in Jesus Christ (1 John 5:4)!

And yet, Mormonism continuously teaches that there are sins that put us beyond the saving power of Jesus Christ—as if we could possibly limit God. Brigham Young, the second president of the Mormon Church, publicly preached what is known as the 'blood atonement' doctrine—that a man might be killed to save his soul. President

Young even went so far as to claim that his blood atonement doctrine fulfilled Jesus' command to 'love thy neighbor as thyself.'

Read it for yourself:

Excerpt of a Sermon by Brigham Young delivered in the Mormon Tabernacle, Feb. 8, 1857

"Now take a person in this congregation...and suppose that he is overtaken in a gross fault, that he has committed a sin that he knows will deprive him of that exaltation which he desires, and that he cannot attain to it without the shedding of his blood, and also knows that by having his blood shed he will atone for that sin, and be saved and exalted with the Gods, is there a man or woman in this house but what would say, 'shed my blood that I may be saved and exalted with the Gods?'

"All mankind love themselves, and let these principles be known by an individual, and he would be glad to have his blood shed. That would be loving themselves, even unto an eternal exaltation. Will you love your brothers or sisters like-wise, when they have committed a sin that cannot be atoned for without the shedding of their blood? Will you love that man or woman well enough to shed their blood?

"I could refer you to plenty of instances where men have been righteously slain, in order to atone for their sins. I have seen scores and hundreds of people for whom there would have been a chance (in the last resurrection there will be) if their lives had been taken and their blood spilled on the ground as a smoking incense to the Almighty, but who are now angels to the devil...I have known a great many men who left this church for whom there is no chance whatever for exaltation, but if their blood had been spilled, it would have been better for them, the wickedness and ignorance of the nations forbids this principle's being in full force, but the time will come when the law of God will be in full force.

"This is loving our neighbour as ourselves; if he needs help, help him; and if he wants salvation and it is necessary to spill his blood on the earth in order that he may be saved, spill it. Any of you who understand the principles of eternity, if you have sinned a sin requiring the shedding of blood, except the sin unto death, would not be satisfied nor rest until your blood should be spilled, that you might gain that salvation you desire. That is the way to love mankind."[42]

What dangerous doctrine! Wouldn't such a belief be the motivation for murder itself? If you killed someone trying to give him salvation, would this not be murder? You certainly can't call it a mercy killing. Mormons naturally are big on capital punishment. Since the person is beyond saving grace, he might as well be executed. Only I wonder how they feel about electrocution or lethal injection since no blood is actually spilt? Would beheading be more appropriate to the necessary requirement of shedding the sinner's own blood?

As Christians, we believe that anyone can come back to God. Anyone can find the saving grace of Jesus Christ. It is not our place to judge someone. That is left up to the law of the land and God. God gave governments the power to incarcerate or execute (Romans 13). It is not the Christian's job to do any of that. We are just to take the Gospel to every person—even murderers. We are commanded to love them!

Listen to what the Bible has to say about forgiveness:

- **Matthew 5:7** – *"Blessed are the merciful, for they will be shown mercy."*

- **Matthew 7:2** – *"For in the same way you judge others, you will be judged, and with the measure you use, it will be measured to you."*

- **Matthew 18:21-22** (KJV) – *"Then came Peter to him, and said, Lord, how oft shall my brother sin against me, and I forgive him? till seven times? Jesus saith unto him, I say not unto thee, Until seven times: but, Until seventy times seven."*

---

42 Printed in the *Deseret News*, Feb. 18, 1857; also reprinted in the *Journal of Discourses*, Vol. 4, pp. 219-20

- **Mark 11:25** – *"But when you are praying, first forgive anyone you are holding a grudge against, so that your Father in heaven will forgive your sins, too."*

- **Luke 17:3-4** (KJV) – *"Take heed to yourselves: If thy brother trespass against thee, rebuke him; and if he repent, forgive him. And if he trespass against thee seven times in a day, and seven times in a day turn again to thee, saying, I repent; thou shalt forgive him."*

- **Acts 10:43** – *"All the prophets testify about him that everyone who believes in him receives forgiveness of sins through his name."*

- **Acts 13:38-39** – *"Therefore, my brothers, I want you to know that through Jesus the forgiveness of sins is proclaimed to you. Through him everyone who believes is justified from everything you could not be justified from by the law of Moses."*

- **1 John 1:9** (KJV) – *"If we confess our sins, he is faithful and just to forgive us our sins, and to cleanse us from all unrighteousness."*

The Unpardonable Sin

In the *Miracle of Forgiveness* by Spencer W. Kimball, he writes, "Eternal life hangs in the balance awaiting the works of men. This process toward eternal life is a matter of achieving perfection. Living all the commandments guarantees total forgiveness of sins and assures one of exaltation through the perfection which comes by complying with the formula the Lord gave us....Being perfect means to triumph over sin. This is a mandate from the Lord. He is just and wise and kind. He would never require anything from his children which was not for their benefit and which was not attainable. Perfection therefore is an achievable goal."[43]

He says that perfection is an achievable goal, yet he goes on and states that if a person sins against the Holy Ghost and/or commits murder, he cannot *ever* achieve perfection. Therefore there is a point where it is *not* achievable. Here is what he says, "All sins but those

43 Spencer W. Kimball, *Miracle of Forgiveness*, pp. 208.

excepted by the Lord—basically, the sin against the Holy Ghost, and murder—will be forgiven to those who totally, consistently, and continuously repent in a genuine and comprehensive transformation of life....This earth life is the time to repent. We cannot afford to take any chances of dying an enemy to God."[44]

He mentions here the sin against the Holy Ghost...the unpardonable sin. Here are the verses from the Bible:

"And so I tell you, every sin and blasphemy will be forgiven men, but the blasphemy against the Spirit will not be forgiven. Anyone who speaks a word against the Son of Man will be forgiven, but anyone who speaks against the Holy Spirit will not be forgiven, either in this age or in the age to come."

— Matthew 12:31-32 (NIV)

Jesus spoke these words in response to an accusation made by the Pharisees. Envious of Jesus' power to heal and cast out devils, they accused Jesus of casting out the devils by the power of Satan. Jesus responded with a dire warning about blasphemy of the Holy Ghost. So exactly what is the blasphemy of the Holy Spirit?

To understand it, we need to examine exactly what it is that the Pharisees did.

1. They wanted to discredit Jesus in the eyes of those following Him. In effect, they were trying to recapture their power base from Jesus. Jesus was stealing much of their influence, and they wanted it back (Mark 15:10).

2. They knew that Jesus was doing these miracles in the power of the Holy Spirit. They knew He was true and taught truly (Mark 12:13-14, Luke 4:14). Yet they intentionally tried to deceive the people into believing that He was not.

3. They attributed the work of the Holy Spirit to Satan (Matthew 12:24).

---

44 Ibid, pp. 14-15.

4. They intentionally and deliberately did this even knowing full well it was wrong.

The blasphemy of the Holy Spirit is when you, knowing better, either attribute a work of the Holy Spirit to Satan or a work of Satan to the Holy Spirit. In order to do this, a person has to consciously reject Jesus Christ. Salvation is by grace through faith (Ephesians 2:8-9). If you have no faith, then it is impossible for you to be saved. We must believe Jesus Christ, who He is, and what He is in order to allow Him to save us. This is what the Pharisees were doing. They were deliberately rejecting Jesus Christ who was a work of the Holy Spirit.

> "As he considered this, an angel of the Lord appeared to him in a dream. "Joseph, son of David," the angel said, "do not be afraid to take Mary as your wife. For the child within her was conceived by the Holy Spirit."
>
> — Matthew 1:20 (NLT)

Jesus' birth, ministry, and life were works of the Holy Spirit. To reject Jesus as the Messiah, as our Savior, as our only way to Heaven is unpardonable. You will not go to Heaven unless you trust Jesus as your Savior. The Pharisees were denying this by their words and actions. How can they find forgiveness if they do not want forgiveness? If they would turn to Jesus, accept Him as their Savior—as the Messiah—then they too can find salvation and forgiveness.

The scary part about all this to me is that Mormon doctrine seems to reject Christ as our means to Heaven and focuses on our works to get to Heaven. How is this different than what the Pharisees were doing? The Pharisees wanted control over people's lives. They didn't like Jesus' teaching and the simple trust of Him to attain salvation. Mormon Doctrine seems to be very much in line with Pharisee Doctrine.

God's Forgiveness Versus Man's Works

Mormon Doctrine teaches that forgiveness must be earned. They believe that you must prove your worthiness for salvation and forgiveness. Christians, on the other hand, believe that forgiveness is something that you get when you seek it. It is freely given to those that want it.

Here are some of the Mormon views from Kimball's *Miracle of Forgiveness*:

1. "The reason is forthrightly stated by Nephi, '. . . There cannot any unclean thing enter into the kingdom of God . . .' (1 Ne. 15:34). And again, '. . . no unclean thing can dwell with God . . .' (1 Ne. 10:21). To the prophets the term *unclean* in this context means what it means to God. To man the word may be relative in meaning—one minute speck of dirt does not make a white shirt or dress unclean, for example. But to God who is perfection, cleanliness means moral and personal cleanliness. Less than that is, in one degree or another, uncleanliness and hence cannot dwell with God."[45]

2. "No one can repent on the cross, nor in prison, nor in custody. One must have the opportunity of committing wrong in order to be really repentant. The man in handcuffs, the prisoner in the penitentiary, the man as he drowns, or as he dies—such a man certainly cannot repent totally."[46]

3. "One of the most fallacious doctrines originated by Satan and propounded by man is that man is saved alone by the grace of God; that belief in Jesus Christ alone is all that is needed for salvation."[47]

4. "Perfection really comes through overcoming...Christ became perfect through overcoming. Only as we overcome shall we

---

45 Ibid, pp. 19.

46 Ibid, pp. 19.

47 Ibid, pp. 206-207.

become perfect and move toward godhood. As I have indicated previously, the time to do this is now, in mortality."[48]

5. "Your Heavenly Father has promised forgiveness upon total repentance and meeting all the requirements, but that forgiveness is not granted merely for the asking. There must be works-many works—and an all-out, total surrender, with a great humility and 'a broken heart and a contrite spirit.' It depends upon you whether or not you are forgiven, and when. It could be weeks, it could be years, it could be centuries before that happy day when you have the positive assurance that the Lord has forgiven you. That depends on your humility your sincerity, your works, your attitudes."[49]

This Mormon Doctrine takes salvation out of God's hands and puts it in man's hands. It takes any hope we have in a loving and forgiving God and places it in the ability of a man to do the proper works at the proper place and in the right time—an impossible task according to Scripture. Jesus did not come to judge or condemn the world (John 3:17). He came that, through Him, we all might be saved!

The Mormon view as expressed in Kimball's *Miracle of Forgiveness* has left a lot of people bereft of hope. How can a person ever be that perfect? And for many, who look back on a life spent outside of God and indulging the flesh, they are left wondering how could they ever dig themselves out of such a deep pit? This brings on depression and a sense of helplessness.

Christians, on the other hand, do good—not to earn forgiveness, but because they are already forgiven! They *get* to go to Church. They *get* to pray. They *get* to be a blessing to others. They *get* to serve God with their life. They don't have to. They *get* to. They do from a thankful and praiseful heart. They do good not to impress a holy God, but out of love for that Holy God. There is a huge difference. They continue to improve and deepen their repentance in the pursuit of a greater holiness. They know that the repentance that brings forgiveness is

---

48 Ibid, pp. 209-210.

49 Ibid, pp. 324-325.

simply a brokenhearted cry for hatred of sin, love for God's holiness, and trust in the God who 'justifies the ungodly' by faith apart from works (Romans 4:4-5). First John is written that "you may know that you have eternal life" (1 John 5:13).

> *"For by grace you have been saved through faith. And this is not your own doing; it is the gift of God, not a result of works, so that no one may boast. For we are his workmanship, created in Christ Jesus for good works, which God prepared beforehand, that we should walk in them."*
>
> — Ephesians 2:8-9

> *"Truly, truly, I say to you, whoever hears my word and believes him who sent me has eternal life. He does not come into judgment, but has passed from death to life."*
>
> — John 5:24

Ironically, Kimball robs his readers of the very thing that would most empower them to pursue holiness. With Jesus Christ, we have immediate and permanent forgiveness and eternal life. Sin is what separates us from God and, if we don't turn to Jesus, it will send us to Hell. It is sin that must be dealt with and it is for our sin that Jesus died on the cross.

Your works can never make up for a sin. You can't murder a man, run across the street, and save a child from drowning and expect the police not to arrest and prosecute you for the murder. A good deed never erases a bad deed. Sin must be paid for. This is what Jesus did on the cross for you and me.

He voluntarily went to a cross and suffered pain, yes, but more importantly, suffered rejection by God just so you and I could have the hope of salvation. Our sin debt was paid for on the cross; it is now just up to you to accept it.

Let me see if I can explain this. Let's say you did something wrong, it doesn't matter what it is, and the judge says you owe five trillion dollars in recompense. That seems excessive, but like sin, the debt is far beyond what you or I could ever pay while we are here on this earth. If, however, a man walks in and says, "Judge, I have a briefcase here with five trillion dollars in it. I would like to pay his debt and have you forgive his trespass." Two things would immediately have to happen before my money could pay off your debt.

First, the judge would have to accept it. He could say, "No. This is his fault. He has to pay." If that happens you would be stuck. God is the judge in this analogy, and He *did not* turn down what Jesus did on the cross for you and me. He accepted it! This is evidenced by the very fact that God raised Jesus from the dead. This shows that the judge (God) accepted the payment for our sin. So, let's say that the judge instead replies, "Very well. The debt must be paid and I'll accept your five trillion dollars as payment." If that happened, then there is one more thing that has to happen.

You have to accept the gift. You could say, "No. It's my fault. I want to pay it." This is something you will never be able to do. But, if you receive the man's gift and the judge accepts it, then your debt is wiped clean and you have found forgiveness.

It is as simple as that. There is no work that you could do to erase the debt of sin. It has to be paid for by someone able to pay for it. For sin, this could only be Jesus Christ. God accepted what He did on the cross and so must you. This and this alone will get you to Heaven. His righteousness is given to you and thus so has eternal life.

King David recognized the forgiving power of the Lord when he wrote in Psalm 103:3 (KJV), "Who forgiveth all thine iniquities; who healeth all thy diseases." The world starves for grace. Since leaving the Mormon Church, it has been amazing to see the difference in myself and my family. My world has been enlarged in ways that are difficult to explain. I now look at people so differently. I realize that there are people in prison that have done horrible things and want forgiveness. They are more broken and humble than the self-righteous religious people that I know. "I tell you, her many sins have been forgiven- for she loved much. But he who has been forgiven little loves little" (Luke 7:47).

People can and do change. If we do not believe in change, then we make God out to be a liar. God can make all things new. He can and does give people new hearts. Grace comes free of charge to people who do not deserve it, and I am one of those people. I think back to who I was in the Mormon Church. I thought I knew God, but I remember feeling self-righteous, resentful, unforgiving, and impatient. All of which are sins in God's eyes.

Experiencing God's grace and how He loves me just because I am me has changed me from the inside out. It has given me the peace that people do not understand. I feel loved. I am unafraid of judgment, because now I know my God is not here to judge me. He came to show me the way in a kind and loving way. I am so much more in love with my God because of His grace. I know that healing, forgiveness and any source of goodness and grace comes solely by the grace of God. No one can deserve or earn this. There is not one righteous, not even one according to Romans 3:10.

God says He forgives our sins and removes them as far away as the east is from the west. I love the following verses from the New King James Version:

- **1 John 1:9** – "If we confess our sins, He is faithful and just to forgive us our sins and to cleanse us from all unrighteousness."

- **Isaiah 43:25** – "I, even I, am He who blots out your transgressions for My own sake, and I WILL NOT REMEMBER YOUR SINS."

- **Jeremiah 31:34** – "For I will forgive their iniquity, and their sin I WILL REMEMBER NO MORE."

- **Hebrews 8:12** – "For I will be merciful to their unrighteousness, and their sins and their lawless deeds I WILL REMEMBER NO MORE."

- **Psalm 103:12** – "As far as the east is from the west, so far has He REMOVED OUR TRANSGRESSIONS FROM US."

When we refuse to forgive, the greatest damage is to our own heart. It is an indictment against our own soul since we must cast judgment from a position of condemnation and guilt infliction. We become self-righteous as if we have never done wrong. The Scriptures are correct on this issue. In Romans chapter 3, our guilt is determined. Verse 10 says that there is none righteous. Verse 12 teaches that in God's eyes there are none that are good, that all have gone out of the way. Verse 23 reminds us that everyone has sinned, no exceptions, that all have fallen short. But verse 19 really brings it home when it says that everyone is guilty before God. Everyone. You. Me. Everyone. How can we judge and condemn when we are already guilty? What damage does that do to our own hearts when we judge others already being guilty ourselves?

It is better to forgive. It is better to love.

Forgiving and Forgiven

We all must deal with forgiveness in some capacity. To begin with, we are all in need of forgiveness. Secondly, we will all find ourselves in a position when we need to grant forgiveness.

If you think about it, forgiveness is a form of worship. Not just any form, but a truer form of worship than we often recognize. The Lord wants us to learn this very important principal in our life as we will be faced with it at some point. Notice the following verse:

"Therefore, if you are offering your gift at the altar and there remember that your brother has something against you, leave your gift there in front of the altar. First go and be reconciled to your brother; then come and offer your gift."

— Matthew 5:24

Notice how this verse puts it. It isn't about your hurt or if a wrong has been done to you. It is about someone else's feeling of pain and injury that they *think* was your fault. To God, reconciliation is more important than worship. Before we go to God to worship, we need to be right with each other. God knows that unforgiveness blocks our ability to hear from Him. It does not matter who has done the offending, or who *thinks* they are in the right, if at all possible, go and reconcile.

Notice one other very important factor here. It never said how bad the sin or the wrong had to be in order to either seek or grant forgiveness. According to Scripture, forgiveness should be sought for any wrong...and granted for any wrong. Remember, the unpardonable sin spoken of in Mark 3 and Matthew 12 was ultimately about rejecting whom Jesus was. There is no sin that should not be forgiven including murder, adultery, and many other horrific and vile deeds.

We are designed by our Creator to worship, and to live our life for Him. We were created as vessels for his glory. Like a straw, we are to be emptied and pure so that the Lord can pour His Holy Spirit into us. We need to do this daily. Worship is not something to do once a year or once a week at church. We need to empty ourselves daily of all the junk and garbage that would keep us from being filled with the love, mercy, and grace of Jesus Christ. Like a light beaming down, Christ pours His love, power and energy into us. We want to be that clear vessel so the Lord can pour all of this into us.

The problem is that sin has gotten in our way. It is interesting that when Christ healed people, He always forgave their sins as well.

"Which is easier: to say, 'Your sins are forgiven,' or to say, 'Get up and walk'?"

— Luke 5:23

To prove that Jesus had the power to heal, he first forgave the man! We want to walk in His light, do we not? We want health in our bodies, energy, radiance and love. So we need to come to Jesus. Forgiveness is healing. It is a process of healing that is necessary for each of us. When there is any area of sin in your life, you will show symptoms physically, mentally, and emotionally. Too often I see physical signs of sin that forgiveness could heal. It is distressing since I know there is true healing. There are three parts to this healing process:

1. In order to be healed, the first thing we need to do is come to Jesus. This is always the first step. How can we seek healing if we never seek the great Physician?

2. We need to recognize our sin, and repent—turn from it. If we do not turn from our sin, our healing will be lost. 1 John 1:8 tells us, "We deceive ourselves when we say we have no sin." We all sin, and thankfully, Christ's mercies are new every day. So He is telling us that daily we need to receive His mercies.

Healing Exercise: Come to Jesus for your forgiveness and healing (2 Timothy 2:23). How? Write down any sins that you can think of on a piece of paper.

Once you have done this, take five minutes to realize how destructive your sins are. By themselves, even the least of them, is a death sentence to Hell without Jesus Christ. Our God who loves us so much took these sins upon Him so that we could be free. Romans 5:8 tells us, "But God demonstrates his own love for us in this: While we were still sinners, Christ died for us."

These sins block the light from going into our vessel. Something had to be done to remove them so we could have life. Take the time to come to Jesus. Mediate on the cross and God's love for you. Seek forgiveness for each one of your sins. After you have done this you are forgiven! Your vessel is clean from your own sin, including unforgiveness. Be warned, any unforgiveness you hold in your heart for other people will block God's blessings in our life (Matthew 6:14-15).

3. After we are healed, we need to forgive and heal others. If you cannot forgive, it is impossible to properly seek forgiveness for yourself. It is like being stranded on a deserted island and refusing to get aboard a rescue boat because you don't like the people on it.

Healing Exercise: Now, on a separate sheet of paper, write the name of the person or event you have forgiven—or need to forgive. Place the paper with your sins on top of their name. Write the word love on top of both papers. 1 Peter 4:8 says, "Above all, love each other deeply, because love covers over a multitude of sins."

Do you realize when you call for blessings on another person that you bring those same blessings to yourself? This is true whether it is a blessing or a curse. God says that He causes the sun to rise on the just and the unjust (Matthew 5:45).

Another helpful tool in forgiving others is to understand that everyone has a story. We really have not walked in someone else's shoes, and until we do, we can't pretend to understand them. Hurt people, hurt people.

To use an extreme example, I will tell you a story that took place during the 1994 Genocide in Rwanda where the Hutus killed about 700,000 people, mostly Tutsis. The Hutus had not healed from their own past hurts and feelings of injustice. These unhealed wounds contributed to their actions. You see, the Hutus had been slaves to the Tutsis before 1959, and even though it was under Belgian rule, the Hutus perceived their slavery and mistreatment to be the fault of the Tutsis. The Hutus unforgiveness led to the genocide.

Chantal, a Christian woman, suffered the loss of her whole family when a neighboring Hutu murdered them. When she found out who had done it, she went to visit him in prison. And there, she asks *him* for forgiveness for her desire to kill his family in revenge! She is a true follower of Christ! She knew that as a person thinks in her heart so is she in God's eyes (Proverbs 23:7). She forgives this man and brings not only healing to him, but to herself as well. The two of them have even maintained a friendship because Chantal was first willing to forgive and then ask for forgiveness.

Can you imagine the very person that killed your whole family living next door to you? In the documentary *As we Forgive*, the perpetrators are released back onto the streets and will be living as neighbors next to the survivors of the families they murdered and slaughtered out of revenge, anger, pain, and hurt.

Something I want you to remember is that our God is a just God. He does not let the guilty go free like our justice system that fails us so many times. No, He convicts the heart, and many of the perpetrators suffer greatly because of what they have done. The worst thing in life for those who live in guilt is to have to live with who they are...every

WHO CAN BE FORGIVEN?

day. It might look like everything is okay on the outside, but trust your God. He is just.

Prayer of Healing

"Lord, thank You that You are a God of hope and healing. We thank You for your Amazing Grace! We are all lost, but by Your grace, Lord Jesus, we find our way and we are saved. Thank You that You forgive anyone that calls on your name and seeks forgiveness. Thank You for dying on the cross while we were still sinners. I pray for all to find the truth and become *free* by Your grace. Amen."

Do You Trust God?

"And we know that in all things God works for the good of those who love him, who have been called according to his purpose."

— Romans 8:28

D o you trust God? It seems odd to even contemplate such a question. Our natural knee-jerk reaction is to say, "Of course I trust God? What Christian wouldn't?" Yet our behavior and actions often demonstrate a rather stark lack of trust in God.

The Lord God has given us many promises; He is true and faithful and will keep His promises. In Deuteronomy 4:31, He makes this clear, "For the LORD your God is a merciful God; he will not abandon or destroy you or forget the covenant with your forefathers, which he confirmed to them by oath."

The question boils down to this: do we trust God and believe His promises or are we going to treat His grace as meaningless?

"I do not treat the grace of God as meaningless. For if keeping the law could make us right with God, then there was no need for Christ to die."

— Galatians 2:21

Our God is a God we can trust. He has kept His Word. We only need to look to prophecy to understand this. What's more, He came to earth in the flesh to reconcile us to Him (John 1:14). Jesus came as God in human form to establish His church and the new covenant. He founded His church and was pleased with it. This Church did not involve temples or required ordinances in order to get to Heaven. Initially, it consisted of twelve men who shared one thing in common. They believed in Jesus.

Since God has come down and established His church, there would never be a need to restore His church. In fact, Jesus said to beware of anyone who came later proclaiming to be Him or represent Him. He knew that false prophets would arise to lead people away.

Can we trust God to keep His Church? Does God's destiny rest in the hands of man? Or can God preserve His Word and His Church? God does not change His covenants and promises. In His word, the Bible, He never asks, mentions or requires that an individual go to the temple in order to receive these promises.

Some of God's promises are:

- **Psalm 145:18-19** – He answers our prayers: *"The LORD is near to all who call on him, to all who call on him in truth. He fulfills the desires of those who fear him; He hears their cry and saves them. The LORD watches over all who love him, but all the wicked he will destroy."*

- **Romans 8:38-39** – He gives us Assurance: *"For I am convinced that neither death nor life, neither angels nor demons, neither the present nor the future, nor any powers, neither height nor depth, nor anything else in all creation, will be able to separate us from the love of God that is in Christ Jesus our Lord."*

- **Romans 10:12-13** – He Blesses and Saves us: *"For there is no difference between Jew and Gentile—the same Lord is Lord of* *all and richly blesses all who call on him, for, Everyone who calls on the name of the Lord will be saved."*

- **John 1:12** – He calls us His children: *"Yet to all who received him, to those who believed in his name, he gave the right to become children of God"*

- **1 Corinthians 1:7** – He reminds us of His return and tells us we lack nothing: *"Therefore you do not lack any spiritual gift as you eagerly wait for our Lord Jesus Christ to be revealed."*

- **Hebrews 9:28** – He has promised to take away our sins and provide us with salvation: *"So Christ was sacrificed once to take away the sins of many people; and He will appear a second time, not to bear sin, but to bring salvation to those who are waiting for him."*

With all of these promises, we can trust that when God makes a promise He keeps it. If God were on trial, we would find that He has never changed, broken or modified a covenant. No less than Jesus declared this in Matthew 5:17, "Do not think that I have come to abolish the Law or the Prophets; I have not come to abolish them but to fulfill them." You can trust God, because He isn't trying to keep salvation from you. He begs you to come to Him and receive it! Jesus came for the lost—He is our searching Savior! Why then would he return secretly to Joseph Smith or any other prophet and restore a gospel that was never lost? It doesn't make sense.

God is not a respecter a persons. In other words, God is totally sovereign, giving salvation freely to whom He will, based on nothing more than His great love. God doesn't love Moses, Paul, David, or Daniel more than He loves you! His grace is still present and ready to forgive even when His people sin. Paul says in Romans 5:20 that where sin increased, grace increased all the more.

Was the Priesthood Ever Lost?

The Mormon faith believes that God's true church was lost from the earth due to sinful men and needed restoration. In some way, they believe that God's promise in Matthew 16:18 was broken. God promised that hell would not prevail against the Church. If the church had been removed, then His promise has been broken.

The Mormons feel that Elijah was more than a prophet. They believe that He returned to the earth—appearing to Joseph Smith—to restore a lost priesthood. They use Elijah's story as an opportunity to interject their own scripture and their own perceived truth. Although Mormon teaching points to portions of this exchange on Mt. Carmel as proof of Elijah's special status (1 Kings 18), nowhere does God even mention or hint about the priesthood. The Prophet Elijah was bringing a message to the people about God, not about the priesthood.

Furthermore, nowhere in Scripture is Elijah tied to the priesthood in any form or fashion. The Mormon view is a complete fabrication. In fact, Elijah mocked Baal's priesthood with all their rituals, chants, and ceremonies to get Baal's attention. But when it was Elijah's turn to get God's attention, he prayed a very simple prayer, and God heard it.

The attempt by the priests of Baal to get their false god's attention reminds me so much of the foolish Temple ordinances Mormons are required to observe. Why must they do all these silly rituals? Perhaps their god is sleeping? Do they not understand that God is so powerful that He can cause water to be set on fire? God does not need our rituals to enter His kingdom. He desires only a trusting heart. The Mormon interpretation of this story shows that they do not understand the Scripture or Elijah's purpose.

Elijah's name means, "The Lord is my God." And that was his ministry and message. We are to trust God, not add to His Scripture to create a way to work out our salvation with Him. Our God is Big! He is sovereign and limitless. Nothing stops Him. His Word does not return void, nor has it ever left man. His Gospel never needed a restoration because He has never left us. To believe that God needed man to restore His gospel here on earth is to believe that God is not powerful enough to last forever. His true believers know He can do all things.

God does not need "ordinances" to take care of His people. Nor does He require a woman to be married to a priesthood holder in order to be saved—as the Mormons would have you believe. A woman need not worry if she is alone and does not marry. Her salvation is dependent upon her *trust* in her God.

Look at Esther who was very much alone and was facing destruction along with all her people. Esther walked in faith, fasted and called upon God for direction. God saved not only Esther, but all of the Jews that would have perished by the hands of Haman. You see, God never leaves his people, man or woman. He is Father to all.

When we do not receive the peace from trusting in Jesus Christ, we will look for it in other places, like trying to "seal" our family together. We have not trusted God's promises or received the peace that only He can give. We try to invent other means and methods to replace what only the Holy Spirit can give (love, joy, peace…etc.).

When God can't be counted upon to preserve His end of the bargain, there must be something else that we cling to, something else we fall back on and place our trust. For Mormons, it is the Mormon Prophet. The following is an excerpt from a Mormon apologist website:

"I believe that this Church is the only Church with authority from God to perform saving ordinances such as baptism.

"Authority given to man by God to act in His name is called the priesthood. Throughout time, God has called special individuals to be prophets. Prophets are given the priesthood authority by God and are instructed to teach the people about the gospel of Jesus Christ. Thus men like Noah, Abraham, and Moses had this authority to act in God's name. But, because we men are silly, these prophets were consistently rejected. When a prophet was rejected, this priesthood authority was lost from the Earth for a time (known as a time of apostasy) until God saw fit to once again call a new prophet to restore what was lost.

"So mankind needed to wait until God saw fit to call a new prophet. The wait lasted until 1820. In spring of that year God and Jesus Christ personally appeared to Joseph Smith to call him as a new prophet – a prophet to restore what had been lost, a prophet specifically given the priesthood authority necessary to once again establish Christ's Church here on the earth.

"And thus it is that Christ's Church was restored (not reformed) and is now on the earth again with a prophet, with apostles, and with the priesthood authority necessary to perform baptisms. The Heavens are still open, God talks to His children in our day."[50]

God has never, never allowed the world to be without Him. Jesus' promise that He would build his church and the gates of Hell would not prevail against it has *not* been broken. The Word of God, in its entirety, has been preserved from the days of Jesus Christ. There has never been a time since Jesus Christ when there has not been a man or woman of God that has stood up and proclaimed the Word of God *from* the Word of God.

Even in Elijah's day, this prophet was not as alone and bereft as he thought. Several times he whines to God about being the only one left who served God. Finally, God slaps him across the face with a cold hard fact. In 1 Kings 19:18, God says to Elijah, "Yet I reserve seven thousand in Israel—all whose knees have not bowed down to Baal and whose mouths have not kissed him." Then to prove that his fears were unfounded, God gave him a mission to find a successor, Elisha. Elijah, a man, couldn't see it, but God did. The priesthood wasn't dead or removed. It continued just as God promised. God is no respecter of persons and will provide for all His children. God calls his Word food and He is our life giving water. He would not take this away.

Just because a prophet is rejected, killed even, does not mean that God removes anything from earth. Our great God says He will never leave us nor forsake us (Hebrews 13:5). Never! To say that He removed the priesthood because people rejected the prophets would be to say our God is a liar. God did not remove Peter because the people had killed Jesus. And even when Peter was killed, God did not remove his influence on others, his converts, and the churches he started. They all continued. It *has* continued to this day.

---

50 Curtis Wiederhold, *Why Mormons*, (www.whatdomormonsbelieve.com/2008/06/why-mormons/)

The author in the above excerpt admits that 'the heavens are still open.' He means from the days of Joseph Smith, but I say from the days of Jesus Christ and even from Adam and Eve. God has never abandoned His creation, taken a vacation, or sulked in a corner of Heaven because some 'silly men' murdered His prophets. He has always been at work and He promised that if at any time we sought Him, He would be found (Matthew 7:7).

The only restoration that was needed was a means to allow people to enter into the presence of God again. Adam blew this. He had direct fellowship with God. He spent time in the presence of God. But he sinned and was separated from God. In Matthew 17:11, Jesus tells us that Elijah would come to restore all things. What things? A way to be in the presence of God. Jesus then said that Elijah had already come, in the form of John the Baptist, and had already been rejected. Yet restoration happened! In John 1:29, John stood on the banks of the Jordan River, saw Jesus, and announced, "Behold! The lamb of God which takes away the sin of the world!"

John did his job! John prepared the way for Jesus, who then in turn died on a cross and thus provided all of us with a means of reconciling (restoration) with God! We can now go to Heaven through our faith in Jesus Christ and stand in God's presence. Even though there were sinful men at that time that rejected John the Baptist and killed him, his message wasn't lost. Just because man's capacity for evil seems limitless, it cannot ever match in power the love, grace, and mercy of our Savior! Man cannot destroy something that God builds unless He wills it. John's tragic death allowed for Jesus to increase because John needed to decrease. Nothing was lost. In fact, it was Jesus' death that was *necessary* for restoration. Salvation was not lost. It was given.

> *"To the only God our Savior be glory, majesty, power and authority, through Jesus Christ our Lord, before all ages, now and forevermore! Amen."*
>
> — Jude 1:25

Mormons are confused because they have discounted the Bible, and they have injected their own scripture. This leads to a belief that was nowhere even hinted at in the Bible: the belief that Elijah came to restore a lost priesthood in order to seal marriages and families. They do not understand scripture. Jesus, God on earth, never sealed marriages or families. God says in scripture that there will be no marriage in heaven. Matthew 22:29-32 says, "Jesus replied, 'You are in error because you do not know the Scriptures or the power of God. At the resurrection people will neither marry nor be given in marriage; they will be like the angels in heaven. But about the resurrection of the dead—have you not read what God said to you, 'I am the God of Abraham, the God of Isaac, and the God of Jacob?' He is not the God of the dead but of the living.'"

You see, Elijah's role and whole purpose was the same as John the Baptist's role. John was to prepare the way and point people to God. Elijah did nothing on his own merit, nor can we do anything on our own merit. Search this out! Nowhere in the Bible is there even a reference on "sealings or sealing power" these are Mormon terms.

Trust God or a Man?

"It is better to trust in the LORD than to put confidence in man. It is better to trust in the LORD than to put confidence in princes."

— Psalm 118:8-9 (KJV)

Paul, another great prophet and teacher, was teaching and healing in Lystra. The people there thought he was more than a prophet and began worshiping him. Startled and worried at such a preposterous reaction to how God was using him, he asks:

"Men, why are you doing this? We too are only men, human like you. We are bringing you good news, telling you to turn from these worthless things to the living God, who made heaven and earth and sea and everything in them."

— Acts 14:15

All great prophets who have come before us, point the way to Jesus, our Messiah. They have taught us to trust in Him alone. They do not teach us about becoming our own god, nor do they teach us to look to our families for our salvation or to the prophets themselves. Paul, one of the greatest prophets, understood Jesus' words to mean that marriage was not mandatory. So in 1 Corinthians 7:8-9 he tells us that there are times when it is better not to marry: "Now to the unmarried and the widows I say: It is good for them to stay unmarried, as I am. But if they cannot control themselves, they should marry, for it is better to marry than to burn with passion." For Mormons, marriage is an essential part of their salvation—particularly having their marriage sealed within their Temple.

Who should we trust? The Mormon prophets who claim that we must be sealed within the Temple to attain salvation or Jesus Christ who pointed the Sadducees back to the Scriptures? Which is more trustworthy?

God gave us a book. We call this book the Bible. The Bible is the Word of God. When God gives His Word, it is something we can trust in.

"And the brethren immediately sent away Paul and Silas by night unto Berea: who coming thither went into the synagogue of the Jews. These were more noble than those in Thessalonica, in that they received the word with all readiness of mind, and searched the scriptures daily, whether those things were so."

— Acts 17:10-11 (KJV)

Apparently, we are to trust what God said more than what man says. We are to search the Scriptures to find out if what man says lines up with what God says. God wants us to trust Him! If a prophet points us in any other direction than that of God's commands and promises, they are a false prophet, not abiding in truth. They are using deception and hiding behind the name of Christ. The truth is not in them. John 1:24 says, "If someone claims, 'I know God,' but doesn't obey God's commandments, that person is a liar and is not living in the truth."

The Mormon prophets point members of the church in many different directions other than resting in God's promises and allowing God to be the sovereign God that He is. To teach that God's true church needed to be restored is to point God's children in a different direction, a direction that does not trust God as the sovereign and great God that He is.

Will God Allow the Church to Be Removed?

The Mormon view is in direct opposition to God's view. God won't allow His church or His people, to be lost or removed from the earth. Let's take a good look at the parable of the Weeds in Matthew 13:

> *"Jesus told them another parable: 'The kingdom of heaven is like a man who sowed good seed in his field. But while everyone was sleeping, his enemy came and sowed weeds among the wheat, and went away. When the wheat sprouted and formed heads, then the weeds also appeared. The owner's servants came to him and said, 'Sir, didn't you sow good seed in your field? Where then did the weeds come from?' 'An enemy did this,' he replied. The servants asked him, 'Do you want us to go and pull them up?' 'No,' he answered, 'because while you are pulling the weeds, you may root up the wheat with them. Let both grow together until the harvest. At that time I will tell the harvesters: First collect the weeds and tie them in bundles to be burned; then gather the wheat and bring it into my barn.'"*

> — Matthew 13:24-30

It says right here that despite sinners growing up alongside those who trust God, He didn't move to destroy these sinners. Instead, He allowed them to grow side by side until the time of the end. He won't remove the church and He hasn't removed the church.

We do not have a God that is like our imperfect justice system where the innocent are punished and the guilty go free. It does not, therefore, depend on man's desire or effort, but on God's mercy (Romans 9:16).

He would not remove His Word or His Holy Spirit from among us when He has promised us that His Holy Spirit would remain with us. God has promised eternal life to all who believe in Christ. As a guarantee that He will keep His promise, He has sent the Holy Spirit to indwell in the believer until the day of redemption. Remember, He has identified you as His own, guaranteeing that you will be saved on the day of redemption (Ephesians 4:30). Our loving Heavenly Father would not remove anything that He has promised. Our God is a forgiving and merciful God. Daniel 9:9 says, "The Lord our God is merciful and forgiving, even though we have rebelled against Him."

God is the loving parent eager to open that door for us when we stop trying to do it through our effort and works and instead accept His help. That requires trust which is closely tied to faith. He won't remove the Church. He won't allow it until He is ready to call *all* of His saints home.

What is Faith in Jesus Christ?

Faith in Jesus Christ believes all of what God has promised. Faith in God does not try to rely on your own merits. 1Timothy 6:21 says, "Some people have wandered from the faith by following such foolishness." You see, we take our faith with us wherever we go. This is how we show we trust in God. We have no fear because we know God is with us. And in Ephesians, we learn it is only through trust in Jesus and not by our works that we are saved:

"God saved you by His grace when you believed. And you can't take credit for this; it is a gift from God."

— Ephesians 2:8

It is important to stop for a bit and look at faith. Trust and faith go hand in hand. You can't have faith and not trust. You can't trust someone and not have faith in them.

Faith (n.) - *confidence or trust in a person or thing: faith in another's ability.*[51]

Trust (n.) - *reliance on the integrity, strength, ability, surety, etc., of a person or thing; confidence.*[52]

This faith was delivered once and for all. The work of our Savior was completed. Jesus said in John 19:30 while on the cross, "It is finished." This means that Jesus set out to establish His victory over the enemy and death. He conquered the grave.

True faith and trust is reliance upon God and Him only. If you trust something else—such as your own power, works, pastor, priest, prophet, or church—you have diminished your trust and faith in God. Can we say that partial faith is faith? If I only trust someone partially, can I truly say, "I trust him?" No. I can't.

If I am to place *all* of my faith and trust in Jesus, how then can I begin to believe that I must contribute to my own salvation? Or how can I trust an ordinance or some other means of salvation if Jesus has all of my trust? Do you see the problem?

Once a man has captured some of my trust for things such as salvation, righteousness, access to God, and service, I have, by default, diminished my trust in Jesus and God. One of the main differences between a true prophet and a false prophet is that a true prophet of God does not require, ask for, or want your trust in him. He only wants you to trust God. He likes for you to check what he says against the Scriptures. He doesn't want you to rely upon his word, but upon God's Word.

A false prophet will try to steal your trust. He wants your faith to be upon his words and his commands. This brings him power over your life and, subsequently, gives him control over your life. This is very dangerous. This is how cults are formed. Even in this book—as much as I want it to be a blessing for you, you should still check it out against the authority of the Bible. Beware of false prophets that seek to inadvertently cause you to distrust the Lord without you even being aware of it.

---

51 www.dictionary.reference.com/browse/faith.

52 Ibid.

"But there were also false prophets among the people, just as there will be false teachers among you. They will secretly introduce destructive heresies, even denying the sovereign Lord who bought them—bringing swift destruction on themselves. <u>Many will follow their shameful ways and will bring the way of truth into disrepute</u>. In their greed these teachers will exploit you with stories they have made up."

— 2 Peter 2:1-3

God demonstrated time and again in the Bible, both Old and New Testaments, that He never leaves His people. He is faithful and quick to forgive. God even said as much himself when Moses asked to see the Glory of God, the Lord proclaimed:

"And he [The Lord] passed in front of Moses, proclaiming, 'The LORD, the LORD, the compassionate and gracious God, slow to anger, abounding in love and faithfulness, maintaining love to thousands, and forgiving wickedness, rebellion and sin. Yet he does not leave the guilty unpunished; he punishes the children and their children for the sin of the parents to the third and fourth generation.'"

— Exodus 34:6-7

Every generation has an encounter with God. That is because He never leaves us. None of these encounters create a new gospel. If they are true encounters, they reinforce God's plan and remind people of His promises. They always point to Jesus' return, not to a man. Until then, we have the promise from Jesus Himself that He will always be with us until the end of the world (Matthew 28:20).

Trust in God, not man, is what we need. The Mormon Church would have you believe that you are not saved unless you go through all their ordinances. If you question whether or not you have eternal life, listen to God's Word and decide who to trust:

1. **Romans 3:23** – God tells us that we have all sinned and fallen short of the glory of God.

2. **Romans 6:23** – Every one of us deserves to die. *"The wages of sin is death, but the gift of God is eternal life through Jesus Christ our Lord"*

3. **Romans 5:8** – Jesus Christ, God in flesh became sin for us so we would not have to die, but have eternal life. *"God demonstrates His love for us in this: while we were still sinners, Christ died for us."* What love! You can trust that kind of love. This is the kind of love that says "I will do whatever it takes to save you, please come follow me."

4. **Matthew 26:32** – The even better news is that this is not the end of the story. Christ rose from the dead proving victorious over the grave!! He promised that and fulfilled it!

5. **1 Peter 1:3** – In His great mercy He has given us new birth into a living hope through the resurrection of Jesus Christ from the dead. We can trust our God. He is good and victorious.

6. **John 3:16** – If we place our faith in Him, trusting His death on the cross to pay for our sins, we will be forgiven and receive the promise of eternal life in heaven. *"For God so loved the world that He gave His one and only Son so that anyone who believes in Him will not perish but have eternal life."*

7. **Romans 10:9** – *"If you confess with your mouth, 'Jesus is Lord,' and believe in your heart that God raised Him from the dead, you will be saved."* Faith alone in the finished work of Christ on the cross is the only true path to eternal life!

You Can Trust Jesus and Know You Are Going to Heaven

If you want to accept Jesus Christ as your Savior, here is a sample prayer you can say to Him—remember, saying this prayer or any other prayer will not save you. It is only "trusting" in Christ and believing in

Him that saves you. This prayer is simply a way to express to God your faith in Him and thank Him for providing for your salvation:

"God, I know that I am a sinner and deserve punishment. I believe Jesus Christ took the punishment that I deserve so that, through faith in Him, I could be forgiven and saved. I place my trust in You, Lord, for salvation. Thank You for Your wonderful grace and forgiveness—the gift of eternal life! Amen!"

It really is this simple with God. It is man and his false doctrine that complicates grace and salvation. All the hard work was done by Jesus Christ on the cross. This is why salvation is a gift. It isn't something you work for or must be deserving of. It is already free. It is already available. We just must accept it!

The word "trust" in the Bible literally means a bold, confident, sure security or action based on that security. Psalms 86:2 challenges us this way, "Guard my life, for I am devoted to you. You are my God; save your servant who trusts in you." Trusting in God holds Him to be true and faithful in fulfilling His promises in all circumstances, even during tough times.

As we walk out our faith daily, we begin to experience His peace, which builds our trust in Him.

"You will keep in peace him whose mind is steadfast, because he trusts in you."

— Isaiah 26:3

"Trust in the LORD with all your heart and lean not on your own understanding."

— Proverbs 3:5

It is the Lord in whom we are to trust, not ourselves, our plans, and certainly not man's plan for us. We trust in the Lord because He and He alone is truly trustworthy. His Word is trustworthy (Psalm 93:5).

Churches have always been corrupted when men steal in and then steal our trust from the Lord. This will undoubtedly continue to be so. Religion, in general, is what Christ despises. There will always be conflict between good and evil and between believers in and the spirit of antichrist. Conflict will arise between these opposing forces all of our lives until our Savior Himself returns and rules during the end times.

You need not fear; God will never leave you. No matter what you are going through, our God is a good God. We can trust Him. He will hold our hand and comfort us no matter what storm is in our life. Throughout the Bible, God tells us to have no fear for He is with us.

"Even though I walk through the valley of the shadow of death, I fear no evil, for You are with me."

— Psalm 23:4

A Prayer of Healing

"Thank You, Jesus, that You are all powerful, that You will never leave us nor forsake us, and that You died for us, even while we were sinning. Lord God, please forgive me for thinking that I could somehow work out my own salvation. You said in 2 Corinthians 6:2, *"Behold, now is the acceptable time, behold, now is the day of salvation."* You are in control, and You have never left Your throne as it says in Daniel 7:9. I come to You, Father, in worship, and I trust You completely, allowing You to take control of my life. I allow You to take control of all the people in my life, Lord, knowing You will work all things out for my good because I love You. Thank You for dying on the cross for me and removing my sin. Thank You for allowing me to cast my burdens on You, for You cause them to be light for me. Please forgive me, Lord, for being involved in any rituals that would cause me to believe that this is what it takes to bring Your life giving water. A simple prayer is all You ask. My prayer is that You come into my life and be my only God. I will put nothing before You. In the name of Jesus, amen."

Freedom versus Control

"There is no fear in love. But perfect love drives out fear,
because fear has to do with punishment. The one who fears is
not made perfect in love."

— 1 John 4:18

Freedom and Love

How would you describe love? If you must continually earn someone's love, would you call it true love? If love is dependent upon your ability to be worthy of it, then love is something different than what is taught in the Bible. Imagine trying to be worthy of the love of a sinless, perfect, holy, and all knowing God. Is that even possible? Even if it were, we would live constantly in fear of wondering if we somehow measure up. How does a person know that he or she is really good enough in the eyes of such holiness?

Jesus loved freely without the need to control us with fear. We are called to be like Christ and therefore love as Jesus loved. What does His perfect love look like?

First of all, His love does not involve the fear of being rejected by Him in any way. Jesus' love is unconditional. So to love as Jesus loves, to walk in His love, requires an unconditional love. In order to love as God loves, we must not make our love dependent upon, or limited to, anything the object of our love does or does not do. In other words, we cannot think or say, "If you do this I will love you, or if you don't do this I will not love you." This is controlling and manipulative.

To follow in the steps of God's love also involves teaching others the perfect way that love operates. If we teach people that God is conditional in His love, we are not teaching pure doctrine unpolluted by man. We see Biblical love demonstrated in Hosea's reconciliation with his wife in Hosea 3:1, "The LORD said to me, 'Go, show your love to your wife again, though she is loved by another man and is an adulteress. Love her as the LORD loves the Israelites, though they turn to other gods and love the sacred raisin cakes.'" God's love wasn't conditional then, and it isn't conditional now.

Manipulation is a subtle type of control intended to make someone do something they would not normally do of their own free will. In order to quietly or secretly manipulate someone, it is imperative that they do not feel controlled. Instead, you manipulate their desires (fleshly and spiritual) to create a fear that pushes them in the direction you want them to go. For example, you can manipulate someone's desire to know God by telling him or her that God wants them to do something in particular and if they don't, something bad will happen. Fearing the 'bad' thing, they will follow your instructions. Control is not from God at all. It is from the enemy.

If God's love depends on ordinances or performance, then when those ordinances or performances are not met His love ceases. If love does not depend on anything, then love never ceases.

Mormons practice this subtle type of control by manipulating the process in which a person can come to God. If a person does not meet all the requirements in order to go to the Temple, and from there remain a perfect follower of the rules, then they might as well not come to the Temple since God will reject them anyway. The fear of rejection is one of the most primal fears that humanity shares. Who wants God to hate them? No one! Boyd K. Packer asks a question and then answers it according to Mormon doctrine: "'Can we not be saved without going through with all those ordinances, etc.?' 'I would answer, No, not the fullness of salvation.'"[53]

On that same page, Packer quotes Brigham Young, "Let me give you a definition in brief. Your endowment is to receive all those ordinances in the House of the Lord, which are necessary for you, after you have departed this life, to enable you to walk back to the presence of the Father, passing the angels who stand as sentinels, being able to give them the key words, the signs and tokens, pertaining to the Holy Priesthood, and gain your eternal exaltation in spite of earth and hell."[54]

Scripture tells us that nothing can separate us from the love of God. "For I am convinced that neither death nor life, neither angels nor demons, neither the present nor the future, nor any powers, neither height nor depth, nor anything else in all creation, will be able to separate us from the love of God that is in Christ Jesus our Lord" Romans 8:38-39.

I also read Packer's book while preparing myself to go to the Temple. My desire to go to the Temple was based on the same desire of all LDS people, and that was to receive salvation. It was only in the Temple where we could receive the secret information required to go to the highest heaven and be with my family and my Savior for eternity.

The fear of not being able to be saved and see my Savior drove me to the temple. It wasn't love; it was fear. I went out of duty, thinking this was the only place I could be close to God and His receive salvation. This is not what the Bible teaches us. The Bible makes it clear that simply asking saves us and that God's presence is with us constantly. We can learn from the story of how God used Moses to set the slaves free in Old Testament times. Moses didn't make anyone come with him. Through God, he offered freedom to all the people. The choice was theirs to make and theirs alone. Salvation is just like that. Coming into God's presence and attaining salvation is something we must simply choose. It is free. In the New Testament, Jesus said, "So if

---

53 Boyd K. Packer, *The Holy Temple*, page 34.

54 Ibid.

the Son sets you free, you will be free indeed" (John 8:36). God hates bondage in any form.

God Wants to Set You Free

God sets His people free.

Beginning in Exodus, we learn how God works to free His people. Exodus chapter one begins with the slavery of the Israelite people. The new king was afraid that the Israelites were too numerous and would possibly join with their enemies in a time of battle. So he put taskmasters over God's people in order to control them. The irony was that this act made the Jews more numerous, not less (Exodus 1:9-11).

Exodus 1:12 it says, "But the more they were oppressed, the more they multiplied and spread." In other words, when we remove freedom from people and try to control them in any direction, the very thing we are trying to prevent will likely happen. Paul teaches us this principal in Romans when he talks about the law.

"I found that the very commandment that was intended to bring life actually brought death. For sin, seizing the opportunity afforded by the commandment, deceived me, and through the commandment put me to death."

— Romans 7:10-11

Christians are not supposed to be a bound up, inhibited, and imprisoned people. The exact opposite should be true. Believers in Christ are supposed to be the ones that walk in freedom. "Then you will know the truth, and the truth will set you free" John 8:32.

It was for our freedom that Christ came to earth and died, conquering death and setting us free. The people in Egypt were set free from their bondage in Egypt by trusting in God. We must learn from this and walk in the freedom given by the power of God. Freedom comes when we are set free, and this will only come when we realize that we are in bondage. We need to walk free from the bondage of legalism, our bad past, fear, guilt, and shame. We have become spiritual slaves because of sin. The Lord has provided a process to set us free. Exodus is all about how the people were set free, but their story is merely a larger version of each of our own. In it, we discover how God wants to set us free.

We get set free when we take a risk with God. Moses' mother had to take a risk when she put her baby in a basket and set him free down the river. The slaves also had to take a risk by listening to God and following Moses into the Promised Land. We must learn and understand that we cannot do this on our own power. We must recognize our need for the power of God to be with us. You must face your fears and obstacles. Moses had to face the obstacle of Pharaoh in order to free the people. He trusted God and realized that God was and still is bigger than any ruler or church organization.

We must face the truth and not be in denial any longer about our situation, whatever situation it may be that God needs to set you free from. There can be no more denial. You will never be set free until you recognize that you are behind bars.

"But I'm not behind bars," you may say. Don't be fooled in to thinking that there is only one kind of bondage. These bars could be anything for you. They could be feelings of unforgiveness, selfishness, fear or lack of faith. For me, when I was in the Mormon faith, I didn't even realize I had been bound. I was simply feeling the symptoms—symptoms of guilt, control, anger and resentment. I didn't understand that the Mormon doctrine of manipulation by rules was causing me to feel the need to control others—such as my own family.

I had no idea that you could be righteous and free at the same time. I thought you needed to be perfect and do all that was required in a church setting to get approval from God. This took away my freedom to find righteousness in Jesus Christ as I sought it within myself and the control mechanisms of the church.

You must decide what your bars are so that you can be set free. Look deeply into your life to see what is causing your depression, anxiety, or fear. Quite possibly you are involved in legalism or a church that is not practicing God's truth. You need the key of understanding and truth to get out of your prison. God says my truth sets you free. "Then you will know the truth, and the truth will set you free" (John 8:32).

In order to be set free by God's truth, you must search His word—the Bible—alone and rely on God's Holy Spirit, and He will bring clarity and truths that will set you free. Only then can you step out in faith and listen for God's direction. The Hebrews did not listen to Moses' message of freedom, even though they were in bondage. They relied on their emotions to direct them. Your emotions alone will not set you free. Moses also let his emotions get in the way when he tried to stop the Hebrews from fighting with each other. His murder of the Egyptian beforehand ruined his influence because he had acted out of emotion. He intended to do the right thing, but emotions will cause us to act outside the will of God. He needed God to guide Him on the right path, which meant being guided in truth, not feelings.

When God called Moses in the desert, he felt inadequate to do what God called him to do—and he was right. It was God's adequacy that caused him to be able to lead the people to freedom. We alone will never be adequate. We are not perfect. "There is no one righteous—not even one" Romans 3:10. Our freedom comes in recognizing our limitations and allowing God to work through us in order to accomplish what He wants us to do.

As Moses has said, "Who am I, God?" He didn't yet understand his purpose or power with God. Moses was afraid, so he escaped to the desert. The way to freedom is not through escape, but with a direct relationship with God. God did not give up on Moses. He used the time Moses spent in the desert to prepare him for the great work of setting the Israelites free.

God also desires to use you to help set others free. If you feel alone in the desert, not understanding your purpose in this life or the power you have in God, pray for an understanding on how God wants to use you to help others. Do not give up on your freedom and God's purpose in your life. Allow God to work in you through His Word, the Bible, so you will gain strength to be set free.

The Hebrews had fear of their own freedom. They had never known freedom. Most of us break down before we break free. As fallible humans, we want to return to old habits when things become difficult. We need God's presence; His presence is what gives us the strength to change things.

Moses had his encounter with God when confronted by God out of the burning bush. You too can have an encounter with God, if you will seek Him. Moses was no different than you or I. God can use anyone. We will find fulfillment in our purpose. Even in the fear, there is excitement in the call. That is the difference between a God call and a person trying to manipulate you.

Satan delights in convincing believers that they are of no use to God, but God delights in making something magnificent out of your life. He can use you regardless of where you are or where you have been. God wants to set you free and then use you to set others free.

"But God hath chosen the foolish things of the world to confound the wise; and God hath chosen the weak things of the world to confound the things which are mighty;"

— 1 Corinthians 1:27 (KJV)

We need God's protection and Gods promise to fulfill our purpose. The Lord gives you strength, hope and confidence. God is already working to set you free whether you were born into this bondage or you chose this bondage. God has compassion on you. He cares. He desires to see you free.

You will come against barriers when you embrace your freedom in Christ, but remember change comes slowly. As you study and learn about Christ, your freedom will increase daily. You may encounter ridicule from people who don't understand your calling or God's path... just like the magicians ridiculed Aaron and Moses as they walked out God's purpose for them. When this happens, remember what Jesus said in John 16:33, "I have told you these things, so that in me you may have peace. In this world you will have trouble. But take heart! I have overcome the world."

In Moses' story, the magicians were selfish in their own right. They were working for Pharaoh and needed to keep their job. Pharaoh had a hard and stubborn heart. He would never admit he was wrong. He would not bow down to God and free God's people, so the magicians gave Pharaoh what he wanted, no matter the consequences.

There were many plagues that came upon the people until Pharaoh was willing to let the people go. God separated the Israelites from the plagues of the Egyptians, protecting them and showing them freedom for the first time. On the last night, the night of the worst plague, their heritage was not enough. The blood of the lamb was the only thing that would protect them, just as Jesus, the Lamb of God, had to shed His blood to protect us and set us free.

God will judge that which is binding His people. The plagues of Egypt were brought on to judge the false gods in Egypt. God was showing them who the false gods were and inviting the people into relationship with Him. This battle was not between Moses and Pharaoh. Each plague showed God's supremacy over an Egyptian god. This was God's battle. He won then, and He will win in the battle to free the Mormons from their bondage to Joseph Smith and his teachings. As with the plagues in Egypt, when we are practicing false teachings we will be plagued by symptoms not of God.

The last plague was the death of the first-born. Only the death of his firstborn finally got through to pharaoh's hard heart. What is dying in your life because of the bondage you are in? Are you in a calling that has been decided for you? Are you giving up a ministry God would have you in because of legalistic rules? Is your marriage suffering due to a counterfeit purity, requiring you to wear garments simply because a religious leader made this a rule? Just as many religions have control over their congregation through rules, Pharaoh had control over the Israelites by placing requirements on them that bred fear. But God is all-powerful. He is the Lord God Almighty. If you are serving the wrong god, you will become stubborn to the point of destruction—destroying yourself, your family and those around you.

Pharaoh wanted to be his own god. This is something the enemy has been using to entice people since the Garden of Eden. We need to repent from this idolatry. We need to honor our one true God. Only then will He give us His power in our life.

What is True Freedom?

Freedom involves more than just breaking the chains of Satan. It is making Jesus lord of your life. Freedom is about experiencing His love, and understanding the sacrifice Jesus made for you by shedding His blood. This perfect man, who was God in flesh, died for you. We could not do this on our own. We are not perfect, nor will we ever be. But we are made perfect through Him. He is the sacrificial Lamb of God.

Just as the Israelites had to eat all of the lamb during the Passover, we must receive all of Christ. It was their faith that brought God's grace. If they did not have faith to place the blood on their door, they would not have been saved.

In addition to the blood, they were required to eat only unleavened bread—bread without yeast. The yeast represents sin and untruth in the Bible. 1 Corinthians says, "So let us celebrate the festival, not with the old bread of wickedness and evil, but with the new bread of sincerity and truth." We must live a life of truth partaking only of that, which represents who Christ is. He gave His body and life so that we would have eternal life. We must not eat from any other bread. If Jesus is the Bread of life and His word the Bible is our daily bread, then we must only partake of His bread, the Bible.

Freedom therefore is choosing to bind yourself to something greater than that which has enslaved you. When you chose to make Jesus your 'lord,' you are freed from other bondages. By being bound to Christ, of your own will, you find great, great freedom!

"Take my yoke upon you, and learn of me; for I am meek and lowly in heart: and ye shall find rest unto your souls. For my yoke is easy, and my burden is light."

— Matthew 11:29-30 (KJV)

Freedom and Righteousness

You can experience both freedom and righteousness at the same time by allowing God to direct your path, not man made rules. You see, some of my religious practices were causing me to be legalistic in my life. I became obedient to the religious rules rather than God. The temple separated me from people that God would not have separated me from, including my own husband. If I had allowed God to direct my path instead of the religious practices of the Temple, I would not have had to go through such disconnect in my marriage. I was under bondage to rules that God had not written.

The word of wisdom was another rule that sought to enslave me. Among other things, it said that I could not drink coffee or wine. Rather than allowing the Holy Spirit to convict me about these things, I only obeyed out of fear—regardless of whether I had a problem with these things or not. I left the church because of the damage these rules caused in my family.

After I left, I had a new sense of freedom, and it was a little scary at first. Now I would be the one responsible for making the choice. For years, the Mormon Church had dictated most aspects of my existence. The Church, through its rules, decided what I could wear, what I could drink, what movies I could watch, what I would do on Sundays, and even the kind of relationship I'd have with my husband and other members of my family.

Paul says in scripture that everything is permissible, but not everything is beneficial for him. So there are times when for me having a glass of wine is actually beneficial. I personally have never had an issue with drinking too much, and so now I am able to minister to someone over a glass of wine that would never go near a church. I am free to have a cup of coffee should I need it to for the energy required to honor God and do His work.

It is how we use our freedom that makes a difference. We should not use our freedom to sin as Paul says in Romans. Everything we do in our life has consequences. God is the ultimate judge and will punish us for behavior that he does not permit under any circumstance. These behaviors are all laid out in the Ten Commandments. The Lord needed to write the Ten Commandments for the Israelites because of their sin and idolatry. The Israelites had been in bondage for so long that they actually could not think for themselves in their new freedom, and they eventually recreated the Egyptian golden calf god. I've see this happen often in religious homes. Religion becomes a false god. It is not God they are in communion with, but a set of rules dictated by man. This results in the suppression of our own internal compass based on the love of the Lord and an inner respect for each other.

Purpose of Commandments

The commandments are designed to protect our families, our communities and us. They're a guide to transforming the way we think, what we do and how we live. They truly are ten keys to a successful and happy life!

The Ten Commandments of Exodus 20:2-17 are:

1. "I am the Lord your God, who brought you out of the land of Egypt, out of the house of bondage. You shall have no other gods before Me.

2. "You shall have no other gods but me."

3. "You shall not take the name of the Lord your God in vain."

4. "You shall remember and keep the Sabbath day."

5. "Honor your father and mother."

6. "You shall not murder."

7. "You shall not commit adultery."

8. "You shall not steal."

9. "You shall not bear false witness against your neighbor."

10. "You shall not covet your neighbor's house; you shall not covet your neighbor's wife, nor his male servant, nor his female servant, nor his ox, nor his donkey, nor anything that is your neighbor's."

The way Jesus loved was in truth and freedom. If we will simply just love God first and then love others, we will walk in the freedom that God has given to us. Matthew 22:37-40 says, "All the Law and the Prophets hang on these two commandments."

Jesus was showing us the *continuation* of God's moral law found in the Old Testament and summing it up as a *Law of Love*, not replacing it. Of course we are talking about the moral law here, not the ceremonial laws which Christ did away with at the cross (Colossians 2:14).

The Pharisees were very meticulous about keeping the laws of God. But they lost sight of the true meaning of their relationship with God—which was love. They completely lost sight of loving God with all their heart, mind, soul and strength (Deuteronomy 6:5), and the law just became something they had to do in order to be saved. They became legalistic in the process. Without that love for God, the external observance of God's Commandments becomes worthless legalism.

That was the truth Jesus was trying to teach them.

Where love is present, a person will automatically set out to order his life in harmony with the will of God as expressed in His commandments (John 14:15; 15:10).

Control Creates Mindlessness

Control, on the other hand, does not allow a person to make their own decisions. Members mindlessly do as they are instructed. Leaders manipulate our fears through rules to control our actions.

Unfortunately, it is easy to manipulate a Mormon's fear of salvation. They love the Lord, but they lack an understanding of His Word. This causes them to be vulnerable to placing their trust in false prophets, and the ordinances they declare as doctrine. Church leaders continue to create and add new rules that will prey on these fears. This carries on for generation after generation as new rules are added. They are not encouraged to walk with God and hear His voice. Instead, they are encouraged to walk exactly as the Church dictates and obey its voice! This promotes control, dependence on rules, fear, and mindlessness.

These rules and ordinances are to be performed and adhered to whether or not it is in the best interest of the individual and their family members. Just as children cannot see from another person's point of view, the elders in the church cannot see the damage that this mind control is doing to an individual or their family.

The mark of maturity is being able to see things from another person's point of view and allowing them to make their own decisions—trusting that they can speak with God on their own. We cannot see another person's heart. We do not always know their intentions, or what is best for them. We need to be mature in the Lord, which requires us to develop our relationship with God. If we rely on another person to dictate God's will to us, it becomes harder and harder for us to discern His voice.

Remember that false ideas enslave and truth liberates.

I came out of a religion that controls and into a deeper relationship with God. I have been set free in Christ! In your situation, if you think it is impossible to be set free from your bondage, then you need to trust God and let Him provide a way. He has a plan for you. You must take the step of faith, knowing God has His hand on you.

The Israelites thought they would die in the desert. They blamed Moses and, to some degree, God. The Lord told them to "move on" and the Lord would deliver them. When they did, they found deliverance and a strengthening of their faith.

When I left the Mormon Church, I was afraid. I didn't know what to do. My family was suffering terribly from the bondage we were in. I wanted to make sure that the Lord knew how much I loved Him. I did not want to betray Him by leaving what I had been taught was the "True Church." I knelt down and asked God what to do. He gave me the peace and comfort I needed to step out and attend my local non-denominational church.

If you desire the peace and freedom that Jesus gives, healthy relationships, and the life that God intended for you to live, then you must take that first step and move forward.

After you are set free, you must remain free. The comfort of slavery kept the Israelites wanting to go back. They didn't have to think. They didn't have to establish a relationship with God. They only had to do what they were told. God had to lead them in a way that made it difficult, if not impossible, to return to Egypt. God took them through the Red Sea. What a miracle! God wants to take you through your own

Red Sea too! He doesn't want you to return to your slavery! Christ set you free. Now you must live free. Continue to praise God for your freedom. The Red Sea has been parted for you, cross it and don't look back!

God will take you the long way around just as He did the Israelites. Often, we do not understand God's path for our life. Keep your faith. He will open new doors for you and nourish you on your journey. He does not want you running back. God will protect you. Following God is a matter of choice. He does not push or control. He invites you to follow. He moves as you move, but He never leaves.

God's provision is in His path. Part of that provision is freedom. While freedom can be scary, it is better than control. Fear is replaced with faith and purpose in God. Walking in His purpose creates joy. The Bible tells us that the joy of the Lord is our strength (Nehemiah 8:10).

A Prayer of Healing

"Lord I need You. Please set me free. Not on my own, Lord, as I can do nothing without You. Help me to see where I am in prison. What spiritual slavery am I in bondage to? Lord, do not allow my feelings and emotions to be my guide. Instead, Lord, I pray that through Your Word You guide and direct me. I thank You, God, that I know it is not garments, passwords or ordinances that save me. Only You can save Lord Jesus. I know that there is no fear in Your perfect love. I thank You that You have set me free, and the only word I need to know to praise You is the name of Jesus. You alone give me joy and dancing in my soul! Who alone is like You God? You are majestic and holy. Thank You. Amen."

Transparency

*"You will open the eyes of the blind. You will free the captives
from prison, out of the prison where they live in darkness."*

— Isaiah 42:7

T he feeling that someone is deliberately hiding something from
you is hard to swallow. Random ill thoughts shoot through
your head. "Why doesn't she trust me?" "Did I do something
wrong?" "What are they hiding from me?" "I wonder if he is doing
something wrong?" These thoughts and feelings are hard to shake.
It becomes even worse when you discover someone with power and
authority intentionally left you in the dark.

God our Father has been very upfront with us about His gospel
and plans for our life. He tells us everything we need to know. He
starts off with the creation and reveals to us how He formed the earth
from nothing (Genesis 1: 1-25). He tells us how He formed man and
woman. He gave them both a very clear commandment and tells us
not only how they fell by disobeying Him, but also helps us to understand why they fell. He makes it clear how the enemy appealed to

them by discounting His word (Genesis 3:1-7), asking Eve "Did God really say?"

Throughout Scripture, God has clearly revealed His character and commands to us. He commands us to worship Him and none other. He is a loving and just God. He is the good shepherd. He wants us to hear and recognize His voice and His goodness. He is looking for a relationship with us and in all great relationships there is love, trust, and communication. Secrets, control, and domination are not elements of a love relationship.

God does not hide or hold out on us. That was the lie Satan tried to get Eve to believe. The enemy convinced Eve that God was holding out on her, that God had more to offer but wouldn't share it. He convinced her that there was something better than the perfection of paradise and the daily relationship with God. He told her that she could also be like God. It wasn't true.

It is Satan that lies (John 8:44). He is the one who does not give us the complete truth. He makes something look good, but does not give us the whole story. If Satan would have told Eve the whole truth, that she would also be kicked out of the Garden, she would not have eaten of the fruit.

Mormon Opaqueness

In much the same way as Satan did with Eve, the Mormon Church hid many of their beliefs and rituals from me. Had they revealed them to me in the beginning, I would have run! They never told me that they believed in polygamy, that they thought God was once a man like us, that human blood atonement was practiced, that we could become gods ourselves. Had they, I would not have been baptized into the church created by Joseph Smith.

You see, I wanted Jesus Christ in my life, but I did not know true Christianity in order to make an informed decision. This is why it was so easy for me to embrace the Mormon Church. They told me the things I wanted to hear, and not knowing that it was only a small, distorted portion of their whole belief system, I jumped on in! Just like Eve did. All because I was not taught the whole truth of what they believe.

Deception is most definitely not a character trait of God. This is characteristic of Satan. Satan lures you into his trap with all kinds of lies and false beliefs. He hides the truth until you are tangled up in something you had not anticipated. For many, they are so tangled that it seems pointless to try to untangle themselves.

Imagine getting married to a man who had intentions and designs for your marriage that he never told you about. He won't tell you because you might not marry him. He doesn't feel you are ready to know, and he only intends to tell you after you are married so you can't back out. This is very much what it is like "marrying" into the Mormon Church. When you are getting baptized into the Church, you are really not making an informed commitment. You really don't know what you are getting into, but since you've put an emotional and timely investment into becoming a Mormon you are less likely to leave after working so hard to join. Just like a bad marriage, you hope you can "change him" or you hope "things will get better in time."

Often, the first thing people do when they sin is try to hide it. Then, when confronted, they outright lie about it. This is what happens in the Mormon Church. I asked about polygamy, and denial happened. When I confronted them, I was lied to about the more obscene parts of the practice. I was told that the men married the women whose husbands had been killed in war. I was not told that girls as young as 15 were taken by Joseph Smith or that he married other men's wives.

God never tells us in Scripture to keep things hidden. No, He tells us to let our light shine.

"No one lights a lamp and then puts it under a basket. Instead, a lamp is placed on a stand, where it gives light to everyone in the house."

— Matthew 5:15 (NLT)

"But the path of the just is like the shining sun, That shines ever brighter unto the perfect day."

— Proverbs 4:18

When Adam and Eve sinned in the garden, the first thing they did was to cover themselves with fig leaves and hide from the Lord. The members of the Mormon Church place a fig leaf on their self during the Temple ceremony. It makes me curious. Why do they want to take us back to the moment of sin hiding from God and creating a separation from Him?

What is the Mormon Church trying to hide? Is it polygamy? Is it racism? Is it that the Book of Mormon has changed many times despite its touted infallibility? Maybe they are hiding the fact that the Garments have changed even though Joseph Smith prophesied that they never would. Perhaps they are hiding from God since they would like to become their own god.

God has made it perfectly clear that we are to have no other God before Him, including ourselves.

Rest assured, the God of the Bible is a God of integrity, and He is our good shepherd. He gives us clear guidelines so we can avoid Satan's traps. David teaches us in Psalm 23 that the heart of a shepherd is toward the welfare of his flock. The Lord Jesus is showing these ruthless Pharisees that they do not have a heart of a shepherd. In Psalms 23:1-3 David says, "The LORD is my shepherd; I shall not want." He immediately attributes to the office of the shepherd that there will be no want. "He maketh me to lie down in green pastures: he leadeth me beside the still waters." Again David is showing the heart of a shepherd. "He restoreth my soul: he leadeth me in the paths of righteousness for his name's sake." Amen!

The Blind Pharisees

The Jewish people were shepherds from the beginning of their history. Jesus is trying to open their eyes about their own blindness by pointing out to them that they really are sheep, and He is the good shepherd. A shepherd knew each of their animals well. He could recognize when one was ill or acting out of character. He knew how to work with each animal to help it stay on the path. He knew the safe routes and was willing to put himself in danger to protect a member of his flock. Sheep, like all rumens, have a very delicate body system and the smallest changes in feed or lack of water can quickly be fatal. A good shepherd watched his sheep for signs of distress. Fly strike happens when biting flies gang up on a sheep. This is painful and can kill an animal. The shepherd watches for this and protects them.

The people listening to Jesus would have recognized all of these characteristics of a good shepherd. They would have remembered the difference in the sheep that were well cared for and those who were neglected.

He said to them in John 9:40-41, "If you were blind, you wouldn't be guilty. But you remain guilty because you claim you can see." In other words, they were not humble or transparent before the Lord or men.

You see, these Pharisees claimed to be the shepherds of the flock of God. They claimed to be servants and disciples of Moses. These Pharisees understood the office of a shepherd and yet they were hypocrites that did not practice what they preached—much like the Mormons. If you have eyes to see and you search out all things, you will notice that just about every doctrine the Mormon's have, they practice the opposite.

Jesus pointed out that the Pharisees had just excommunicated one of God's true sheep, one that was seeking Jesus to see. They were offended that Jesus spoke of their own blindness. They could not see that Jesus was the true shepherd and was standing before them fulfilling the very prophecy they had professed to know. They were hard hearted and filled with bitterness. They had a heart prepared for murder. They were standing there with their hands full of stones ready to kill Jesus, and yet He was the one who had opened the eyes of the blind man.

Look at John 9:34 (KJV). They are talking to this man whose eyes were opened. "They answered and said unto him, 'Thou wast altogether born in sins, and dost thou teach us?' And they cast him out." They threw the man Jesus had healed out of the synagogue—they threw him out of the church. They excommunicated him. Why? He was professing that Jesus was a prophet, and they wanted to label Jesus as a sinner. The Pharisees are not the only ones that would like to label

Jesus as just a man, a sinner like us. The Mormon Church also claims that God was once a man like us, a sinner. "As man is, God once was; as God is, man may be,"[55] said LDS Apostle James E. Talmage. Make no mistake, God was never a man like us; He is without sin and always has been (2 Corinthians 5:21). This belief is not something that they teach you at first. Could it be that the LDS Church knows that if they were to reveal such information right up front that less people will accept the gospel according to Mormonism? They wait until you are baptized, until you are integrated, until you have made vows. By the time you find out, you're already in too deep.

The blind man had an answer for these Jewish hypocrites. He said in John 9:25, "He [the man born blind] answered and said, whether he be a sinner or not, I know not: one thing I know, that, whereas I was blind, now I see." Many Mormon members are born blind merely by being born into the Church; it is when they begin to search for Jesus to restore their sight that they begin to see.

Verse 30 continues, "The man answered, 'Now that is remarkable! You don't know where he comes from, yet he opened my eyes.'" Verse 33 proclaims, "If this man were not of God, he could do nothing." How can a sinner do such great wonders? That is the question the man put to the Pharisees. The Pharisees could not comprehend that Jesus was God in flesh.

In John 9:16, we see the hidden motive behind the Pharisee's accusation. "Therefore said some of the Pharisees, 'This man is not of God, because he keepeth not the Sabbath day.' Others said, 'How can a man that is a sinner do such miracles?' And there was a division among them." The Pharisees didn't really care if this was God in flesh. Their legalism blinded them, so they could not see that Christ was setting this man free from them.

These chief priests, scribes and Pharisees should have understood the scriptures and the prophecies of the coming Messiah better than anyone. The prophecy of God coming in the form of man was being fulfilled before their very eyes, and they didn't see it. This is the case with the Mormons. They do not see the signs of the end times

---

55 Lorenzo Snow, *Teachings of Lorenzo Snow*, compiled by Clyde J. Williams, (Salt Lake City: Bookcraft, 1984), 2.

being fulfilled within their religion nor do they see how deceptive the Church is—a church that is using the name of Jesus Christ but does not know who He really is. This church is stealing the life and salvation of men.

> *"He who has an ear, let him hear. If anyone is to go into captivity, into captivity he will go. If anyone is to be killed with the sword, with the sword he will be killed."*
> —Revelation 13:9-10

This verse says that people place themselves in their own captivity by not hearing and understanding God's Word. His Word is the sword of the Spirit, and by this sword you will die if you do not follow the True Shepherd.

Following Our True Shepherd

Jesus Christ taught that He is the True Shepherd and His sheep will know His voice. They recognize and hear His voice, and He calls them by name. He leads them to green pasture and freedom. The Lord wants to lead you to freedom with Him as well. He will call to you, but He will not use deception or fear to rule over you. He calls His sheep by name and desires a personal relationship with them.

Many claim to be teachers of God but do not understand the parable in John 10:6. They claim to be shepherds of God's flock. Back then, they were the chief priests and high priests of Israel. Today they hold positions in our churches. They claim to be the shepherds of the flock, yet they were spiritually blind to the qualifications of their office.

Then as now, the spiritual shepherds must understand their need of a Savior for their own soul. They must first have had their eyes anointed in order to see Jesus. Jesus must be much more than a mere man. He must be God in the flesh. He must be sinless, holy, and perfect. They need to recognize the one true God and have Him anoint their eyes, washing them with God's Word in order that they recognize their own sinful nature before they can go forth to lead the flock of God. Only after they have opened their eyes to Jesus can they lead a flock to Jesus and none other.

What do we understand by His reference to a 'sheepfold' and what is meant by *"climbing up some other way"* into that sheepfold? The sheepfold is where those who profess themselves to be Christians are sheltered. He is the rightful Shepherd to enter into this fold. Yet, we are told that there are false shepherds that try to steal into the sheepfold. John 10:1-2 (KJV) says, "Verily, verily, I say unto you, He that entereth not by the door into the sheepfold, but climbeth up some other way, the same is a thief and a robber. But he that entereth in by the door is the shepherd of the sheep."

These false shepherds will try to steal the sheep away from the True Shepherd. If anyone comes into the church through a different means than that which is laid out in the Bible, he is a false prophet! The Lord Jesus is showing you and me how to identify the true under-shepherds of the flock whom He has ordained to lead His flock. The sheepfold is not referring to Heaven—robbers and thieves can't get into Heaven! This sheepfold does not illustrate the True Church of Christ either. If it did, He would not lead His flock out of it.

The 'sheepfold' referenced in this parable is the mixed multitude of the professing church. It is to the professing church that the Lord comes with His Holy Spirit; it is where the call of the Lord Jesus Christ comes, and He leads His own out. They can no longer remain in this professing church because they would starve to death. There is no feed in there. They have to come out of this sheepfold and follow the voice of their Shepherd so that he can lead them to green pasture. This is what the Lord is teaching us. The sheep must be called out.

We must see the contrast between those shepherds who enter their ministry by the door and those who choose to add to His word and seek their own glory and praise. This latter group often claims that we need their approval. They are thieves and liars! How do you recognize the difference? You can only do this by knowing Jesus Christ and His Word!

There are many false religions claiming to know Jesus. There are many people who truly love God and want to be closer to Him and are deceived by these false religions. They live a life of struggle and hurt, because they don't realize the love God has in His Word and the deliverance that exists in Christ. We must separate ourselves by knowing our Shepherd and His Word.

Now, our Savior has clearly warned us to be very discerning. We must be wary of those who claim to teach in His name and yet are not sent by Him. If we do not hear of the work of the cross and how we are saved by grace, we are following a stranger to Jesus.

He says in Matthew 7:15-16, "Beware of false prophets, which come to you in sheep's clothing, but inwardly they are ravening wolves. Ye shall know them by their fruits. Do men gather grapes of thorns, or figs of thistles?" These wolves are here to devour you. They don't understand the nature of the work of grace in the soul, and you will know them by their attitudes and their fruits. False shepherds are the thieves and robbers who preach a different gospel. A different gospel will present a lot of nice sounding truth. However, it will deny the work of the cross and will instead demand works to earn grace, obedience to obtain mercy, and subservience to man to gain Salvation.

Jesus is cautioning us about them. They come in sheep's clothing as if they are part of the flock, but Jesus says, "Beware." They are not teaching salvation through Jesus. They teach salvation through man.

In Matthew 7:22-23 (KJV) we read, "Many will say to me in that day, Lord, Lord, have we not prophesied in thy name? and in thy name have cast out devils? and in thy name done many wonderful works? And then will I profess unto them, I never knew you: depart from me, ye that work iniquity." Iniquity is sin. There is much sin done in the Mormon Church hiding behind the Lord's name.

Your true shepherd will lead you out of that sheepfold. He will lead you out of sin and away from false teachings and rituals. When the Lord Jesus gathers His flock, He goes before them as an example for us to follow. It is Jesus that we are to follow. It is His teachings, His Gospel that we are to pattern ourselves after. Can you follow a pastor or a shepherd who has a heart filled with deceit and a desire to be worshiped through legalistic practices? No, but this is what Joseph Smith and those that followed him built. They sought, and still seek, to control you through deception and manipulation. They make it about your ability to be good rather than Jesus' love on a cross.

The Mormon members have pretty much conformed to this method of interaction. You will rarely ever hear a Mormon tell you what a sinful life they lived before they became a member. Mormons have been taught that they must become perfect through rituals, initiations, and outward acts. There is no safety for a person struggling with sin. Bringing to light a struggle that one has with sin is sure rejection. There is no support, no understanding, no forgiveness, and no love. There is only fear and wrath.

The unfortunate part about all this is that God will work *all* things out for the good of those that love him (Romans 8:28). He wants to use your past to help others come to know Him more. To appear perfect is to deny the lessons learned and how much Christ has changed your life. How has He healed you and restored you? This can be used as a source of encouragement and healing for others. In scripture we hear Paul talk quite often how he used to persecute Christians when he was Saul, he tells how Christ changed his life. He freely admits that he was the worst of sinners. And if that is true for him, then there is hope for you and me!

Another testimony that sticks out to me is taken from the book *Save Me from Myself.* Brian Welch explains how God touched his heart to share his testimony of how God freed him from a meth addiction. Bringing light to his addiction not only helped set him free and give him more strength, but it also touched other lives, giving hope to thousands of others who suffer with addictions.[56]

By contrast, a Mormon testimony is more a declaration that Joseph Smith was a true prophet and that they know the Mormon Church is true. It is pretty much verbatim for each testimony. It is almost as if the members are trying to convince themselves that this is where the truth is. It is never about how Jesus set them free. It is always about how true Joseph Smith was.

Jesus is the Christ, and we need not worship Him from behind the dark shadows of false shepherds who would have us believe that Jesus is the author of polygamy, human blood atonement, racism, or a myriad of other corruptions. You see, for Mormonism to be true, Christ Himself must be the culprit behind all the terrible behavior of past

56 Brian Welch, *Save Me from Myself,* pg. 159

Mormon Prophets. According to Mormonism, these prophets did and said only what they were commanded by God. Thus, the blame is not with these men, but with God and Christ. This is foolishness!

To say that the Lord commanded polygamy or any of the other false teachings is to blatantly call our Savior a sinner. The Mormon Church continues to defend these teachings as divinely inspired of God. This is in complete opposition to the character of our sinless Savior. The Church hides behind the name of Christ, but does not represent who Christ is. He and His holy name have been disgracefully used so that self-centered men might gain some measure of power, prestige, and perversion.

To deceive people that wish to have a relationship with the Lord is in direct conflict to how Christ wishes to set us free. Merely stating that one belongs to the Church of Jesus Christ does not make it truth. Nor does calling a book "Another testament of Jesus Christ" make the Book of Mormon true. Truth is not truth unless it meets God's definition of truth. Truth cannot be relative unless it is relative to the God of Truth. Anything less is deception. Truth is a person.

"Jesus said unto him, 'I am the way, the truth, and the life.
No one comes to the Father except through Me.'"

— John 14:6

Any other way and Jesus will say, "Depart from me, I never knew you." Jesus Christ wants a direct and very personal relationship with each and every one of us. He is the good shepherd who has laid down His life so that we might live. He wants you to truly know Him and recognize His voice. There is a sweet and spiritually fulfilling relationship with the Lord Jesus Christ that awaits you as you discard the false teachings of man.

God calls us to be transparent with Him and others. He is a God who has never hidden His plan and desire for us. Whatever it is, whatever part of your life that you've yet to share with God, may I suggest that today is the day to begin to be transparent. When we repent of our sins, God promises forgiveness, cleansing, mercy, and grace. He is trustworthy and fair. He will forgive us, cleanse us, and make us white as snow.

Once this is done, we should then give God all the glory and share with others how God has transformed our life. Be transparent with others too!

> *"Confess your faults one to another, and pray one for another, that ye may be healed. The effectual fervent prayer of a righteous man availeth much."*
>
> — James 5:16 (KJV)

God calls us to be transparent with Him and others. What does it mean to be transparent? It means easily seen through, recognized, or detected, straightforward, showing through, to manifest, and be obvious. Whatever it is, whatever part of your life that you've yet to share with God and others, may I suggest that today is the day to begin to be transparent.

> *"He said to them, 'Do you bring in a lamp to put it under a bowl or a bed? Instead, don't you put it on its stand? For whatever is hidden is meant to be disclosed, and whatever is concealed is meant to be brought out into the open. If anyone has ears to hear, let them hear.'"*
>
> — Mark 4:21-23

A false shepherd believes it is entirely okay to mislead people about the process of leading them to Jesus. The consequences will be that His message is not in us. The message becomes something the leaders of the church choose to make it. It is the message of some man.

I pray that Mormons will follow the true shepherd and come out of the sheepfold. You will die from hunger and thirst from not receiving the truth.

- **Revelation 3:20** – Here I am! I stand at the door and knock. If anyone hears my voice and opens the door, I will come in and eat with that person, and they with me.

- **Psalms 27:1** – The LORD is my light and my salvation; Whom shall I fear? The LORD is the strength of my life; of whom shall I be afraid?

- **Deuteronomy 31:8** – The LORD himself goes before you and will be with you; he will never leave you nor forsake you. Do not be afraid; do not be discouraged.

- **Deuteronomy 4:39-40** – Acknowledge and take to heart this day that the LORD is God in heaven above and on the earth below. There is no other. Keep his decrees and commands, which I am giving you today, so that it may go well with you and your children after you and that you may live long in the land the LORD your God gives you for all time.

- **Psalms 43:3** – Oh, send out Your light and Your truth! Let them lead me;

The Spirit of Anti-Christ on the Earth

Scholars debate on who the person of the anti-Christ is, but one thing they do agree on is that he deceives people in order to gain worship.

> *"This is how you can recognize the Spirit of God: Every spirit that acknowledges that Jesus Christ has come in the flesh is from God, but every spirit that does not acknowledge Jesus is not from God. This is the spirit of the antichrist, which you have heard is coming and even now is already in the world."*

> — 1 John 4:2-3

It is important to realize that what we worship has power over us. Joseph Smith demonstrated that he desired the worship of people. One particularly poignant statement shows his desire to rule over God's people. "...no man or woman in this dispensation will ever enter into the celestial kingdom of God without the consent of Joseph Smith....Every man and woman must have the certificate of Joseph

Smith as a passport to their entrance into the mansion where God and Christ are...I cannot go there without his consent....He reigns there as supreme a being in his sphere, capacity, and calling, as God does in heaven."[57]

We must get Smith's approval to go to heaven? The blood of Jesus is no longer enough?

This is such blasphemy! Mormons must repent of this belief! God clearly tells us in John 10:1-3 that there is only one door to be entered and Jesus Christ is the good shepherd guarding that door.

> *"Very truly I tell you Pharisees, anyone who does not enter the sheep pen by the gate, but climbs in by some other way, is a thief and a robber. The one who enters by the gate is the shepherd of the sheep. The gatekeeper opens the gate for him, and the sheep listen to his voice. He calls his own sheep by name and leads them out."*
>
> —John 10:1-3

Believing that Joseph Smith has the authority to grant a person permission to enter Heaven knocks Jesus off His throne—and this is the spirit of antichrist.

There is only one way to get into the kingdom of God. It is through the atoning blood of Jesus alone. Anyone who does not enter through *that* gate is a thief and a robber. The work on the cross is what secured our entry to Heaven. As much as Joseph Smith would like to think that He is God in flesh, he is not.

Just as the Pharisees did not acknowledge that Jesus was God in flesh, Mormons do not acknowledge that Jesus was the Word made flesh or that He is the only Savior for all eternity. How can they say they are Christians or a church of Jesus Christ when they dismiss Jesus to a secondary and often irrelevant role?

We cannot earn our salvation, and God doesn't want us to try. We cannot control it. We have to accept grace and recognize there is

---

57 Brigham Young, *Journal of Discourses*, vol. 7, p.289.

nothing more we can do to be saved but to accept that He is our Savior sent here to die for our sins. There is no other way.

- **John 14:6** – We are being blinded if we think that there is any other way to enter God's kingdom. God says, *"I am the way and the truth and the life. No one comes to the Father except through me."*

- **Luke 11:9-10** – *"And so I tell you, keep on asking, and you will receive what you ask for. Keep on seeking, and you will find. Keep on knocking, and the door will be opened to you. For everyone who asks, receives. Everyone who seeks, finds. And to everyone who knocks, the door will be opened."* God desires for us to search out all things about Him. He has nothing to hide. He will teach you of His ways and reveal false teachings to you as well as reveal those teachings that are anti-Christ as you continue to search.

- **1 John 4:1 (KJV)** – God's ways cause you to receive clarity and will bring you peace. False teachings and those that dethrone Christ will not agree with the Bible. They will stir up feelings of sadness. They will lead you to idolatry. Finally, you'll be left with the sense that the ways and teachings are unjust. You will gain an understanding just as the man whom Jesus caused to see. *"Beloved, believe not every spirit, but try the spirits whether they are of God: because many false prophets are gone out into the world."*

- **John 9:30** – The Pharisees were indignant that a rule had been broken, and in their righteousness, said they'd have no part of Him. So, they questioned the man who'd been healed as to who healed him. The man said to the teachers of the law, *"Now that is remarkable! You don't know where he comes from, yet he opened my eyes."*

The Lord Jesus Christ opened the eyes of one who was born blind. Jesus had anointed the man's eyes, and then told him to go wash; he did and he came away seeing. He had to wash. When our eyes are anointed to see false teachings, it is by the washing of the Word that our eyes are opened to see clearly the blessed news of the Gospel. Jesus will open your eyes too as you seek Him.

The Pharisees failed to see what Christ was teaching. He told them He was the light of the world. They replied, "Are we blind also?" They did not understand their spiritual blindness. They had hearts that were filled with dead men's bones, and they never understood it. They refused to have their eyes anointed so that they could see the truth.

So, these blind leaders of the blind claimed they could see. What Jesus declares to them is a teaching that demonstrates that He alone is the good shepherd. He will lay down His life for His sheep (John 10:11).

A Prayer of Healing

"Lord Jesus, I am asking You to be my Shepherd, to lead and guide my life. Help me to know the truth, Lord. Show me areas where I have been deceived and bring clarity to me through your Word the Bible alone. I pray, Lord, that You go before me, Lord, and bring me peace and uphold me through the challenges I face. Give me courage, Lord, and help me not to become discouraged as I face those that have deceived me. I will fear no evil for You are with me. I will worship no one but You, Lord. Today I claim that You are the only way, and that I need no one's approval but Yours. Set me free, Jesus. Take me out of the sheepfold into Your sweet embrace. In Your holy name, Amen."

14 *Identity*

*"For you created my inmost being; you knit me
together in my mother's womb. I praise you because
I am fearfully and wonderfully made; your works
are wonderful, I know that full well."*

— Psalm 139:13-14

From our early years, we struggle with trying to figure out who
we are. Teenagers seem to be particularly prone to identity cri-
ses and the essence of a midlife crisis is also that of identity.
This search for identity is important. Identity lends itself to purpose
and purpose gives life to living.

Control, on the other hand, to be effective must strip away this
identity and force you into a type of cookie cutter mentality. On a
small scale, the military does this by giving everyone the same clothing, teaching him or her to walk the same way, talk the same way,
and react the same way. This is how they exercise control over unique
individuals on a large scale.

Hitler, with his Hitler Youth, actually followed a pattern of control
that King Nebuchadnezzar first employed in the Bible (Daniel 1). This

method stripped candidates of their identity in order to be remade and controlled. Daniel was stripped of his name, his native language, his customs, his normal diet, and his religion. He, along with a bunch of other Hebrew young men, was then given a new name, a new language, a new diet, and a new religion. We only know of Daniel because he bucked this system and was able to retain his identity when all but three others lost theirs.

So in this search for identity, people turn to many different things. Here is a casual list that historically people have turned to in order to establish a personal identity:

1. **Materialistic Possessions** – The thinking says that the more you have, the more people must take note of you...perception of success.

2. **Power and Position** – The thinking here is much the same as #1. It is about building a perception that others buy into.

3. **A Cause** – Many people spend their life trying to save the whales, feed the poor, or create world peace. Although noble, their identity becomes that of association to something often intangible. Outside of the chosen association, there is no identity.

4. **A Religion or Cult** – For many of the same reasons listed above, people turn to religion to establish their identity. The problem here is that identity becomes bound to the power structure and system. Control becomes the norm.

5. **A Person** – Sometimes people desire to be like someone else. Call it a 'fan' or hero worship, or even envy, people often identify themselves with another person.

6. **An Idea** – I would say that atheism is more a religion than not, but for the sake of an argument, we'll call it an idea. Many people chose to identify with an idea in their quest to find a purpose. Ideas, important as they might be, do not provide purpose or true identity. Ideas are most valuable to those who already know who they are.

7. **Relationships** – This one is very common. We often say 'I am a mother," or "I am a husband," etc. This is how we often identify ourselves to other people. It becomes important and significant. At times it becomes everything and can lead to an identity crisis when the relationship falls apart.

Knowing your identity is important. God didn't mistakenly create you. He never said, "Oops! I didn't mean to make that guy!" You were created for a specific purpose and reason. You are indeed unique, a designers model. Determining what that purpose is will be among the greatest joys of your life.

Mormon Identity

During my time as a Mormon, I did my best to identify as a Mormon. The pressure is intense to do so since Mormon doctrine requires one to be a Mormon to achieve the highest level of Heaven. I took a "new name," wore Garments, tithed, went to the Temple, followed the Prophet's edicts and so forth. I fulfilled all the roles they wanted me to. I did this because I was searching for God's love and forgiveness, and this is what I was told I had to do to get it. Like a child, I looked to them to guide me instead of to my Heavenly Father to guide me. This was the only option presented to me.

It quickly became about finding my place within the Church instead of finding my place with God. This robbed me of a personal identity that allowed for a real relationship with God. Don't misunderstand me. A lot of Mormons want to find God. They want to know God, do the right thing, and be a good person. But when religion, of any sort, becomes your identity, you must conform to their concept of who you are or should be.

Because religion is not a relationship, but a system, your identity becomes lost in the masses of public opinion and action. Eventually, the entity (or the system) seeks to establish its own identity by assimilating individuals into a corporate thought process. In short, you become an extension of the religion's will instead of God's will.

I had to yield control of my life to the Mormon Church in order to identity with it. For me, this ended up damaging those relationships that should have been yielded to God instead of a system.

This is in no way unique. Religious systems stemming from well before Christ was born have sought to exercise control over people by incorporating their identity into their system. In Jesus' day the Pharisees, Sadducees, Herodians and the Zealots all vied with one another. Even within the Christian Church this identity problem became apparent. In 1 Corinthians 1:12-13) we read, "What I mean is this: One of you says, 'I follow Paul'; another, 'I follow Apollos'; another, 'I follow Cephas'; still another, 'I follow Christ.' Is Christ divided? Was Paul crucified for you? Were you baptized into the name of Paul?"

Even the group claiming to identity with Christ was doing so only within a system or group mentality. It wasn't about Christ for them. It was about identifying themselves with what others were doing within an individual church. This identity to a system or group created division and turmoil within the church and relationships. Paul goes on and says:

"For when one says, 'I follow Paul,' and another, 'I follow Apollos,' are you not mere men? What, after all, is Apollos? And what is Paul? Only servants, through whom you came to believe—as the Lord has assigned to each his task. I planted the seed, Apollos watered it, but God made it grow. So neither he who plants nor he who waters is anything, but only God, who makes things grow."

— 1 Corinthians 3:4-7

Did you notice what Paul said? He said he was nothing except where his identity is in God. It can't be in a system or religion. It took me years to finally understand this and see the damage that placing my identity in Mormonism was doing—not just in my own personal family, but to the cause of Christ in general.

In Christ, however, there can be true identity.

Establishing Your Identity

First, we must ask, what is an identity? What constitutes what a person is? The following is a basic definition of what an identity is:[58]

1. A set of characteristics by which a thing is definitively recognizable or known.

2. The set of behavioral or personal characteristics by which an individual is recognizable as a member of a group.

3. The quality or condition of being the same as something else.

4. The distinct personality of an individual regarded as a persisting entity—individuality.

5. The relation established by psychological identification—in other words, what is in our mind about who we are.

I would like to add a few more ideas to the concept of personal identity. Certain religions and even societies themselves often place a huge emphasis on family and marriage. Many times our spouse or significant other becomes our identity. More than that, friends, children, jobs, health, youth, financial status, country, houses, church, religion, and even emotions become our identity.

But all of these things are temporary. What happens when you lose one of them? When people lose a sense of their identity, they are set adrift, cut off even from themselves. This is not good. Paul understood this when he mentioned that he had learned to be content in any situation (Philippians 4:11). His identity was not wrapped up in temporal things. He could suffer their loss and still retain his identity and purpose. He had to *learn* to put his identity in something more stable, something that would last.

I've seen many marriages break up because the identity of the marriage was the children. As soon as the children grew up and left home, the marriage fell apart. I've watched Mormon friends lose their identity in the rubber stamp of religious practice and laws. I've had

---

58 Taken from the *World English Dictionary*

my own identity manipulated by fear and rejection. My daughter's identity was destroyed completely and I almost lost her—praise God for His grace in restoring her. People reach middle age and their own image is shattered the day they realize, "I'm not young anymore." Suddenly they are plunged into a midlife crisis. The list seems endless.

As long as our identity is wrapped up in temporal things, we risk the loss of that identity. We think of ourselves as something, and so we all have said things like:

- I am a mother.

- I am sad.

- I am an attorney.

- I am a Mormon

- I am a Catholic

- I am a brother.

- I am happy.

- I am an American.

- I am a Protestant.

- I am rich.

- I am poor.

- I am an atheist.

- I am an optimist.

- I am good.

- I am bad.

- I am healthy.

The list continues on and on. This is how we typically establish an identity, yet all of these things are merely temporary. Our emotions change like the tide. Our situations, positions, financial status, all change. Relationships evolve, change, and sometimes go separate ways. Even our life on this Earth is merely temporary.

So our identity needs to be in something eternal, something everlasting.

God is eternal.

He becomes our True Identity when we are adopted into the family of Jesus Christ (Ephesians 1:4-5). Having our identity placed in Jesus Christ gives eternity to our lives. Because Paul knew of his eternal destiny he could be content in all circumstances, and in only this way could he glory in his weaknesses (2 Corinthians 12:9).

Anything that we place above Christ becomes idolatry. Christ isn't a hobby or a weekend job. He is our all in all.

"For to me to live is Christ, and to die is gain."

— Philippians 1:21 (KJV)

What an amazing thought. For me to live *is* Christ! Look at the rest of these verses:

"But whatever was to my profit I now consider loss for the sake of Christ. What is more, I consider everything a loss compared to the surpassing greatness of knowing Christ Jesus my Lord, for whose sake I have lost all things. I consider them rubbish, that I may gain Christ and be found in him, not having a righteousness of my own that comes from the law, but that which is through faith in Christ—the righteousness that comes from God and is by faith."

— Philippians 3:7-9

To establish the identity that Christ has for you, you need to know that you are unique. We are not to imitate one another and be clones. God purposely made us unique! He is an infinite God with limitless possibilities. We are precious and special to God. Psalm 139:13-14 says, "For you created my inmost being; you knit me together in my mother's womb. I praise you because I am fearfully and wonderfully made; your works are wonderful, I know that full well."

Jesus wants you. He formed you. Even if you were born somewhere in the world where no one knows who you are—God knows you. He does not need records for He holds the very book of life. He does not need man to do genealogical work to find your name—He knows it!

In the Mormon Temple, you are given a secret "new name." What is comical about this to me is that the Temple often gives the same name to each group of people looking to get a "secret" name that day. It is less of a "secret" naming and more of a "batch" naming. They cannot possibly come up with billions of new names, and so they don't even try. In fact, they typically rotate which names they use on any given day.

God isn't like that. God knows you intimately—on a level that neither you nor I could possibly comprehend. Not only does God know your name, He knows your spirit and keeps track of every hair and cell in your body. You are not going to surprise God with your presence in Heaven. You have a purpose that only you can really know, although others might be able to help us figure out what that is—ultimately God will give that information to you. Not a man. Not a Bishop. Not a Prophet. Only God.

"The simple song by Tommy Walker, *He Knows My Name,* proclaims that He, the Almighty, who is also your Father in Heaven, knows your name and everything about you. In fact, I encourage you to quiet your spirit, even now, and listen to Him call your name.

Establish your identity with your creator. Take for example some other aspects like that of a painting. Why is a painting valuable? Because of the painter. Where does a song originate? From its composer. What makes a book or movie possible? The writer. The identity of any creation is intimately intertwined with its creator. This is certainly true with us. God created us, so our value, importance, purpose, and identity are tied back to Him. In our true identity, in Christ alone, we find who we are, our value and our purpose.

How Does God Identify Us?

This is an interesting question. Take a look at the following verse:

"For those God foreknew he also predestined to be conformed to the likeness of his Son, that he might be the firstborn among many brothers."

— Romans 8:29

God identifies us with His Son. Can there be any greater honor? Imagine a king taking a poor child, homeless, hungry, and alone off the streets and saying, "I want to make you like my son. I want you to have from me what he has from me. I want you to know my love and care." This is essentially what God is doing for each of us. God identifies us as His children.

- **John 1:12 (KJV)** – *"But as many as received him, to them gave he power to become the sons of God, even to them that believe on his name."*

- **2 Corinthians 6:18 (KJV)** – *"And will be a Father unto you, and ye shall be my sons and daughters, saith the Lord Almighty."*

- **Galatians 3:26 (KJV)** – *"For ye are all the children of God by faith in Christ Jesus."*

- **Galatians 4:4-7(KJV)** – *"But when the fulness of the time was come, God sent forth his Son, made of a woman, made under the law, To redeem them that were under the law, that we might receive the adoption of sons. And because ye are sons, God hath sent forth the Spirit of his Son into your hearts, crying, Abba, Father. Wherefore thou art no more a servant, but a son; and if a son, then an heir of God through Christ."*

- **Ephesians 1:5 (KJV)** – *"Having predestinated us unto the adoption of children by Jesus Christ to himself, according to the good pleasure of his will."*

233

These verses make it abundantly clear that God identifies us as His children. The marvelous part about this is that this identity is created through our faith in Jesus Christ. It isn't given according to man's creed, dictation, grant, sufferance, or whim. It is how God has chosen to identify us, and it is not subject to man's control. This is so important and so amazing at the same time!

When you have placed your identity in Christ, God identifies you in the same way. No flesh will ever be glorified in the presence of God (1 Corinthians 1:29). The flesh is often associated with our own personal perception of our identity. Your likes, dislikes, passions, and lusts are wrapped up in the flesh (identity). You will never stand before God and say, "I was pretty impressive down there, wasn't I?" No, when we trust Jesus Christ as our Savior, we are identifying with Him. It is His Spirit that then lives within us. It is His Spirit that gives us life and identity (Romans 8:11).

> *"Before I formed you in the womb I knew you, before you were born I set you apart; I appointed you...."*
>
> — Jeremiah 1:5a

> *"He chose us in Him before the foundation of the world, that we would be holy and blameless before Him, in love."*
>
> — Ephesians 1:4 (NASB)

Identity and Fruits

When we are walking in our True Identity in Christ, we will bear the fruits of His Grace: love, patience, kindness, and so on. This happens merely because we are connected to the life giving water of His love. When you are in a true relationship with Christ these fruits come naturally. You cannot make them on your own; they are born as a result of being adopted into His family.

It is hard to bring forth fruit if you aren't sure what you are. Imagine a plumber, hired to do an electricians job. He is a plumber not an electrician. It is hard to be productive when you are trying to be something that God didn't create you to be.

Once you have your identity settled, the fruits become a natural byproduct of who you are. Others around us begin to identity us by these fruits.

> *"Wherefore by their fruits ye shall know them."*
>
> — Matthew 7:20 (KJV)

The wonderful thing about having a True Identity in Christ is that our fruits not only come naturally, but they identify us to those around us. They will know us by our fruits. You won't have to tell people you are a Christian, they'll know. You won't have to make people believe you are happy, they'll know.

Identity and Forgiveness

Something that I didn't realize when I first began going to the Mormon Church was that by placing my identity in Christ, I would find the forgiveness I was seeking. Forgiveness is something that any true seeker of God desires. There is no feeling in the world that quite matches the one you have when you know you have been forgiven.

God wants to forgive us. And He has forgiven us. But until we identify with Christ, we won't feel we have access to that forgiveness. Identity is association of self. When we associate with Christ in a relationship with Him, then we begin to understand the following verses:

> *"He was pierced for our transgressions, he was crushed for our iniquities; the punishment that brought us peace was upon him, and by His wounds we are healed."*
>
> — Isaiah 53:5

How can we receive the forgiveness of God when our identity is in something else? This was my problem. I kept looking for forgiveness, living in fear that I would never get it, until I finally identified with Christ. Once I did that, I *knew* I had found forgiveness! When you understand that God is also identifying you as His son or daughter, you recognize His forgiveness, love, grace, and mercy.

When God promises never to leave you or forsake you, you will believe that all the way to your soul. It will resonate with your spirit and bring healing and peace. Nothing else will ever bring this type of satisfaction or peace. God's choice to identify you as His child is proof of His acceptance of you.

Acceptance is part of forgiveness. If we feel God does not accept us, we won't feel forgiven. If we feel that God can't accept us for whatever reason, then we will feel that we aren't forgiven. But when you identity yourself with Christ, God accepts you, makes you His own in a personal relationship with Him.

Acceptance automatically grants forgiveness. The two go hand in hand.

> *"If we say that we have fellowship with him, and walk in darkness, we lie, and do not the truth: But if we walk in the light, as he is in the light, we have fellowship one with another, and the blood of Jesus Christ his Son cleanseth us from all sin. If we say that we have no sin, we deceive ourselves, and the truth is not in us. If we confess our sins, he is faithful and just to forgive us our sins, and to cleanse us from all unrighteousness."*
>
> — 1 John 1:6-9 (KJV)

But it is more than just forgiveness and acceptance. Jesus goes to bat for us too. This is where your walk with God becomes something more than an exercise and becomes a true relationship. Identifying with Christ means you are accepted with God (He identifies you as His child), you find forgiveness, and you have an advocate!

> *"My dear children, I write this to you so that you will not sin. But if anybody does sin, we have one who speaks to the Father in our defense—Jesus Christ, the Righteous One. He is the*

*atoning sacrifice for our sins, and not only for ours but also for
the sins of the whole world."*

— 1 John 2:1-2

You have God in your corner, on your side, and He has more than
your back, He holds you in His hand!

Consider the most fearful situations in your life—where real people cheat, are unkind and possibly even hurt you. Maybe you have not
been as good at something as someone else or you are smaller and
weaker. You might dread certain events in your life or you are still
haunted by painful memories. It is really great to know that when we
are identified as His own, we have someone on our side that is bigger,
stronger and more powerful than any of these situations. God tells us
to 'Fear Not' over 365 times in the Bible.

*"So do not fear, for I am with you; do not be dismayed, for I
am your God. I will strengthen you and help you; I will uphold
you with my righteous right hand."*

— Isaiah 41:10

This is exactly how I felt when I came out of the Mormon Church
and began identifying with Christ. I suddenly felt I had an army on
my side, upholding me, walking beside me, fighting for me. I felt loved,
accepted, forgiven, and empowered!

So can you. He is standing at the door knocking waiting to be let in.

A Prayer of Healing

"Lord Jesus, I thank You that You are eternal, and that You are my
Father. You are my constant Rock in this ever-changing world. Lord,
help me not to be moved by the flesh, any idea, religion or person that
is temporal. Lord, You are my forever love and I will place my identity
in You. Guard me constantly, Lord, and bind my will to Your will.
Amen."

Does God Love Everyone the Same?

"There is neither Jew nor Greek, there is neither bond nor free, there is neither male nor female: for ye are all one in Christ Jesus. And if ye be Christ's, then are ye Abraham's seed, and heirs according to the promise."

— Galatians 3:28-29 (KJV)

You would think that this is a question that has an obvious answer—*Does God love everyone...the same?* Most Christians, and even Christian spinoffs, would agree that God loves everyone, but the second part of the question seems to be a source of some degree of controversy: *the same?*

For some reason, there are people and groups, even so called religious groups that don't really believe that God loves everyone the same. This idea exists not just in a comparison between *saint* and *sinner,* but has largely been waged on a battlefield of *skin color!*

Racism is not reserved just for the KKK, but can be found in many places and among many people. The Mormon Church in particular hides an insidious racist belief under a cloak of love and grace. Many Mormons do not learn—or they would probably leave—that the LDS

Church has for most of its existence barred black people from ever attaining the priesthood. This in turn kept them from participating in many of the Temple rites such as Temple Endowment, family sealings, and other ordinances that are necessary, according to Mormon doctrine, to reach the highest level of salvation.

Since its inception by the 'Prophet' Joseph Smith, the Mormon Church has taught that black people are an inferior race. In 1838, Joseph Smith answered a question about freeing black slaves while en route from Kirtland to Missouri as follows: "Are the Mormons abolitionists? No...we do not believe in setting the Negroes free."[59]

Such racism was echoed by many of the future church leaders, including Brigham Young who, upon commenting on the appearance of black people, said, "Cain slew his brother...and the Lord put a mark upon him, which is the *flat nose and black skin...*"[60] Another prominent Mormon leader, wrote, "Not only was Cain called upon to suffer, but because of his wickedness *he became the father of an inferior race.*"[61] Later, he would expand upon this opinion when he wrote, "There is a reason why one man is *born black* and with *other disadvantages*, while another is born white with great advantages. The reason is that we once had an estate before we came here, and were obedient; more or less, to the laws that were given us there."[62]

The underlying teaching is that God loves black people less than He does white people! This is not a statement that can be found in Scripture, nor is it a concept that is ever endorsed by God. On the contrary, the Bible is clear:

- **Romans 2:11** – *For God does not show favoritism.*

- **Galatians 3:28-29** – *There is neither Jew nor Greek, slave nor free, male nor female, for you are all one in Christ Jesus. If you belong to Christ, then you are Abraham's seed, and heirs according to the promise.*

---

59 *Smith* 1977, p. 120.

60 *Journal of Discourses*, Vol. 7, pp. 290-291.

61 Joseph Fielding Smith, *The Way to Perfection*, p. 101.

62 Joseph Fielding Smith, *Doctrines of Salvation*, Vol. 1, p. 61.

- **John 3:16**– *For God so loved the world that he gave his one and only Son, that whoever believes in him shall not perish but have eternal life.*

Even with these few verses, we can see that God is not racist at all! He neither endorses encourages, or supports such a notion. If this is true, then why does anyone perpetuate this idea? Luke 6:45 tells us that only out of the abundance of the heart does the mouth speak. This means that what someone is really feeling in their heart will come out with the words that they speak. Many will try to camouflage their true and underlying belief with words that their audience wants to hear—but eventually, the truth comes out in their own words.

This has been the case with Mormons, they would like people to believe that they are not racist, but their own words will convict them of their true belief. Make no mistake in thinking this was a command from God, as they will tell you, instead listen to their words and observe the fruit of such words in discerning right and wrong through God's word, the Bible. He wants you to know that He loves all people and desires all to come to Him. People have a choice as to whom they will follow, God or man.

Racism in the Mormon Church is not obvious at first. However, due to underlying doctrine, a subtle seed of judgment and the fear that blacks are born sinners occurs in most members. I hadn't realized that this was a doctrine I believed. Without knowing why, a sort of caution and wariness raises its ugly head when it comes to dealing with black people—this happens subconsciously without even realizing it.

I had never even considered this before becoming a Mormon, but the Mormon scriptures crept in, creating an unconscious judgment that I was unaware of until I left the church. I have since gained an enormous amount of compassion for all people. I have gained an understanding through the outreach programs of the Christian Church I attend. All races are in need of outreach. Compassion for circumstances regardless of race, and an awareness of an individual's life story is not a common sermon in the Mormon Church.

The reiteration of "white and delightsome" causes a sense of supe-riority. I often wondered what I did that was so *obedient* in order to be white. How grateful I am that my eyes have been opened! I did nothing! I am a sinner just like everyone else—no matter the color. My God-given nature to love everyone the same and to see through the eyes of others has been restored. I have been humbled by God with the knowledge that there is no one righteous, not even one (Romans 3:9-19).

Like I was, most Mormon members are ignorant as to what is happening unconsciously by attending a church that has subtle rac-ist beliefs. Surprisingly, a few black people have even been lulled into the Mormon faith. Like me at the time, I didn't know the belief, and because I thought this church would bring me close to my Savior, I joined. The smooth speaking of the leaders would cause you to believe that this was a God given command. Romans 16:18 says, "By smooth talk and flattery they deceive the minds of naive people."

Even the leaders themselves do not recognize the problem, unfor-tunately. They should take a look at Scripture, because all Christian leaders and teachers will be held accountable at the judgment seat of God (Matthew 12:36, James 3:1, Timothy 1:7). The problem is not with the individual; it is with the entire belief system itself. Mormon-ism began with this concept of racism and then perpetuated it until 1978 when they finally caved into pressure and allowed people of any color to attain their priesthood. This does not mean, however, that they have rebuked the doctrine or ever called it an evil practice. They stand behind this doctrine as something God commanded at the time. Apparently, God must have changed His mind and relented in 1978.

However, the ramifications of this initial doctrine are still ongo-ing. This instilled belief that God commanded something so evil has created an underlying belief that God is a racist. You can't sim-ply discontinue a major doctrine without rebuking it as an evil and ungodly belief. Since Mormons believe that edicts are given directly to their prophets from God, it becomes problematic when they want to change something. When they do, they are either saying God can't make up His mind or He is indecisive in His commands. Listen to this quote: "Negros in this life are denied the priesthood; under no circumstances can they hold this delegation of authority from the Almighty. The gospel message of salvation is not carried affirmatively to them.....Negroes are not equal with other races where the receipt of certain spiritual blessings are concerned...."[63]

So, when they changed this policy, how does this make Mr. McConkie look? And if the Mormons are willing to admit he was wrong, then that puts a question mark on everything that not only McConkie stated, but on all that other supposedly "godly" and inspired Mormon leaders have said as well. As Christian leaders, God himself will judge them for teachings that go against what He taught. God says something entirely different in His Word. Philippians 2:5-7 says, "Your attitude should be the same as that of Christ Jesus: Who, being in very nature God, did not consider equality with God something to be grasped, but made himself nothing, taking the very nature of a servant."

Of course, they can just claim that God changed His mind, which is quite common in the Mormon faith, making it possible to justify sin. Make no mistake, God sees all and will judge those that practice a doctrine other than the doctrine of His grace and love.

Understanding the Priesthood of Jesus Christ

Taking Scripture out of context often results in confusion, misdirection and, as a result, sin. Is there ever Biblical justification for Sin? No, there is not. But that hasn't stopped many people down through the centuries from trying. The following is taken from the LDS.org website: "Ever since biblical times, the Lord has designated through His prophets who could receive the priesthood and other blessings of the gospel. Among the tribes of Israel, for example, only men of the tribe of Levi were given the priesthood and allowed to officiate in certain ordinances. Likewise, during the Savior's earthly ministry, gospel blessings were restricted to the Jews. Only after a revelation to the Apostle Peter were the gospel and priesthood extended to others (see Acts 10:1–33; 14:23; 15:6–8)."[64]

---

63 Bruce R. McConkie, *Mormon Doctrine*, 1958, p. 477.

64 www.lds.org

There is a profound lack of understanding regarding the Scriptures referenced. To begin with, the Levitical Priesthood was indeed restricted to a certain group of people, but not to a race. It was restricted to a specific tribe of one race—the Levites. These were the descendants of Levi who were the only ones to come and stand with Moses (Exodus 32:26) when Moses asked, "Who is on the Lord's side?" Because of this, God chose the Levites to be the priesthood. This wasn't about race! This was about identifying with God and receiving His priesthood.

Secondly, Jesus did indeed come to minister to the Jews, but He went out of His way to touch the lives of many Gentiles, including the Woman at the Well, the Centurion, the woman whose daughter was possessed, and many others just to demonstrate His love to *all* people. Jesus cared for *all* mankind. He came to the Jews because the Jews were God's chosen people, prophesied to murder and kill Him, thereby breaking the covenant and allowing God to establish a New Covenant with *all* people and *all* races!

Thirdly, Jesus did indeed appear to the Apostle Peter to get him to take the Gospel to Cornelius and other Gentiles. However, Peter's reluctance to go to the Gentiles had nothing to do with a law of God, but rather with a law of man which contributed to Peter's own racism. Peter, in Acts 10 verse 28 confirms this when He said to them, "You are well aware that it is against our law for a Jew to associate with a Gentile or visit him. But God has shown me that I should not call *any* man impure or unclean."

God's laws in the Old Testament about intermarrying were not about racial superiority. Rather they were set in place to protect His people. He didn't want those that were followers of Him to marry those that were not—those that worshiped a false god. He was trying to protect His people from being pulled into idolatry as Solomon was. It wasn't a racial problem, it was an idolatry problem. Jesus' appearance to Peter wasn't about changing something God had done; it was about getting Peter to let go of the racism he had been taught while growing up so he could do what God had always intended—give the Gospel to all people!

So, in regards to the priesthood, the Bible clearly states that as Christians we are all welcomed to be his holy priests. Notice the following verses:

*"You are coming to Christ, who is the living cornerstone of
God's temple. He was rejected by people, but he was chosen
by God for great honor. And you are living stones that God is
building into his spiritual temple. What's more, you are his
holy priests. Through the mediation of Jesus Christ, you offer
spiritual sacrifices that please God."*

— 1 Peter 2:4-5 (NLT)

This passage is directly referencing all Christians. Many of these
Christians were Gentiles of various races, colors, and cultures.
According to Old Testament doctrine and practices, they would
never be allowed into the priesthood—rejected by men. But God,
through Jesus Christ, has chosen every believer to be part of the
priesthood.

The purpose of the priesthood even in the Old Testament was
to bring sinful man back to a Holy God. The purpose and aim of the
priesthood hasn't changed even in the New Testament. Only this
time, instead of a tribe of people who had chosen to stand with God
to be His priests, He now wants *anyone* who has chosen to stand
with Him (through faith in Jesus) to be His priests. Now, each and
every Christian has a priestly mission: the ministry of reconciliation
(Hebrews 5:18).

And just to make sure He was clear on this, God had Peter pen the
following verses as well:

*"But you are a chosen people, a royal priesthood, a holy
nation, a people belonging to God, that you may declare
the praises of him who called you out of darkness into his
wonderful light. Once you were not a people, but now you are
the people of God; once you had not received mercy, but now
you have received mercy."*

— 1 Peter 2:9-10

Gentiles of any race can now be named among the chosen people
of God. Every Christian is part of this priesthood. We are all called to

service. We are all given the job of preaching the Gospel and sharing our Savior, Jesus Christ. Jesus is our High Priest (Hebrews 3:1). He is called the High Priest of our profession. What profession? The priesthood! Into this priesthood, every believer is called.

We need to get back to what Jesus taught in 1 Corinthians 12. In this chapter, we learn that there are many different members. Regardless of color, gender, race or ethnicity we are one body of Christ. Here are some things we should bear in mind:

1. No two people are ever the same, so everyone matters (1 Corinthians 12:4-11).

2. No one can be considered irrelevant (1 Corinthians 12:21-24).

3. If we are in Christ we are part of Him (1 Corinthians 12:12, 27).

4. God determines where we best fit in the body, where we are most needed (1 Corinthians 12:11, 18).

5. Not everyone has the same gifts, but everyone is important to the function of the body (1 Corinthians 12:8-11, 28-30).

6. The purpose of one person is different than the purpose of another so we can't really compare the two. We can't say one is better (1 Corinthians 12:22-25).

7. Our relevance is not in association to a group of people but in the body of Christ (1 Corinthians 12:19).

8. Division is a work of the Devil, not the work of God (1 Corinthians 12:25).

9. More important than any gift, ability, position, or honor is that of love. If you don't have love, then you don't have anything of value (1 Corinthians 13).

Wasn't Cain's Curse that of Black Skin?

We don't know that. No one does. The Bible doesn't say what the mark was; however this is a belief in Mormonism. Joseph Fielding Smith wrote, "Not only was Cain called upon to suffer, but because of his wickedness he became the father of an inferior race."[65] The Mormon prophet Brigham Young when commenting on the appearance of Africans said this, "Cain slew his brother....and the Lord put a mark upon him, which is the flat nose and black skin..."[66]

Here is the actual reference found in Genesis 4:15, "But the LORD said to him, 'Not so; if anyone kills Cain, he will suffer vengeance seven times over.' Then the LORD put a mark on Cain so that no one who found him would kill him."

What was the mark? No one knows. So it is foolish to insist that the mark was black skin. But, for the sake of argument, let us suppose it was. Where is the evidence that this mark would be passed down to his children? The mark was to protect Cain from vengeful wrath. It wasn't for punishment. It was for protection. Why would this protection need to be passed down to his children? Secondly, if all of man died in the flood except for Noah (who was descended from Shem) then how did this 'inferior' race survive? Shouldn't they all have died out in the flood? To explain away these two issues means you have to reinvent the Bible—which, in essence, is exactly what the Mormon Church has done when Joseph Smith wrote the Book of Mormon.

Here is what the Book of Mormon has to say about it in 2 Nephi 5:21- 24, "And he had caused the cursing to come upon them, yea, even a sore cursing, because of their iniquity. For behold, they had hardened their hearts against him, that they had become like unto a flint; wherefore, as they were white, and exceedingly fair and delightsome, that they might not be enticing unto my people the Lord God did cause a skin of blackness to come upon them. And thus saith the Lord God: I will cause that they shall be loathsome unto thy people, save they shall repent of their iniquities. And cursed shall be the seed of him that mixeth with their seed; for they shall be cursed even with the

---

65 Joseph Fielding Smith, *The Way to Perfection*, p. 101.

66 *Journal of Discourses*, Vol. 7, pp. 290-291.

same cursing. And the Lord spake it, and it was done. And because of their cursing which was upon them they did become an idle people, full of mischief and subtlety, and did seek in the wilderness for beasts of prey."

Since they could not rightly justify this belief Biblically, they invented it within their own scriptures. This is no evidence at all that Cain's curse was that of black skin. There is no evidence that Adam and Eve were even white! They were most likely brown. There is an interesting passage that follows the Biblical flood. It refers to Ham, one of Noah's children. It says in Genesis 10:6, "And the sons of Ham; Cush, and Mizraim, and Phut, and Canaan." Notice the names 'Mizriam' and 'Cush.' Mizriam's name means Egypt—it's the same word. Cush means 'Ethiopia' or 'black.' He was most likely born with black skin.

This is interesting because the very first Gentile in the Bible that God specifically sent someone to witness to was an Ethiopian—a black man (Acts 8). In fact, God pulled Philip from a great revival to go way out into the desert and find one man—a black man—to give the Gospel to. Isn't it great that God does not show favoritism? God loves everyone, no matter what the color of his or her skin is.

A little girl asked her mom, "Mom, what color is Jesus?"

"Sweetie," her mom replied, "Jesus is the light of the world, and pure light is made up of every color in the rainbow."

Amen!

Hasn't the Mormon Church Recanted This Doctrine?

Following Joseph Smith's death, the church through the Prophet Brigham Young taught that 'Negroes' were black due to the mark of Cain. Mormonism, not God, determined that most black people of African descent were disqualified automatically from being ordained into the Priesthood. This policy lasted for a century.

Then, in 1978, church leaders claimed that they received a revelation that the time had come to now accept 'Negros' into the priesthood. The following is taken from the LDS.org website: "In June 1978, President Spencer W. Kimball received a revelation extending priesthood ordination to all worthy males of The Church of Jesus Christ of

Latter-day Saints (Official Declaration 2). Before that time only worthy male members who were not of black African descent were ordained to the priesthood. With the revelation to President Kimball in 1978, the priesthood is now available to all worthy male members regardless of race or ethnicity (see Official Declaration 2). Each candidate for ordination is interviewed by priesthood leaders to ensure that he understands and agrees to live by established principles of righteousness (see Doctrine and Covenants 84:33–44; 121:34–46)." [67]

Despite this reversal of policy, no acknowledgement has ever been made that either the doctrine or practice of racism was actually wrong. To the contrary, the idea that black people are a product of a curse is still taught within Mormon circles. They may let them into the priesthood, but there will always be the underlining belief that they are somehow inferior due to their skin color and ancestry.

Could it be that Mormon Church leaders merely stopped 'the practice' of denying priesthood on the basis of race due to the current state of America at the time? After all, Utah was denied statehood because of the practice of polygamy and the Mormon Church suddenly got a 'revelation' to stop that practice. The Civil Rights movement had hit America hard and governmental and workplace policies were all changing. The pressure on the church would have been immense. How convenient to get a sudden 'revelation' to change the policy.

The policy may have changed, but has the doctrine? No. They can't change the doctrine without admitting their most sacred prophets—Joseph Smith being one of them—was wrong. If their founding fathers were wrong then the entire religion is wrong! It is my prayer that one day they will come forward and declare the truth.

This doctrine still exists. Africans and African Americans still have their beautiful black skin and characteristics, and so what are we to make of the words spoken in Book of Mormon, Mormon 9:6, "O then ye unbelieving, turn ye unto the Lord; cry mightily unto the Father in the name of Jesus, that perhaps ye may be found spotless, pure, fair, and white, having been cleansed by the blood of the Lamb, at that great and last day."

---

67 www.lds.org

What are members to make of the words "white and delight-some?" The association of white and pure and black as impure is hard to miss. It is an association that to this day people outside of the Mormon Church try to do away with. It is unfair and it is racist. In the Book of Mormon, 4 Nephi 1:10, all the people of Nephi had become "an exceedingly fair and delightsome people." In other words, they became white-skinned. The Mormon Church still teaches this association of white with perfection and black skin with sin.

It is still taught within the church today that white people did not sin in some form of their previous life and therefore that is why they are born white. With this teaching, how then can the leaders no longer view the black skin as loathsome? In the meantime, it appears that this so called 'curse of Cain' still remains on the African race even though the Mormon Church extended the Priesthood to them in 1978. This curse has not been removed—for their skin is still dark.

What does this do to the mentality of both white and blacks? What about all the other races and ethnicities in the world? There has never been a recantation of this evil doctrine or an apology for the racism. Please note, I am not writing this to invoke "racism" towards Mormons or any other creed—but to bring the Truth and Love of Jesus to *all* mankind.

Racism versus the Command to Love

Since we are all to be part of the body of Christ, there must not be any division. "If a kingdom is divided against itself, that kingdom cannot stand," Mark 3:24 teaches us. When we place a cursing or label on another individual, whether it is about their skin color, power, position, or any other way, we categorize them. We place the same cursing on ourselves whether we realize this or not.

We will not experience the Power in the Priesthood that we have been given by being in the body of Christ if we have any form of racism or prejudice. Jesus taught us to "Go into all the world and preach the good news to all creation. Whoever believes and is baptized will be saved, but whoever does not believe will be condemned. And these signs will accompany those who believe: In my name they will drive out demons; they will speak in new tongues; they will pick up snakes with their hands; and when they drink deadly poison, it will not hurt them at all; they will place their hands on sick people, and they will get well." (Mark 16:15-18). We are literally cursing ourselves and blocking the blessings of Christ if we have any form of racism or prejudice.

A lawyer came to Jesus and asked Him a question, "Teacher, which is the great commandment in the law?" Jesus said to him, "You shall love the Lord your God with all your heart, with all your soul, and with all your mind. This is the first and great commandment. And the second is like it: You shall love your neighbor as yourself. On these two commandments hang all the Law and the Prophets."

Jesus gave us the command to Love one another (John 13:34). It is important to each of us to feel like we matter in this world. It breaks my heart to think that I was ever a part of something so against God's desire to love and accept *all* men. We hurt others and ourselves when we do something God does not want us to do.

Let us use our life, our words and our actions to be a blessing to others by accepting and loving *all* men. Solomon was an example of this to the Shulamite woman. She was insecure about her appearance. When she first met Solomon, she said, "Do not look upon me, because I am dark, because the sun has tanned me" (Song of Solomon 1:6). But after she had been around Solomon for only a short time, she called herself "the rose of Sharon, and the lily of the valleys" (Song of Solomon 2:1). That is quite a change of perspective! How did it happen? In spite of herself, Solomon's word pictures made their way around his bride's defenses.

When we lose sight of God's intention, we begin to hate instead of love. This is not of God. Look at these verses:

*"Anyone who claims to be in the light but hates his brother
is still in the darkness. Whoever loves his brother lives in the
light, and there is nothing in him to make him stumble. But
whoever hates his brother is in the darkness and walks around
in the darkness; he does not know where he is going, because
the darkness has blinded him."*

— 1 John 2:9-11

"If we love our Christian brothers and sisters, it proves that we have passed from death to life. But a person who has no love is still dead."

— 1 John 3:14 (NLT)

"If anyone says, "I love God," yet hates his brother, he is a liar. For anyone who does not love his brother, whom he has seen, cannot love God, whom he has not seen."

— 1 John 4:20

Do you get the idea? It is important that we feel as if we mattered. But you get this feeling, not by being better than someone else, but by loving the brethren. In this way, as listed in 1 Corinthians 12 and 13, you not only matter, but you also begin to understand that everyone matters.

Without this, we place a curse on ourselves from God. Racism and division does more than just cause you to hate, it causes separation from God and others. This is the danger of racism. Jesus Christ's whole ministry was about reconciliation. He came to reconcile us to God and others. How can we love God when we don't love our brothers and sisters?

There is no fear in love!

Perfect love casts out all fear (1 John 4:18). God loved us and that casts out the fear of rejection, of bigotry, of prejudice, and of racism. He trusted us enough to allow us imperfect humans to become parents and to go and make disciples of all nations. He never said you must get it right and become perfect before He would trust you enough to have priesthood power. He allowed us to learn and grow into becoming like Him. Every one of us is a sinner, regardless of our color.

Let us become like Christ and love one another. It does not matter whether you are black, white, Hispanic, Asian, or any other color or ethnicity. God made you, and you're perfect in His sight. Don't let racism stop God's blessing in your life and others. Reconcile with one another. Help one another. Love one another, and in this way we will be not only hearers of the word, but we will do what it says (James 1:22).

A Prayer of Healing

"Father, we come to You right now in the name of Jesus. We break every curse that has ever come upon on us in the body of Christ through Racism either knowingly or unknowingly. Lord, our eyes have been opened and we choose to love as You loved. Lord, we renounce and rebuke any form of hatred. We ask for Your forgiveness. We ask that You remove any curse that has been placed upon us through racism and not treating others equally. We release and claim Your blessings on us by the blood of Jesus. Amen."

Is the Church Safe or Judgmental?

"Let he who is without sin cast the first stone."

— John 8:7

God did not come to judge, but to show the way. The Bible says in John 3:17, "God sent his Son into the world not to judge the world, but to save the world through Him." Jesus' great love for all mankind is evident in all He says and does. He does not want anyone to perish (1 Timothy 2:3-4). Jesus lived a life of forgiveness and mercy. He is so quick to forgive, and if He possesses any judgment at all, it is on those who refuse to forgive (Matthew 6:14-15). He requires that we forgive others as well. You can see that in 1 John 1:9, Ephesians 4:32, and Colossians 3:13.

Jesus was safe to be around when He walked the Earth—not just physically, but emotionally and spiritually. He never condemned anyone. He came to bring truth and light, to show others the way. The only people Jesus ever criticized were those of His own religious group who were condemning the prostitutes, murderers, tax collectors, gluttons, drunkards, and other "sinners." Jesus criticized the religious leaders of His day who were making it hard for the "sinners" to experience the love, grace, and forgiveness of God. He wanted to make it easy for the Kingdom of Heaven to reign in people's lives, not more difficult. Those who set up roadblocks received His harshest words.

"There is therefore now no condemnation to them which are in Christ Jesus, who walk not after the flesh, but after the Spirit."

— Romans 8:1

Love as Jesus Loved

We should not criticize sinners and people who do not "measure up" to our idea of righteousness. Jesus never did this. He loved the prostitutes. He forgave murderers. He invited greedy tax collectors to join Him. He shared food and drink with gluttons and drunkards.

We need to help people, not condemn them. Jesus criticized the Pharisees, not to gain power or prestige, but to help the common people who labored under the oppression of the Pharisees. We should include everyone and love them into the light. Judgment and exclusion causes resentment and rebellion.

Jesus taught with love and loved the people He taught. He made everyone feel like each day was a new day. He taught that His mercies are new every day. "Because of the Lord's great love we are not consumed, for His compassions never fail. They are new every morning; great is your faithfulness" (Lamentations 3:22-23). Jesus makes all things new (2 Corinthians 5:17). He has not changed since He was resurrected and became our intercessor from Heaven.

When Jesus met with the woman at the well, He did not judge her but instead offered her living water. He was her defender then and He is our defender now.

"My dear children, I am writing this to you so that you will not sin. But if anyone does sin, we have an advocate who pleads our case before the Father. He is Jesus Christ, the one who is truly righteous."

— 1 John 2:1

256

Did you see what that scripture said? He said that Jesus is our advocate. That means He is our lawyer in God's court. He is on our side, pleading our case and, when we have guilt, taking the punishment for us.

Jesus calls us to follow His example and care for His flock. "Then I will give shepherds after my own heart, who will lead you with knowledge and understanding" (Jeremiah 3:15). When Paul was speaking to the Ephesian Elders, he admonished them, "Pay careful attention to yourselves and to all the flock, in which the Holy Spirit has made you overseers, to care for the church of God, which he obtained with His own blood" (Acts 20:28).

To be appointed to care for Jesus' flock one would need to take great care not to harm them. God gave specific instruction on how to do this. One of the commands that He gave was in Deuteronomy 12:32, "See that you do all I command you; do not add to it or take away from it." This means that every word that comes out of your mouth as a leader, apostle, prophet, and so forth needs to be what Christ spoke in the Bible. At the very least, they must be words that convey His heart. Read it again!

> *"Then I will give shepherds after my own heart."*
>
> — Jeremiah 3:15

Despite this, the Mormon Church issues guidelines that are very judgmental and require us to pay for the sins of others. A Mormon prophet made this statement on a woman's virtue, "Also far-reaching is the effect of loss of chastity. Once given or taken or stolen it can never be regained. Even in forced contact such as rape or incest, the injured one is greatly outraged. If she has not cooperated and contributed to the foul deed, she is of course in a more favorable position. There is no condemnation where there is no voluntary participation. It is better to die in defending one's virtue than to live having lost it without a struggle."[68]

---

68 Spencer W. Kimball, *The Miracle of Forgiveness.*

This is not the heart of Christ at all! Have they studied what is in the Bible? Do they understand that there is no condemnation in Christ whether voluntary or not (Romans 8:1)? We can't pay for the sins of another; therefore we have no power of condemnation. Only the righteous, only the holy Son of God can condemn. But He did not. He came to save. He died on the cross for our sins and paid our price. There is no place for our condemnation. Statements like those made by Mr. Kimball hurt a person who is seeking relationship with Christ. How many of us have sinned? How many people have sinned, and then came to Christ later? How many Christians have sinned and then sought forgiveness and cleansing from God? Who are we to deny them that?

Here are more statements made by Apostles and leaders of the Mormon Church:

- "There is no true Latter-day Saint who would not rather bury a son or daughter than to have him or her lose his or her chastity — realizing that chastity is of more value than anything else in all the world."[69]

- "The victim must do all in his or her power to stop the abuse. Most often, the victim is innocent because of being disabled by fear or the power or authority of the offender. At some point in time, however, the Lord may prompt a victim to recognize a degree of responsibility for abuse. Your priesthood leader will help assess your responsibility so that, if needed, it can be addressed. Otherwise the seeds of guilt will remain and sprout into bitter fruit. Yet no matter what degree of responsibility, from absolutely none to increasing consent, the healing power of the atonement of Jesus Christ can provide a complete cure."[70]

Never, never, never does God say that we must accept responsibility for the sin of another person! Even throwing in the last line saying

---

69 Heber J. Grant, quoted in *The Miracle of Forgiveness* by Spencer W. Kimball

70 Apostle Richard G. Scott, *Healing the Tragic Scars of Abuse*, (General Conference, Ensign, May 1992).

that Jesus Christ provides a complete cure is more an afterthought to the focus of this article. The point being, from Apostle Richard Scott's point of view (see above quote), is that we bear *some level* of responsibility for the sins committed against us. What kind of message does this send to the perpetrator? That the burden of sin also falls on the victim? Victims have a hard enough time with blaming themselves and trying to overcome the emotional trauma inflicted upon them. They do not need additional guilt and responsibility heaped upon them by these designated spiritual authorities in their lives.

When Christ was crucified, the Romans did everything they could to humiliate and torture the Son of God. According to Matthew's Gospel, Jesus was stripped of his clothes and mocked (Matthew 27:35). No one knows for certain whether or not Jesus himself was raped. What we do know is that in the Gospel accounts of Jesus' flogging, it is entirely possible that Jesus was naked while he was beaten. We also know that sexual violence was used in the ancient world both by the Romans and by other ancient cultures. There was an element of sexual humiliation in the torture Jesus went through.

Remember, the Bible says that Jesus was without sin (2 Corinthians 5:21). Jesus willingly surrendered; He did not fight; yet He remained without sin. The Word of God does not say in any way that what He endured was His fault. Nor did His father say to Jesus that someone would show Him which responsibility was His in this violation! No, Jesus suffered through no fault of His own. He chose to take this upon Himself solely because He loved us and wanted to save us.

Recognizing a Safe Church

When you belong to a judgmental church, guilt becomes your new companion. Remember, the enemy is the one that comes to condemn, not Christ. Safe churches do not condemn, inflict guilt or use control. They allow you to keep your free agency and make decisions for yourself based on your own conviction from the Holy Spirit.

A safe church will not cause fear of judgment. Fear is not of God. When you are hearing truth from your church, you will experience His grace. You will not be afraid to make mistakes or voice your opinion when they differ from your leaders. Your leaders will respect your individuality and boundaries. We are not perfect and there will be disagreements, therefore the Bible even shows *how* to handle disagreements within the body.

"If your brother or sister sins (against you), go and point out
their fault, just between the two of you. If they listen to you, you
have won them over. But if they will not listen, take one or two
others along, so that 'every matter may be established by the
testimony of two or three witnesses.' If they still refuse to listen,
tell it to the church; and if they refuse to listen even to the
church, treat them as you would a pagan or a tax collector."

— Matthew 18:15-17

This shows that we are to try to work together in a safe place. The church is to be a place where we have mutual trust, respect and caring. It doesn't distinguish whether the disagreement is between members or members and the leadership. If there is a conflict, God provides a way to work it out.

People in a safe church will know that God can speak to you directly, without having to go through the authority of the church. Members of a safe church will not expect perfection of you because they realize that you are human and live in a fallen world. Their goal for themselves and for you is the pursuit of God and a relationship with Him. They know that we all sin and fall short of the glory of God. They will not try to look or act perfect, but instead will be transparent with their own imperfections.

Prophets, leaders and any position of authority are held to a higher standard and commanded to practice what they preach. Leaders who did not live to this standard were to be removed from office. They were not to use their power to justify their actions or manipulate people into satisfying their own lusts. Joseph Smith was having sex with young girls he wasn't married to. Was he concerned about these young girls losing their "virtue?" The leader is not outside the rules. They are to be an example of the rules in action. Hypocrisy in any leader results in a poor organization. Hypocrisy in church doctrine and practice is a sign of a false leader. Even David repented when called on his sin; he didn't try to justify it.

Safe churches will offer comfort. They don't blame the victim. They bring hope to you and help you to understand that God wants to restore you. They are a source of support in any healing process. They will not judge you, but will instigate a healing process by whatever resources are available, both in and outside of the church. There must be a profound recognition of the fact that *all* Christians are part of the body of Christ and are working towards the same goal: Christ!

In safe churches there are outreach groups, support groups and small groups to help the members grow. They offer different ministries, including counseling, post abortion, divorce care, special needs care, and so on. The teaching recognizes brokenness, struggle, and inability as normal parts of the sanctification process.

Jesus offers comfort to those who suffer, for He knows our every suffering. "I have told you these things, so that in me you may have peace. In this world you will have trouble. But take heart! I have overcome the world" (John 16:33).

The quotes I gave you from the Mormon Prophets are not words that Christ would ever speak! They are hurtful and wounding words. This is dogmatic, puffed-up arrogance and ignorance. It also closely resembles the Islamic faith where a raped woman is stoned to death for enticing the man into a sexual frenzy. These people are so judgmental and brainwashed that the family "gets" to throw the first stone.

What Jesus Wants to do for You

The condemnation of the Mormon leadership is a far different characterization from the Jesus of the Bible who teaches, "Let he who is without sin cast the first stone" (John 8:7). Remember, stones come not only in the form of rocks, but in words and in attitude, showing the reflection of the heart.

> *"Those things which proceed out of the mouth come forth from the heart; and they defile the man."*
> — Matthew 15:18

I wonder if the Lord would consider the prophet defiled because of the words he spoke that showed a lack of compassion. These judgmental statements made by people who have no right to declare someone guilty or to impose punishment are not the heart of compassion for the hurting. They are not the words Christ would speak. No, Christ says words like:

- **Psalm 34:18** – *"I will heal the brokenhearted and save those who are crushed in spirit."*

- **Psalm 147:3** – *"He will bind their wounds."*

- **2 Samuel 16:12** – *"It may be that the LORD will see my distress and repay me with good for the cursing I am receiving today."*

Please look to the Lord Jesus Christ for your comfort and safety. Go to His Word, the Bible, and find the words He longs to say to you. When you begin to understand His word, you will have peace. "Peace I leave with you; my peace I give you. I do not give to you as the world gives. Do not let your hearts be troubled and do not be afraid" (John 14:27).

Remember, Luke 1:37 tells us "nothing is impossible with God!" He can raise the dead and He can certainly give a woman back her virtue and purity. Look at the examples God gives in his word:

- **Ephesians 5:25-27** – "Husbands, love your wives, just as Christ loved the church and gave himself up for her to make her holy, cleansing her by the washing with water through the word, and to present her to himself as a radiant church, without stain or wrinkle or any other blemish, but holy and blameless."

- **Revelation 21:9-11** – "One of the seven angels who had the seven bowls full of the seven last plagues came and said to me, 'Come, I will show you the bride, the wife of the Lamb.' And he carried me away in the Spirit to a mountain great and high, and showed me the Holy City, Jerusalem, coming down out of heaven from God. It shone with the glory of God, and its brilliance was like that of a very precious jewel, like a jasper, clear as crystal."

In both of these verses, we see that God loves us. Husbands can, through their love and through speaking God's Word over their wives, cleanse her. She radiates in his love, not his judgment. She serves in love. In Revelation, we see that the wicked city, Jerusalem, which Jesus wept over, was purified and came down from Heaven. Again, it was love, not judgment, which brought the city to Christ.

God is a God of Hope. God wants us to love life. He came that we might live life to the fullest and have joy (John10:10). John 3:16 shows us that the love of God has provided a way for each and every person to be saved through their faith and trust in Jesus Christ. Verse 17, however, shows WHY God did it:

> *"For God did not send his Son into the world to condemn the world, but to save the world through him."*
>
> — John 3:17

God didn't send Jesus to judge, but to draw them to the safety of His loving embrace. If that is why God came to earth in the form of a man, how can we then say that His true church—His representation on earth—should be a place of ritual, rules and judgment? Likewise, how could it be a place of hypocrisy and control since Jesus criticized that very trait among the religious leaders of His day? Notice that He did not condemn the person, but He did criticize the trait. Had the religious leaders turned their life to God, He would surely forgive them.

Here is the truth of God's Word: even if you chose to be involved in a sexual violation such as prostitution, Jesus still wants to offer you a new life and a chance to be made new. Not just one time either, but continually, for the rest of your life. You see, He is not just a God of second chances, but He is a God of forever forgiveness—if you will just come to Him. He also desires that we treat others with this same forgiveness. Perfect love keeps on loving even after being betrayed.

Take, for example, Hosea. In his case, this perfect love meant buying back his prostitute wife from those she has sold herself to. God even commands it.

> *"The LORD said to me, "Go, show your love to your wife again, though she is loved by another man and is an adulteress. Love her as the LORD loves the Israelites, though they turn to other gods and love the sacred raisin cakes." So I bought her for fifteen shekels of silver and about a homer of barley. Then I told her, "You are to live with me many days; you must not be a prostitute or be intimate with any man, and I will live with you."*

— Hosea 3:1-3

Hosea's steadfast love in the face of such unfaithfulness parallels God's love for His people in the midst of their idolatry. God restores Israel even after all of her betrayal to Him. Jesus healed and restored people both physically and spiritually. He restores purity. When prophets put such a heavy emphasis on virginity as the standard of purity that, once lost, is gone forever, they are not offering what Jesus offered, which is the hope in Him. "This truth gives them confidence that they have eternal life, which God who does not lie, promised before the beginning of time" (1 Titus 1:2).

In the Book of Mormon, there are verses that place purity of the physical body above the love of Jesus. An example can be found in Moroni 9:9, which says, "For behold, many of the daughters of the Lamanites have they taken prisoners; and after depriving them of that which was most dear and precious above all things, which is chastity and virtue." What should be most precious to us is our Lord Jesus Christ. God told us not to put anything above him. Anything that we do put above Him becomes idolatry. Mormon thinking causes victims of sexual abuse and those that have sinned to believe they have lost all that was precious to them. When what should be most precious to anyone is forgiveness of our sins, our salvation and the hope of eternal life (Titus 1:2, Titus 3:7). Call on the Lord and you will be saved (Acts 2:21).

God does not judge our outward appearance. He looks on our heart. We do not know what causes some people to walk in certain patterns in their life. In the case of Hosea's wife, Gomer, we do not know if she was sold as a child prostitute. Perhaps she lived such a bad life that anything else, like what Hosea offered her, was so far out of her comfort zone that she may have felt she didn't deserve it. Her betrayal, in her eyes, may have been the only gift she could give to her husband—freedom from her. It would take time before she realized what love really was. We cannot judge others. We have not walked in their shoes.

When I was Mormon, no one ever knew the path I had walked before Christ came into my life. Having a new relationship with Jesus and my salvation should have been enough to be allowed to become part of their Christian fellowship. Instead, ridiculous expectations were placed on me. These included having lots of children, not going for walks with my husband on a Sunday because it was breaking the Sabbath, not drinking ice tea and other outward actions that some-how demonstrated purity in their eyes. These actions had nothing to do with the condition of my heart.

These things were so inconsequential and of no importance to my salvation, but I felt such pressure and judgment from others to wear clothing like them, go to the Temple and then enforce these rules on my family. They kept trying to make me become like them. I was never accepted for who I was and what I was created to be. Therefore, in my efforts to conform, I became judgmental too.

I started to become like them and to expect others to become like me. God tells us to spend time meditating on His word and to spend time in the presence of other believers. This is because we begin to become like those we spend the most time with. This is a better way to change into what we can become! Instead of being forced to conform, we are accepted and the time we spend with loving people changes us. If we are with kind people, we will be kind and so on. However, if we are with people who condemn, we will condemn even if we obey all the rules.

Instead, if we trust in Jesus and rest in His safety, we too will become safe people. When we are shown grace we show it to others. We need to allow Him to be the one that convicts our hearts and the hearts of other people.

"Do not judge, or you too will be judged."
— Matthew 7:1

I experienced judgment in many forms against myself, my family, and my friends while I was a Mormon. One time in particular stands out to me. I was serving in the nursery and my youngest of three children was only one year old. Sunday was always a difficult day since my youngest took his nap at 1 p.m., but because the ward we were assigned to always met at 1 p.m., my child had to forgo his nap. As any parent knows, this makes for a very cranky child. I served in the nursery during this time for over a year! My mornings were busy with family. My afternoon was spent serving in church and my evenings were spent catching up for the week to come. I dreaded Sundays.

Finally I built up enough courage to go ask the bishop to be released from this calling—a ministry assignment of the church—as I was exhausted and losing my mind. Instead of being met with gratitude from the bishop for serving for over a year in the nursery, I was met with criticism and judgment. I was made to feel guilty as if I was turning my back on the Lord.

"Many people say they would die for the Lord and yet they can't even hold a calling," He said. To say that I felt belittled, underappreciated and overwhelmed would be an understatement.

This is just one example of the lack of understanding and compassion the Mormon Church has. After I left the Mormon Church and attended my local non-denominational Christian Church, I served in the first grade class a couple of times. I was shown such gratitude and appreciation for my services that I was overwhelmed. I felt so loved and important...like what I did mattered.

Since I left the Mormon Church, I have gone to church where I experience God's grace every time. I am loved and accepted for who I am and how I was created. I feel safe and loved, not judged. Whether I am in jeans or a dress, it does not matter. I am still accepted and loved. I feel welcomed and at peace. I know that if I needed help for anything in my life—be it my own sin or someone else's—I have someone to turn to for help and healing.

Search out for yourself if what I am telling you is true. Some Mormons, even family members, say that my family and I go to the "feel good church." Our response is "Yes, and we feel good." It is amazing how the safety and love of our Savior can be felt in hearing His truth. It is truth that brings peace and freedom, safety and comfort. Jesus is calling you to come and experience His truth and rest in His peace, freedom, comfort and safety.

A Prayer of Healing

"Lord Jesus, I come to You now and ask Your Holy Spirit to fill me with wisdom. I want to rest in Your peace and safety, Lord. I want to be set free, Lord, and experience Your grace. Lord, I am tired of the judgment placed on me by men, and You have commanded me not to judge others. I give You that position, Lord, and ask that You forgive me for ever trying to take Your place in judging. Judging others causes separation, and I know that You have called us to be in the ministry of forgiveness and reconciliation. Show me the way, dear Lord. Open my eyes that I might see. Thank You, Jesus, in Your precious name. Amen."

Your Calling and Outreach

"Go ye therefore and make disciples of all nations, baptizing them in the name of the Father and of the Son and of the Holy Spirit."

— Matthew 28:19

For some reason, there seems to be some confusion about who gets to call you into the ministry. It seems obvious, on one hand, that the only person able to call you to anything is God. But, how often does that really happen? How often is the call really from a man or woman in a church somewhere? Who really called you? I would agree that God could use a man or woman to provide you with the opportunity to fulfill His call, but in the end the only person who can call you to serve God is God.

But more and more we bend to the call of man and his ideas in how we are to serve. Jesus faced the same problem. Look at the following verses:

"For John the Baptist came neither eating bread nor drinking wine, and you say, 'He has a demon.' The Son of Man came

269

*eating and drinking, and you say, 'Here is a glutton and a
drunkard, a friend of tax collectors and sinners!'"*

— Luke 7:33-34

Here is a group of religious people who had lost control of both
Jesus and John the Baptist. As a result they attacked both Jesus' calling and His ministry. After all, Jesus didn't have any formal training.
He didn't have a diploma or a license to preach. John certainly didn't
even dress appropriately as befitting a proper Pharisee. Because neither man had been ordained and appointed by the Jewish Counsel,
they were attacked. At one point, the Pharisees accused Jesus of casting out devils by the power of Satan!

I found this to be true in the Mormon Church as well. Mormon
missionaries must follow very strict rules. Their mission is quite different than the call to go and make disciples in all nations as the Bible
calls for. Unfortunately, these young men have not been given a clear
meaning to what Jesus was asking for. The control of their mission
keeps these young men from finding information and forming their
own opinion.

They are not allowed to access the Internet or to search out answers
to their own or seekers' questions. They are not allowed their own discernment to find out exactly who the Lord wants them to reach and in
what way. They cannot question the Mormon faith. Their reading mate-
rials are monitored and follow strict church standards. They must have
their hair cut short, wear specific clothing, be to bed and arise at a certain time, and many other rules. Their individuality is removed as they
become more like Mormons and less passionate about the call God has
placed on their heart. Had they been allowed to form their own opin-
ions and discover what area of ministry God was really calling them to,
they would not only be more informed, but they would have been able
to walk in their true identity and calling. This is how they could make
a true difference in the world by caring for the people that they could
relate to and, in the process, reach many souls. And yet, these are the
men that are coming *equipped* to mold you into a carbon copy of them.

My own experience of losing my identity and not serving in my true calling has reinforced this opinion. I was 'called' by the Mormon leadership to do things that I wasn't good at, that stressed me out, and that eventually caused resentment. I was asked to head up the Emergency Preparedness Team, for example. I didn't have a gift or a desire for this task. I tried to get out of it, but was made to feel so guilty for not wanting to by the Mormon leadership that I continued to do it. I was even 'called' to be a Boy Scout leader! These definitely were not my gifts or talents!

Now that I am out of the Mormon Church, I get to use the talents God has naturally gifted me with to serve Him! I have a passion and the training for counseling the hurting and the lost. Now I look forward to church and to serving God, knowing that I am doing what God has called me to do!

Whenever or in whatever capacity we serve God, we need to make sure we are called by God and not doing so out of a sense of guilt or according to man's will. Many people in leadership simply should not be there. They are not good at what they do because it is not a calling from God. Most are bitter because of being made to feel guilty for not accepting this "call" that came from man and not from God. In the Mormon Church, you are taught that refusing a calling is basically saying 'no' to God.

Who Can Be Called?

We do not need special requirements in order to serve God and bring people to Him. God calls everyone to go and spread the Gospel. The Gospel literally means "good news." Jesus declared that He had come to "preach good news to the poor" (Luke 4:18). But what good news, what gospel, does the Mormon Church have for the poor? There are so many needy people outside of a church building. The church should be there to help people learn how they can help and serve others. Unfortunately, not everyone hears Jesus' call or they are too busy with man's call.

*"The Spirit of the Lord is on me, because he has anointed me
to preach good news to the poor. He has sent me to proclaim
freedom for the prisoners and recovery of sight for the blind, to
release the oppressed, to proclaim the year of the Lord's favor."*

— Luke 4:18-19

*"Serve wholeheartedly, as if you were
serving the Lord, not men,"*

— Ephesians 6:7

God calls each and every one to join Him and serve in His mission. The only prerequisite you will need is willingness. When you yield to God's will and allow Him to further develop the desires, talents and abilities He has given to you in the first place, your life will be very fulfilling.

*"But in fact God has arranged the parts in the body, every one
of them, just as he wanted them to be."*

— 1 Corinthians 12:18

Having a willing heart and volunteering on your own accord is what makes the difference to the calling. You just need to be willing. Without this willingness, you will not hear the call of God. It's not about being willing to do something specific, but rather a willingness to do what God wants you to do. Don't fall for the trap of doing what a man wants you to do. God can use man to offer you opportunity, but only God can call you. When you feel called of God, it changes the way you serve. Having the desire come from your heart instead of out of guilt and obligation is what sets the outstanding apart from the bitter. God has placed this passion inside of you. When someone else gives you something that is not your calling, it only embitters you and causes stress. This is why God says that He likes a cheerful giver (2 Corinthians 9:7). One that is giving of their time out of desire is what pleases Him.

Different Seasons, Gifts and Talents for Service

While in the Mormon Church, I served in the nursery. I had three small children and dreaded Sundays for the amount of work that I would be 'called' to give. I was stressed, tired and my family felt it. I wanted a break, but felt incredibly guilty for even considering such a thing. Finally, after my 13 month of service, I could not take it anymore; I went to my bishop to ask to be released and told him I needed time off.

But instead of gratitude for all the time I did serve, I was reprimanded and told that many Mormon pioneers were willing to push a handcart and yet I could not hold to my calling. What position was he in that he could tell me what I needed in my life? Wasn't the body of Christ supposed to help (1 Corinthians 12:25)? I left that day feeling very inadequate, underappreciated and sad. There is a season for everything (Ecclesiastes 3:1) and it is important that we be in a position to serve and have a desire to serve.

In sharp contrast, when I attended the Christian church, I felt ready and had the desire to serve the children along with my young son. I only served one day and was given so much gratitude and appreciation that it furthered my desire to serve even more. This is exactly the way God would want us to treat one another.

The visiting teaching program is another legalistic approach to friendship that I discovered within the Mormon Church. This is a program that every member is assigned to. The men are given a specific man to befriend and visit monthly and the women are given specific women to befriend and visit monthly. To have someone "called" to be my friend never demonstrated to me what true friendship was all about. Every visiting teacher I have ever had never touched my life like the Christian women that have since come into my life. Having a bishop decide who was going to be my friend in the position of "visiting teacher" instead of allowing God to lead someone's heart to be friends with me and do life with me certainly never felt like a call from God. My visiting teachers, cloaked in the guise of friendship, brought me a lesson from their scripted Mormon magazine—The Ensign—each month. But when it came time, when I really needed a friend, someone I could be honest with and reveal my needs to, I felt very alone.

Friendship is something that exists between two people that loves us because they have a desire to help and fellowship—not out of obligation. This causes people to be so busy doing jobs that are given to them that they never get around to asking God what He wants.

Another point I would like to bring out is in regarding these so 'called' leaders. Should these leaders really be in the position of leadership that they are in? Should people be put in positions of trust over children without a background check? I served in many children leadership positions and was never trained or given any form of background check.

How skilled are they? Have they been equipped and prepared for this calling? Was it on their heart or were they obligated with a call from another man? Ephesians 4:12 tells us we are to equip the body of Christ. "Their responsibility is to equip God's people to do his work and build up the church, the body of Christ." My experience with seeking help from my leaders never brought me the help I needed. Most of the time, it just brought more damage to my life.

On one particular time, I sought parenting advice for one of my children. So naturally, I went to someone who had been 'called' to work with children in the Church. In this case, I sought the advice of the bishop's wife. Her advice to me was to try slapping my daughter in the face in the vague hope this would stun her into thinking about what she was doing! Now that I have had enough training and years of experience behind me, I am shocked at the council I received. Slapping a child is so completely detrimental to a child, and to have someone in a position of authority tell you to do this it is very confusing—not to mention unhelpful for everyone involved.

The point is, when we listen to man's calling over God's calling, we find ourselves in positions that we neither have God's grace to do, God's power to see through, or God's blessings to succeed in. When God calls you into the ministry, He will equip you. In the Christian church that I attend now, they equip servant leaders through training in the callings that God has gifted the individual in.

Who Are We To Reach?

God first instituted the church so that the talents and abilities of every individual would be used to bless the world. Outreach is a task that God has called every Christian to do. We are all given the commission to go and tell others about the "Good News" of Jesus Christ and to serve the poor regardless of their faith. This outreach can and does take on so many different forms. In order to do this, we must equip the body of Christ to reach more souls. It takes transformed people to transform lives.

1. We must first build and strengthen individuals along with their families.

2. Then we must equip them with knowledge and understanding in order to equip them to reach out to their own community, nation and then the world.

We must first start with the individual, then strengthen their family, our community, nation and then the world. In order to make a difference in our world both steps are necessary. In the process of doing as Jesus commanded us of feeding the poor and helping the lost and broken, many souls will be won for Christ.

> "The third time he said to him, "Simon son of John, do you love me?" Peter was hurt because Jesus asked him the third time, "Do you love me?" He said, "Lord, you know all things; you know that I love you." Jesus said, "Feed my sheep."
>
> — John 21:17

> "Therefore go and make disciples of all nations, baptizing them in the name of the Father and of the Son and of the Holy Spirit, and teaching them to obey everything I have commanded you. And surely I am with you always, to the very end of the age."
>
> — Matthew 28:19-20

If we would obey the truth of what Jesus taught, we would have the compassion and love necessary to bring about the change in an individual's life. In turn, they will gain the ability to turn around and feed His sheep too. Jesus cared not just for their spiritual condition, but also for their physical well-being also. He healed the diseased, showed empathy for the poor, fed the hungry and literally restored sight to the blind. You see, it is more than just reaching those who do not know Jesus; it is transforming them to wholeness so they too can be disciples. This involves proper teaching and training. And since every person is different with different needs, problems, issues, and struggles, we need to have many different outreach opportunities to help meet their needs.

One of the greatest ministries I discovered in the Christian church was the MOPS ministry, Mothers of Preschoolers for these new moms. What an amazing ministry for mothers of preschoolers! To go outside of church and have someone watch your preschooler while you study God's word and learn to be a better mother and wife would be a blessing for every woman! Wow, what had I been missing all these years? I always thought it would be wonderful for moms to get together and study God's word, and I often wondered why the Mormons didn't have this. After leaving the church and discovering that this was available, I was so overwhelmed by the amount of support and help available to me. I certainly wished that I had something like that for all those years of raising my children alone.

> *"They helped every one his neighbor; and every one said to his brother, Be of good courage."*
>
> — Isaiah 41:6

I believe God desires for us to be a help to one another during trying times in our lives. Having a new child in the home is an opportunity to minster to that new mother. What mother wouldn't want to become a better mom? Providing her with resources, teaching, and training to become a successful mother, particularly when she doesn't have other family members around, is something that will impact her and her child for the rest of her life. Christ will greatly benefit, not only in this generation, but in the next generation as well.

Church should be a place of healing as well as service and worship. The doors of the church should never be closed to anyone who is seeking God or who needs a helping hand. When someone needs marriage counseling, there should be competent Christians with years of experience willing and able to help. Instead of shunning drug addicts, the Church should have a program in place to help them defeat drugs in their life. Bible studies and small groups should be offered to keep people in God's Word. I often wondered why this was never offered in the Mormon Church. Parents should be able to get godly advice on child rearing. There should be someone constantly available to pray for the emotionally injured, for the weak, the outcast and the hopeless. Many Christian churches have an area for prayer after services for this exact purpose. There should also be a call from the pulpit offering, anyone the opportunity to accept Christ into his or her life. This is one of the main reasons there is a sermon given.

I attend a large Christian church that has a program for practically everything. Not every church has every program; it is in this lack that an opportunity is born. Be willing to listen to God's call and be prepared to grow in order to meet the needs of other Christians...and so fulfill the law of Christ!

"Just as each of us has one body with many members, and these members do not all have the same function, so in Christ we who are many form one body, and each member belongs to all the others. We have different gifts, according to the grace given us. If a man's gift is prophesying, let him use it in proportion to his faith. If it is serving, let him serve; if it is teaching, let him teach; if it is encouraging, let him encourage; if it is contributing to the needs of others, let him give generously; if it is leadership, let him govern diligently; if it is showing mercy, let him do it cheerfully."

— Romans 12:4-8

In all of this, there is a place for you and I. God gives strengths and talents to each of us according to His pleasure and needs (1 Corinthians 12:4-11). Our job is to use these strengths for the cause of Christ.

According to Romans 12:1-2, the will of God is good, acceptable, and perfect for you. Some take this to mean that God actually has three different wills for you, but that is not what the verse is teaching. It is saying that God's will is good for you...like eating vegetables is good for you. It is spiritually healthy; it is spiritually uplifting and strengthening to you! It is also acceptable, or well-pleasing. In other words, the will of God will *always* be something that you will like to do. You will enjoy it. You will have a passion for it. In addition, the will of God is perfect for you. Given who you are, your circumstances, your personality, who you know, where you live, your skills and talents, and so forth, God has designed a plan for you that is a perfect match to you! It is perfect! Don't ever forget that God uses broken and imperfect people to inspire others.

Rick Warren said, "If God only used perfect people, nothing would get done. God will use anybody if you're available."

We need to remember that there are two parties involved in outreach. There is the person we are trying to reach, but then there is us, the ones who are trying to do the reaching. Because of our experiences, we are then able to relate better to them. We must be able to see through their eyes.

Paul understood this concept as he was once under the law and could relate to those under the law. Look at these verses:

> *"Though I am free and belong to no man, I make myself a slave to everyone, to win as many as possible. To the Jews I became like a Jew, to win the Jews. To those under the law I became like one under the law (though I myself am not under the law), so as to win those under the law. To those not having the law I became like one not having the law (though I am not free from God's law but am under Christ's law), so as to win those not having the law. To the weak I became weak, to win the weak. I have become all things to all men so that by all*

possible means I might save some. I do all this for the sake of the gospel, that I may share in its blessings."

— 1 Corinthians 9:19-23

Paul had to become the right person to reach the right person. This is why there is such a need for servants for God's glory—but not just any servant, the right servant for the right person in the right situation. That is why all of us are called, but then we are chosen and placed by God to fulfill His will—and help the people that only we can help! If you want to get a perfect example of what it means to become all things to all people consider Christ himself becoming one of us.

"Because God's children are human beings—made of flesh and blood—the Son also became flesh and blood. For only as a human being could he die, and only by dying could he break the power of the devil, who had the power of death."

— Hebrews 2:14 (NLT)

"You know the generous grace of our Lord Jesus Christ. Though he was rich, yet for your sakes he became poor, so that by his poverty he could make you rich."

— 2 Corinthians 8:9 (NLT)

Jesus points to His self-sacrificial death as the example of what it means to become a slave to all. What drove Jesus to do all that He did? Paul tells "the Messiah did not seek to please Himself" (Romans 15:3). What drove Jesus? Was He driven by self-consumed desire? No! He was driven by a love for sinners and a desire to please His Father. The Messiah became a slave to all (Philippians 2:5-10).

"But it must not be like that among you. On the contrary, whoever wants to become great among you must be your servant, and whoever wants to be first among you must be

*a slave to all. For even the Son of Man did not come to be
served, but to serve and to give His life—a ransom for many."*

— Mark 10:43-45

Who are you to serve? You are to serve those that God has called
you to serve. Your strengths, weaknesses, talents, skills, personality,
circumstances, family, location, and church have all been taken into
consideration when God designed His will for your life. When you
find it, you'll know it, because it will be good for you, something you
have a passion for, and a perfect match for who you have been created to be. Bill Hybles said, "Every follower of Christ was made for
a purpose and that our most important task is to discern what that
purpose is."

The Role of the Church in Outreach

*"The Lord says: 'These people come near to me with their
mouth and honor me with their lips, but their hearts are far
from me. Their worship of me is made up only of
rules taught by men.'"*

— Isaiah 29:13

During my time as a Mormon my daughter tried to commit suicide one time by taking an entire bottle of aspirin. Fortunately, I was
told about the attempt by one of her non-Mormon friends and she was
taken to the hospital. Not one of her Mormon friends that knew of it
took it seriously enough to tell me. I do not fault the children, but I
believe when you grow up in a Mormon household, you are not taught
the compassion that you need to help others. Our bishop knew of
my daughter's attempt to take her own life, but he never once offered
comfort, counseling or even a kind word for our daughter. Instead,
he told us, her parents, that she was "just trying to get attention and
was being dramatic." Wow, was I ever shocked at the lack of compassion and understanding. I didn't know enough to leave the Mormon
Church at the time, but I remember thinking, "If she is seeking atten-

tion, isn't that what we should be offering her? She is hurting; doesn't anyone see that?" No one in my family understood that the lack of compassion was a direct result of the legalistic, controlling environment that permeated throughout the Mormon Church.

Because Mormonism expects a life of perfection, they have a tendency to ignore anything that isn't. They either overlook it or merely condemn it. They overlook it when it comes from authority within the church and they condemn it in anyone who is outside the church. But they don't have anything in place to try to heal it, to help these people.

Where are the ministries for addictions—porn, alcohol, anger, drugs, workaholics, and so on? I have seen people in the Mormon Church become an outcast because there was nowhere for them to go for help. They are taught they need to suck it up, toughen up and just go to the Temple. They become superficial and are expected to just sweep all their problems under the rug. They do not deal with them because there is nowhere for them to turn for help. I have seen divorce happen because there was a problem with porn or other addiction in the marriage. These issues were never dealt with simply because a Mormon is expected to conquer them on their own—it is part of their spiritual progression. So they never get the help they need.

Mormons are not addressing the root problem. Instead of trying to help someone overcome their sin or problem, they simply condemn them for being evil and wicked. It is easier to dismiss someone as unworthy than it is to put programs in place or provide resources that will help them conquer their sin or problems. They need to discover the root problem. These are real problems that need real solutions and attention specifically for the related problem.

Scriptures teach us to mourn with those that mourn (Matthew 5:4). Adulterers mourn, drug addicts mourn, alcoholics mourn, and the homeless mourn. There are lots of hurting people out there. It does not say that we should act like those that mourn or avoid those that mourn. No, God's Word is telling us not only to have compassion for those that are struggling with addiction or any stronghold, but to gain an understanding of their problem, offer resources, support and help (Proverbs 4:7). To mourn is not just about shedding tears and crying together—although this shows great love and compassion—but it is an action of sympathy, understanding, and love. God blesses those that mourn for they shall be comforted.

What does it really mean to comfort these individuals? The dictionary tells us to comfort means to give strength, to give hope to someone, to ease the grief or trouble of someone.[71] I believe that as Christians, we are to have knowledgeable people on our team ready for action to help people that need it when they need it.

How can we as Christians comfort those that mourn if we do not have anywhere for these people to turn? Where can any of these people go for help in the Mormon faith? There is certainly nothing listed in the Mormon program for alcoholics, addicts or the hurting to go to. They are simply outcasts. There are no ministries or resources for them. We are all in need of help at one time or another in our lives. For even Paul said, "I do not understand what I do. For what I want to do I do not do, but what I hate I do" (Romans 7:15).

An outcast is a person that does not fit into the mold. They are rejected. They are not accepted into the church until they do and act certain ways. An outcast is someone that is not wanted, not needed, and one that is avoided by others. The people of the Mormon faith avoid contact or communication with an outcast for fear of "falling" or becoming like them. This is where trained and gifted counselors are needed within the body of Christ.

There are many charities to become involved in. Not just through church, but everywhere. One of my favorite charities is World Vision. I didn't even know World Vision existed while in the Mormon Church. "World Vision is an international partnership of Christians whose mission is to follow our Lord and Savior Jesus Christ in working with the poor and oppressed to promote human transformation, seek justice and bear witness to the good news of the Kingdom of God."[72] After leaving the Mormon Church, many opportunities for service opened up to me as I began to associate with Christians.

---

71 www.merriam-webster.com/dictionary/comfort

72 World Vision Mission Statement (http://srilanka.wvasiapacific.org/about-us/our-vision-and-core-values)

When you are in the Mormon bubble, the comforts of your home and church are the only thing you know. God's true charities need your support! We must feed the hungry and clothe the naked.

Jesus commanded us to love our neighbor (Luke 10:27-37). That neighbor is anyone that crosses our path that we are in a position to help. We are to love God and our neighbor. Everything revolves around these two commands. These two commands should spark every program and resource we make available to our 'neighbors' who so desperately need them.

When you belong to the Mormon Church, however, you are basically serving the Church, not the other way around. This is the opposite of what Jesus demonstrated when he knelt down and washed his disciples' feet. The church should be serving the people. When we are truly serving God, we will be serving people on the outside, glorifying God and bringing others to Him.

> *"But if serving the LORD seems undesirable to you, then choose for yourselves this day whom you will serve, whether the gods your ancestors served beyond the Euphrates, or the gods of the Amorites, in whose land you are living. But as for me and my household, we will serve the LORD."*
>
> — Joshua 24:15

Reaching the World

Bill Hybles said something truly profound, "If Church leaders do not have an outward vision to become salt and light in our world, to promote social and spiritual transformation, pursue justice, and proclaim the whole gospel, then the Church will fail to realize its potential as an agent of change."

Where are all the mission trips in the Mormon Church? The only way you can go on a mission trip, as a Mormon, is to be a 19-year-old boy, a 20-year-old girl or a grandparent. Even then, you are assigned where you will go. And these are not the kind of mission trips that offer help to a hurting world. There are no trips for the average member to go to Africa, the Ukraine, on relief missions during disasters, and so on. The Mormon mission trips are very legalistic and controlled, so that the only ones able to serve are the ill equipped young missionaries that live a controlled environment. Their aim is not to demonstrate the love of Jesus Christ through word and deed, but to convert people to Mormonism. They aren't interested in helping the poor and needy. Their only mission is to convert people.

I will never forget the time that my husband and I were building homes in Mexico with our kids, we were covered in dirt and working to build this family a home. I saw two Mormon missionaries walking by in their clean shirts, carrying their Book of Mormon. I thought to myself, what they are doing is not love. These people need you to get in the dirt with them. They need a home. Love in action. People that are hungry need to be fed before they can receive what you have to say.

Jesus says, "Faith, hope and love, but the greatest of these is love" (1 Corinthians 13:13). Love is demonstrative. Love is shown when you do something for someone!

> *"Dear children, let us not love with words or tongue but with actions and in truth."*
>
> — 1 John 3:18

In true Christian fellowship, there is always a place where you are needed and wanted. You should have a place where you are able to fulfill your God-given purpose on this earth. There should always be a child to sponsor or some sort of charity to do. God tells us in Scripture that we will do greater things than even He did, if we have faith in Him and a heart like His.

> *"I tell you the truth, anyone who has faith in me will do what I have been doing. He will do even greater things than these, because I am going to the Father."*
>
> — John 14:12

You must remember, however, that it is faith in Jesus that allows us to do these great works. You must also remember that these great works are always in service to others, and not to glorify an organization or us. Jesus did these great works among people and for the people. He did not do them to serve the church, but to build up the body of Christ.

I was never exposed to any of these charities or opportunities to serve outside of a church building while I was Mormon.

With so many rigorous rules that have nothing to do with God's grace and love for all mankind, I found myself seeking to establish my own salvation instead of bringing the light of salvation (Jesus Christ) to others. This is exactly what Satan hopes will happen—that you hide your light under a basket. Satan wants to keep you so busy that you will not have time for the poor, the oppressed or the needy.

Outreach for the poor is one of the last things to get done, if it gets done at all in the Mormon Church. Never did I serve the poor through the church as a Mormon; the opportunities to do so where not offered or available. I sometimes served these people on my own, because that was my heart. I did it alone, however, with no support or help.

I will never forget attending a Christian church for the first time and seeing all the ministries available for anyone to serve. There were houses to build for the homeless, established food rooms for the poor, counseling ministries for all types of pain, addiction, and need, worldwide missions, and on and on. I was blown away. I remember thinking this is exactly what God wants us to be doing, serving the least of these.

> *"He will reply, 'I tell you the truth, whatever you did not do for one of the least of these, you did not do for me.'"*
>
> — Matthew 25:45

Look at what the Bible says,

> *"Not everyone who says to me, 'Lord, Lord,' will enter the kingdom of heaven, but only he who does the will of my Father*

who is in heaven. Many will say to me on that day, 'Lord,
Lord, did we not prophesy in your name, and in your name
drive out demons and perform many miracles?'
Then I will tell them plainly, 'I never knew you.
Away from me, you evildoers!'"

— Matthew 7:21-23

The church is supposed to be for the people. It is a hospital for the sick, training for the weak, prayer for the hurting. Mark 2:17 Jesus came to save people in every way: "On hearing this, Jesus said to them, 'It is not the healthy who need a doctor, but the sick. I have not come to call the righteous, but sinners.'"

Just because a church does 'works' in the name of the Lord, doesn't mean they are serving Jesus. You are only serving Jesus when your 'works' are to help the poor, the needy, the downtrodden, the contemptible, the dishonorable, and the hurting. It is not about the building, the ordinances, or convincing others how holy and righteous you are.

Find a place where you can use the talents that God has given to you. He does not want you to hide them. He will equip you in every way.

"My grace is sufficient for you, for my power is made
perfect in weakness."

— 2 Corinthians 12:9

"As Christians, we all have a part in this great work of caring for one another and reaching the lost and the outcast. We are dominos in the chain reaction set off by Jesus 2,000 years ago. The amazing thing about dominos falling is that the chain reaction always starts small- with just one, seemingly insignificant domino."[73] Whatever your talent or gift may be, if we use it to bless others, then you are doing what is pleasing to God and He will multiply your faithfulness.

---

73 Richard Stearns, *World Vision*, (2011).

"You are the light of the world. A city on a hill cannot be hidden. Neither do people light a lamp and put it under a bowl. Instead they put it on its stand, and it gives light to everyone in the house. In the same way, let your light shine before men, that they may see your good deeds and praise your Father in heaven."

— Matthew 5:14-16

A Prayer of Healing

"Lord, please forgive me for being so preoccupied by ordinances and callings from man that I forgot what it really meant to serve one of the least of these. Lord, I pray that You will guide me to the body of Christ where I can serve beside them and bring others unto You. There are many people that need our compassion and service. Lord, I want to serve others as if I were serving You. I want to do the great things You tell me I will do in Your name. I will worship you, God, and no one else. Thank You, Lord, for giving me eyes to see the lost, the hurting and confused. Lord, let me glorify You in serving others. In Jesus' name, Amen."

18

Will I Ever Be a God?

"For I am God, and there is no other; I am God, and there is none like Me."

— Isaiah 49:6

Wondering what we will become after this earthly life is a question that we have all rightfully pondered. The answer of which often determines the particular faith you decide to follow. Many times, however, the answer is rather convoluted or distorted so that those following a particular faith don't even know if their belief is actually Biblical or in line with the will of God or not. In order to have a clear understanding, God has made it perfectly clear through His Word who and what we are to become.

While I was a Mormon, I didn't quite understand God's will for my life on earth or in eternity. Embracing the Mormon doctrine introduced me to many new concepts and ideas. Although I didn't give much thought to these ideas at first, I would soon expand my imagination in ways I had never thought about. One of these concepts is that of 'eternal progression.' In the beginning, this seemed like a harmless idea. After all, aren't we supposed to progress and become like Christ? To answer this question, God has given us different examples of His will in our spiritual progression. Before I get to that, let's examine some of what the Mormon belief teaches. Regardless of your faith, however, you might find areas in your own beliefs that need correcting. Mormons believe that every individual person can spiritually progress to the point of becoming their own god. In fact, Mormon doctrine teaches that the god of this planet, earth, was once a man on a planet somewhere under the rule of another god.

If this doctrine is true, then there is the possibility of trillions of gods and trillions of planets around the universe that are all experiencing similar states of growth and progression as earth does. But this brings up some rather bizarre questions. Questions I wish I had asked myself when I was adopting these beliefs instead of merely embracing them. Who first created the world? Wasn't there an original creator? Who decides which planet I will go to? If each and every person gets to be a god of their own planet, then where will my children go? If God wrote His Word in the Bible, will I eventually write my own word? Who will fill me with the Holy Spirit; will I have my own Holy Spirit?

It is important to understand the Mormon view. Examine the following quotes:

- "God is an organized being just as we are who are now in the flesh. He is a progressive being, and possesses the capacity of eternal increase. Perhaps once a child and mortal like ourselves."[74]

- "Every man who reigns in celestial glory is a god to his dominions."[75]

- "There never was a time when there were not Gods and worlds."[76]

---

74 *Gospel Doctrine*, p. 64, *Articles of Faith*, p. 529, *Journal of Discourses*, 1:123

75 McConkie, *Mormon Doctrine*, p. 322.

76 Brigham Young, *Journal of Discourses*, pp. 22-23.

- "Each god, through his wife or wives, raises up a numerous family of sons and daughters."[77]

- "The doctrine of a plurality of Gods is prominent in the Bible. The heads of the Gods appointed our God for us."[78]

- "The eternal Father is a progressive Being...the capacity of eternal increase."[79]

- "I wish to declare I have always and in all congregations when I have preached on the subject of Deity, it has been the plurality of Gods."[80]

- "In the beginning, the head of the Gods called a council of the Gods; and they came together and concocted a plan to create the world and people it."[81]

- "If we should take a million of worlds like this and number their particles, we should find that there are more Gods than there are particles of matter in those worlds."[82]

- "Mortality is the testing or proving ground for exaltation to find out who among the children of God are worthy to become Gods themselves, and the Lord has informed us that 'few there be that find it.'"[83]

- "When the servants of God and their wives go to heaven there is an eternal union, and they will multiply and replenish the world to which they are going."[84]

---

77 Pratt, *The Seer*, I, no. 3, p. 37.

78 *Teaching of the Prophet Joseph Smith*, p. 370.

79 Talmage, *Doctrine and Covenants*, p. 529.

80 Prophet Joseph Smith, Jr., *History of the Church*, v. 6, p. 306.

81 Ibid. pp. 307-308.

82 Apostle Orson Pratt, *Journal of Discourses*, (February 18, 1855) v. 2, p. 345.

83 Joseph Fielding Smith Jr., *Doctrines of Salvation*, Vol.1, pp.69-70.

84 Orson Hyde, *Journal of Discourses*, (October 6, 1854), Vol.2, pp. 85-86.

This is just a sampling of how we as humans can really get away from God's will if we do not fully understand the Bible. If we are reading words that are not His, our mind and imagination can get away from us and we will be deceived. This is exactly Satan's intention. This is why God commands us to read from His Word daily and really get to know Him and His will for our life.

While I was a Mormon, I remember one morning when I got up early to meditate on what I thought was God's Word. It was not the Bible; it was the Ensign Magazine, which is doctrine only to Mormons. I began to contemplate what it meant to reach perfection like God. I needed to become perfect. This was a scary thought, but also very exhilarating. After all, I thought God would deny me nothing, right? Even to become a god in my own right.

This is an underlying lie from the enemy. He is seeking to get you to worship anything but God, even your own self. We were never meant to be in charge or worshipped. Not now, and not in eternity. When we become Christians, we surrender that right to be in charge of our own life. We surrender to new management, the management of Jesus Christ.

We are to Worship God Alone

The relationship that God invites us into is not one to be equal with Him. His very first command to us from the very beginning is: "You must not have any other god but me" (Exodus 20:3). He desires us to rely on Him—not to become equal to Him. God has breathed the very life into us. It is by His sheer mercy that we breathe each and every day. His desire is that we stay near to Him in relationship so He can fill us with His Holy Spirit. Having an awareness of your constant need for Him is your greatest strength. Paul gave us an example of this:

> *"To keep me from becoming conceited because of these surpassingly great revelations, there was given me a thorn in my flesh, a messenger of Satan, to torment me. Three times I pleaded with the Lord to take it away from me. But he said*

*to me, 'My grace is sufficient for you, for my power is made
perfect in weakness.' Therefore I will boast all the more gladly
about my weaknesses, so that Christ's power may rest on
me. That is why, for Christ's sake, I delight in weaknesses, in
insults, in hardships, in persecutions, in difficulties. For when
I am weak, then I am strong."*

— 2 Corinthians 12:7-10

We must keep our eyes constantly on Jesus. This is how we show
our trust in Him. If we have our eyes on ourselves becoming a god, we
have taken our eyes off of Jesus. This is a choice and God offers you
this choice. He will never force you to become His child, but when you
do, it pleases Him greatly.

God invites you to present yourself as a living sacrifice to Him
(Romans 12:1). This is your spiritual act of worship. God views this as
one seeking to exalt himself when we try to become a God, in other
words idolatry. True worship is humility.

"For by the grace given me I say to every one of you: Do not think
of yourself more highly than you ought, but rather think of yourself
with sober judgment, in accordance with the measure of faith God has
given you" (Romans 12:3). We are not to think highly of ourselves, and
as long as we worship God as the only true God, we will stay humble.

To be a god or even like God requires worship from someone. God
is so against anyone receiving worship but Him. God understands our
nature—a nature that craves attention (worship). The temptation to
do as Satan did is one each and every one of us struggles with. This
is exactly why God commanded no one to receive worship but Him.

Isaiah expands on the cause of Satan's fall: "You said in your heart,
'I will ascend to heaven; I will raise my throne above the stars of God; I
will sit enthroned on the mount of assembly, on the utmost heights of
the sacred mountain. I will ascend above the tops of the clouds; I will
make myself like the Most High'" (Isaiah 14:13-14).

When the Apostle John tried to worship an angel, the angel rebuked
him for it (Revelation 22:8-9). When Cornelius tried to worship Peter,
Peter rebuked him (Acts 10:25-26). Paul preformed a miracle and the
people proclaimed him to be a god and went about worshiping him.

Paul rent his clothes and ordered the people to stop, claiming that he was just a man and not God (Acts 14:11-15). God understood that his people loved Moses and would have a desire to worship him so He hid the body of Moses after he died (Deuteronomy 34:5-6, Jude 1:9).

King Nebuchadnezzar built a vast empire that came to dominate the known world. The Bible records his thinking process. We are told that he became proud of his accomplishments and gave himself all the glory. Daniel 5:30 tells us Nebuchadnezzar's words, "'Is not this the great Babylon I have built as the royal residence, by my mighty power and for the glory of my majesty?' The words were still on his lips when a voice came from heaven, 'This is what is decreed for you, King Nebuchadnezzar: Your royal authority has been taken from you. You will be driven away from people and will live with the wild animals; you will eat grass like cattle. Seven ties will pass by for you until you acknowledge that he the Most High is sovereign over the kingdoms of men and gives them to anyone he wishes.' Immediately what had been said about Nebuchadnezzar was fulfilled."

He had become arrogant in his ways of thinking and glorified himself instead of God. God never, never condones idolatry, even when the idolatry is ourselves.

We serve a holy God, who is an all-consuming fire. Let's come before Him each day with humble hearts. If we were to stand before God in our present state, we would be consumed. We would not be able to bare the sight of His glory and majesty. This is a God that angels bow down to and worship, crying holy, holy, holy!! The image of God that John saw in his vision was this:

> *"And immediately I was in the spirit: and, behold, a throne was set in heaven, and one sat on the throne. And he that sat was to look upon like a jasper and a sardine stone: and there was a rainbow round about the throne, in sight like unto an emerald....And out of the throne proceeded lightnings and thunderings and voices: and there were seven lamps of fire burning before the throne, which are the seven Spirits of God....And the four beasts had each of them six wings about him; and they were full of eyes within: and they rest not day*

and night, saying, 'Holy, holy, holy, LORD God Almighty, which was, and is, and is to come...' the four and twenty elders fall down before him that sat on the throne, and worship him that liveth for ever and ever, and cast their crowns before the throne, saying, Thou art worthy, O Lord, to receive glory and honor and power: for thou hast created all things, and for thy pleasure they are and were created."

— Revelation 4:2-11 (KJV)

Behold your God!

I plead with you to give your all to Jesus and worship Him in spirit and truth, and to be humble before God. It is only because of God that we are alive. He is our King!

Didn't Jesus Say We Are All Gods?

Nowhere in the book of revelations does it even claim that those that were exalted became a god like our God.

Taking Scripture out of context and then redefining it to justify a belief is going against what God has really said. This is a sin. God never said *anywhere* that we can become a god. A misinterpreted scripture relating to gods by Mormons is John 10:34. Jesus said, "Is it not written in your Law, 'I have said you are gods?'" He is referring to Psalm 82. But a cursory examination of the entire Psalm 82 is very revealing:

1. The reference to 'gods' are always lower case in contrast to *the* God (capitalized).

2. These 'gods' judge unjustly (verse 2) and are far from achieving any sort of divine power.

3. These 'gods' were human judges living as flesh and blood on the earth. They would be equivalent to our court judges today. They were instructed to deliver the poor and fatherless and to do justice where there is injustice (verses 3-4).

4. These 'gods' or men are all children of God—humans, not divine beings (verse 6).

5. They will all die like any other man (verse 7) and are no better than any one else.

The reference to gods was about civil rule and the ability to make decisions of right and wrong. Jesus was chastising the Pharisees for their hypocrisy in deciding that what Jesus was doing was wrong. They didn't consult God; they just made a decision. Jesus pointed out that their system was flawed and they had no right to judge His judgments.

This isn't about becoming a god. This is about man's usurpation of judgment.

The possibility of man becoming a god is a manmade promise that the true God will not honor. It was His plan that we become His children by faith in Jesus Christ, to live with Him throughout eternity as His people (not fellow gods). In and of ourselves, we can do nothing to earn our way there. That debt was paid by the death and resurrection of Jesus Christ Himself. Because our good works on their own are like filthy rags in God's sight (Isaiah 64:6). It is only faith in Christ alone that we receive salvation.

The full concept of gods is one created by Satan. In Genesis chapter 3 Satan comes to Eve and tells her that if she eats of the Tree of the Knowledge of Good and Evil she will be as God, knowing good and evil. One of the powers that God has given to all is the ability to choose whom they will listen to. This same ability was given to Adam and Eve. They were tricked by Satan, not understanding that God had already given them this ability to know right from wrong through His word when He said "You shall not eat of the tree." He even forewarned them what would happen. The same way He forewarns us today through His Word what will happen if we think we can become a god. God says "The LORD will terrify them as he destroys all the gods in the land. Then nations around the world will worship the LORD, each in their own land" (Zephaniah 2:11, NLT).

Adam and Eve listened to Satan instead of God, a common problem today. If you think you can become your own god and not see God's wrath you are sorely mistaken.

By believing you can become a god you are exalting yourself and you are practicing idolatry. Yes! Idolatry! What really matters is not what we think we perceive, or what others tell us is the truth, but what God says in His Word. And in His Word, He tells us that there is only one God—Him!

Qualities of God

God has certain innate qualities that He has always had. No other 'being' can ever achieve these qualities.

1. **God is the Great I AM** – He is the beginning and the end. "I am the Alpha and the Omega, the First and the Last, the Beginning and the End" (Revelation 22:13).

2. **God is Holy** – Holiness is not a quality God achieved. It is a description of His very nature. God cannot be less than holy, and by definition, something that is holy is sacred, set apart, and essential. Where God *is* holy, we are commanded to *be* holy (1 Peter 1:16). God *is* holy and has always been holy. We are to *become* holy since we are not holy. For us, holy living is a quality we assume. For God, it is His very nature. It is completely different.

3. **God is Omniscient** – Omniscient means to know everything (Hebrews 4:13). Imagine trillions of beings who are omniscient. What utter chaos would that bring? And if God has a limited omniscience that is limited to our own planet, then, by definition, He is *not* omniscient. But He is, and He is the only One.

4. **God is Omnipotent** –There is only one God and that God is *all* powerful. If there were more than one being, then by definition He cannot be *all* powerful.

5. **God is Omnipresent** – Mormons don't believe this. As Christians we believe His Word that tells us that God can see all. He is everywhere. His Spirit is in every believer, His presence in every atom in the universe (Psalms 139:8-10).

6. **God is the Savior** – In the human form of Jesus Christ, God died for us and provided a way to Heaven (Isaiah 43:11, John 3:16). Not a single one of us has ever lived a perfect life as Jesus did. Only Jesus could die for our sins (Hebrews 4).

7. **God is to Receive Worship** – The consequences of receiving worship have been stated. We are to worship Him and Him only.

Man can never achieve these qualities of God. And any similarity of achievement, such as being holy, is based solely on the Holy Spirit within us and not on our own merits and abilities.

What then Are We to Become?

Nowhere in the Bible are we taught that we will become a god. We can only become perfect through Jesus Christ, meaning only by relying upon Him can we achieve anything close to perfection. Since this is an impossibility, we must always and continually rely on Him to fill all the gaps.

> *"'My grace is all you need. My power works best in weakness.'*
> *So now I am glad to boast about my weaknesses, so that the*
> *power of Christ can work through me."*
> — 2 Corinthians 12:9 (NLT)

> *"My old self has been crucified with Christ. It is no*
> *longer I who live, but Christ lives in me. So I live in*
> *this earthly body by trusting in the Son of God,*
> *who loved me and gave himself for me."*
> — Galatians 2:20 (NLT)

You see, it will always be Christ living through us. This is *how* we become perfect—through Him. Once we remove Jesus, there is no more of us. We die and we remain dead. This is why if you put your identity in Jesus Christ you will have eternal life. Take Jesus away, and you will not have life in eternity. It was Jesus who conquered the grave, not us. We were bought with a price and we are not our own (1 Corinthians 6:19).

All of our worship must be directed towards God. Without Him, we are nothing and will never be anything. If our faith is in ourselves, instead of Jesus, then we violated the absolute core of Christianity and Biblical doctrine. Jesus was clear. He is the way the truth and the life (John 14:6). No one, absolutely no one will get to Heaven except through Him.

We must fix our eyes on Jesus Christ who is the Author and Perfector of our faith (Hebrews 12:2).

Surrendering to God is Worship

We are taught to worship God. In order to worship Him, we must surrender. Instead of trying to be like Him, or to become equal to Him, we are to surrender our will in favor of His will. When we do so, we gain:

1. A Manager of our lives

2. His discernment and wisdom

3. Protection

4. A Comforter

5. Power

6. Fellowship with Him

7. Love, joy, peace, longsuffering, gentleness, kindness, meekness, and temperance

8. Patience

9. Hope

But if our mentality is that we will become like God or equal to God, then we are left on our own without the blessings of having God be God.

> *"I am the vine; you are the branches. If a man remains in me and I in him, he will bear much fruit; apart from me you can do nothing."*
>
> — John 15:5

> *"But since he has no root, he lasts only a short time. When trouble or persecution comes because of the word, he quickly falls away."*
>
> — Matthew 13:21

God is Preparing a Place for You

> *"No eye has seen, no ear has heard, no mind has conceived what God has prepared for those who love him."*
>
> — 1 Corinthians 2:9

> *"Don't let your hearts be troubled. Trust in God, and trust also in me. There is more than enough room in my Father's home. If this were not so, would I have told you that I am going to prepare a place for you? When everything is ready, I will come and get you, so that you will always be with me where I am. And you know the way to where I am going."*
>
> — John 14:1-3 NLT

It is comforting to know that when you meet with God He will have already prepared a place for you. This should bring great peace to you. Knowing that it is finished and that someone else is going to be there in charge is pure heaven! This is equivalent on a very small scale of knowing that you get to be the child! You do not have to be the boss. Each and every moment on this earth that we try to be the boss, we place heavy burdens on ourselves. With Jesus, He is the boss! Hallelujah! Praise God! We get to be free because He paid the price. This should make you fall in love with Him all over again. Just imagine the peace! The place that is prepared for us is where Jesus already is! On earth we describe heaven loosely when we say something is heavenly, or peaceful. We will be praising God because we are so in love with His peace! This amazing place of rest! Some get this picture in their heads that we will be slaving away for a narcissist God that desires all of our praise and instant servitude. This is not the reality at all. In truth, we will be praising God because we will be unable to stop ourselves because of how great we feel. We will serve Him because we *get* to, not because we have to. How happy we will be. In heaven we will be in a perfect world with one God, the true and living God.

I do not know what choice you will make…"But if serving the LORD seems undesirable to you, then choose for yourselves this day whom you will serve, whether the gods your forefathers served beyond the River, or the gods of the Amorites, in whose land you are living. But as for me and my household, we will serve the LORD" (Joshua 24:15).

If we only realize what God has and is doing for us, our attitude would change. God is inviting you, a sinner, into His home. He is even willing to make it so that you can come into His home by trusting Jesus as our Savior. This is comparable to a King choosing to adopt homeless beggars as sons and daughters, and then inviting them in to live in his kingdom, and then they think that they too will be king. There can only be one king, and our Great God is that King.

"Before me no god was formed, nor will there be one after me.
I, even I am the Lord, and apart from me there is no savior."

— Isaiah 43:11

Thy kingdom come! It is His kingdom and He is coming! We all need to ask ourselves if we really think we could do everything Jesus did. He is God in flesh.

"The Word became flesh and made his dwelling among us. We have seen his glory, the glory of the One and Only, who came from the Father, full of grace and truth."

— John 1:14

A Prayer of Healing

"Lord Jesus, please forgive me for ever exalting myself. I was lost and confused, thought I could control things on my own and somehow work out my salvation. I confess, Jesus, that it is only through You and Your sacrifice and death on the cross that I am saved. Lord, I could never do what You did, nor will anyone else ever be able to. I put You in charge of my life and I trust You, Lord. I know that You will work all things out for my good. Help me to die to myself and live through You, Lord. Thank You, Lord, for being my God, for being in charge of my life. It is an honor to worship You. I thank You that I am Your child and that I can give my burdens to You, Lord. Thank You that You make them light for me. I love You, Lord Jesus. You are my only God. Amen."

His Great Love

"We love him, because he first loved us."

— 1 John 4:19 (KJV)

T he above verse is very powerful in so many different ways. In one sense, unfortunately, it pinpoints our human frailties, because too often we only have reciprocal love. In other words, we only love those that love us first. It's like the playground mentality of, "I'll be your friend, if you'll be mine." But on so many other levels, the verse demonstrates the love of God in a way that surpasses every possible imaginative quality of love that we cling to in all of our fantasies and paradisiacal dreams.

God loved us first.

Amazing. What exactly does that mean? Honestly, I can't begin to explain it. I know what it means to me, and I know that as I get older, it means more and more. But the love of God is a bottomless spring. It can't be qualified or quantified. It is beyond science. It is beyond our full understanding.

Nevertheless, I will attempt, in some small meager way, to try to get you to understand the vastness of God's love for you.

This book, while exposing many of the false teachings of Mormonism, also sheds light on how we can access the love of God. You see, this is the main thing: God loves everyone, regardless of who or what they are. Yet not everyone is able to experience the love of God. This is not God's fault. This is our own. The reasons we don't bask in God's love is because we have not yet experienced it and so choose not to come to Him. Much of this is because of the false doctrine of man that keeps us in condemnation. This book has brought to light many of the ways we have kept ourselves away from God. The calling has been given for you to come back into His loving embrace. He is waiting for you with open arms.

I want to summarize some of the main points that have been given in this book, but I also want to tie each truth to the love of God. Interestingly enough, if you can't tie it to the love of God, then it is not truth.

"You were cleansed from your sins when you obeyed the truth, so now you must show sincere love to each other as brothers and sisters. Love each other deeply with all your heart."

— 1 Peter 1:22 (NIV)

"A new command I give you: Love one another. As I have loved you, so you must love one another."

— John 13:34

Truth and love are irrevocably tied together. Each of the following truths is shown in such a way as to demonstrate more fully the love of Jesus Christ for each and every person.

1. **God's love is self-sufficient.** No matter what the reason for Adam's transgression, he didn't need to sin for God to manifest His love or His will to us. God's will and love are already self-sufficient, and He certainly doesn't need our help to demonstrate that love. He has given us very clear commands and wants us to trust Him and follow Him to safety and green pastures. His desire for us is an abundant life. This is an act of love!

Each command is given out of love for our safety and protection. We do not need to violate God's commands in order to receive His blessings and love! If you want to <u>feel</u> His love and receive His blessings, simply follow His Word!

2. **God's love is shown in the Message.** Trusting God's Word brings blessings into our lives. He would not let His word become corrupted. If He did, then His love would have failed us. Romans 8:38-39 teaches us that nothing can separate us from the love of God. And His love is demonstrated to us in His Word! He would never let it be lost...and He has not allowed it to be lost. He loves us too much for that.

3. **God's love is an action!** Too many times we think love is some sort of warm fuzzy feeling. But the Bible doesn't say that God so loved the world that He had a warm and fuzzy feeling for it. It says He *gave* His only begotten Son (John 3:16)! Love is an action. Remember, the true church is about love. It is about the action of sharing the love of God with anyone and everyone! Their social status matters not. Their education, skin color, current spiritual state, or even their popularity matters not. God's love is for everyone and the true church shares it with all. If there is no giving, there is no love.

4. **God's love does not flow through one conduit.** Other people and leaders will try to get you to listen to them. They will try to funnel any love through them down to you. These voices in this world will try to control your mind and try to get you to follow them as the only way to find God's love. But God loves you directly, not through a representative. You must learn to discern God's voice for yourself. Look to His Word—His love letter to you—to be sure. Remember, God's sheep know His voice and His Word and they follow only Him. What a powerful representation of love! God wants to walk and *talk* with you—directly with you!

5. **God's love is defined by His will for you.** The Bible teaches us in Romans 12:1-2 that the will of God is good, acceptable, and perfect. It is good for you in the sense that it is healthy

physically, mentally, emotionally, and spiritually for you. This is love! It is acceptable in that it is something you will love doing! In fact, it will be perfect for you, who you are, your circumstances, and your personality. If you want to really know the love of God, then listen to what He wants you to do. You'll never be happier in life than doing that! Be careful that you don't fall prey to man's will instead. If this happens, you won't feel God's love, only the guilt man places on you for failure.

6. **God's love is to be shown in our marriage.** God's rules are born out of love. Man's rules are born out of control and power. Many manmade rules such as polygamy place a wedge in your marriage. Marriage that is designed by God is a replica of the trinity with one man, one woman and God. God's love is to be revealed in marriage, not squelched. Garments squelch a marriage by placing a barrier in the middle. Marriage is a microcosm of how incredible our relationship with God can be. Manmade rules, however, bury the love of God and hurt relationships by placing them in an iron box of control. That is not love.

7. **God's love is absent in manmade rules.** Place God above all rules. He does not work in a box of control. Manmade rules are born out of a need to control others. God is not looking to control you. He is looking to have a relationship with you. God's laws are born out of love, out of a need to protect us. You feel safety when you obey His rules. Only then will you know protection, care, and love. Following manmade rules will make you feel guilty for every single failure. But God loves you. Place Him above all rules.

8. **God's love washes you clean.** When you trust Jesus as your Savior, His blood washes you clean of all sin (1 John 1:7). Baptism is something we do for God to show our love for Him. It doesn't actually wash away your sins. It is an act of obedience. But if you are looking for God's love, then know that when you turned to Jesus, you were made clean (1 John 1:9)! God washes

you with His spirit in order to receive your full inheritance into His family. If that isn't love, then what is?

9. **God's love is always with you.** God listens and hears your prayers—He is always with you. There is no need to go anywhere or perform any special ordinance to find the love of God. The veil (the barrier to God) has been split. You can find the love of God in church, in your home, on a mountaintop, or in your car. If you think that you must do this or that for God to notice and love you, you will never feel loved. Imagine your parents treating you this way. If you had to earn their love, would you really consider it love? Of course not! God's love is always with you!

10. **God's love forgives all sin.** There is no one on the face of this planet that is so far removed from the love of God that they can't find forgiveness. There is no greater act of love than to forgive. Can anyone doubt Jesus' love when He forgave those who were crucifying Him? Did they do anything to deserve that forgiveness? No, but Jesus loved them nevertheless. That's good news for you and me! We can find forgiveness with God without needing the approval of man. Why? Because God loves you. With this in mind, and with the knowledge that we are to love others (even our enemies) maybe we should forgive others—all others—as well.

11. **God's love is trustworthy.** When we trust God and believe everything He says, the enemy has no power over us. It is an aspect of God's love that you can bank on. Satan is not omnipresent, and he does not know everything. We give Satan power when we demonstrate that we are not trusting God by relying upon His love. When we try to work things out with our own understanding, we invariably turn to other practices that often times are cultish filled with rules and rituals. At such a point, the measure of a person is not about the love of God, but about trying to be better or superior to someone else—something that dismisses love. But God is trustworthy. We can rely upon His love in even the darkest of times.

12. **God's love is freedom.** Unconditional love is true freedom, and when you experience such love spiritually, you'll never want to settle for anything less. Control, on the other hand, is not about love, it is about power and who has it. Fortunately for us, God doesn't feel the need to prove He is bigger and tougher than we are. His focus is on deliverance and freedom in love. "For the Lord is the Spirit, and wherever the Spirit of the Lord is, there is freedom" (2 Corinthians 3:17 NLT).

13. **God's love is transparent.** There are many things about God that remain a mystery, not because God fears to share them with us, but because we are incapable of understanding them. However, the love of God is not one of those mysteries. His love is apparent and it is not shrouded in rituals, obscure ordinances, or secret symbols. God wants to fill our minds with wisdom. He wants to use our brokenness as our strength to help others. He's not trying to hide from us and He doesn't want us to hide from others. Love is transparent. Love is open and obvious!

14. **God's love is a calling.** 1 Peter 2:9 tells us, "We are a chosen people, a royal priesthood, a holy nation, a people belonging to God, that you may declare the praises of him who called you out of darkness into his wonderful light." We love God *because* He loved us first. That is a calling. His love is what calls us to serve Him! I don't do things for God because I have to. I do them because I get to! If someone saved your life, but ended up in the hospital as a result, you would do things for that person, not so that he *would* save you, but because he *did* save you. That person's act of love *called* you to service! This is where love is so powerful. When you finally know the love of God, as you should, you will react in love—and that's the only way to walk with God!

The Love of God and Knowing Him

One incredible aspect of God's love is revealed in the fact that God wants you to know Him. This is not a casual acquaintance, either. God wants you to *really* know Him. Psalms 46:10 tells us to be still and know that He is God. The word 'know' is to experience. It is a very powerful word used to describe the closest of relationships, such as between a husband and wife. In these relationships we are able to experience love. To really know God is to experience His love!

I want you to know *all* about your God—who He is—everything. We need to reestablish God as truly the God of our lives. We must trust Him and follow His Word for everything He has created us to be. God loves you for who you are, not for what you do. We cannot, however, fully understand Him as this is what makes Him God—He is beyond us. Part of our journey of love must involve trust. Your love for someone only grows when you can trust that person. We are to trust Him and enjoy the journey with Him. It is in coming to 'know' God and developing a close relationship with Him that we begin to experience His love.

We have taught people that God cannot be where sin is. This is not the truth of what God says. He tells us there is nothing that can separate us from His great love—God is in everything and is everywhere.

"For I am persuaded, that neither death, nor life, nor angels, nor principalities, nor powers, nor things present, nor things to come, Nor height, nor depth, nor any other creature, shall be able to separate us from the love of God, which is in Christ Jesus our Lord."

— Romans 8:38-39 (KJV)

Even during the most atrocious acts, God is there. He sees. He knows, and His heart breaks. He is there protecting those that call upon Him and even those that don't. He has given free will to every human being so that we can choose to get to know Him. We have the freedom to call upon Him or not. Often when you think God did not protect you, He was there protecting you from what could have been a worse result. While on this earth, you can never be beyond His great love.

Often people get really stuck wondering why something bad happened. We must remember that in all things, God works it out for the good of those that *love* him. There's that word again. When we know Him, we love Him. We are not victims. With God, we are victorious! Even though we do not understand certain things, we must trust in Him who loves us.

Trials and tribulations come to all Christians—and all people, Christian or not. The advantage that Christians have is a God who will be with them through any tribulation. We do live in a fallen world and unfortunate things do happen, but God will be with you, holding your hand and delivering you in each and every situation. You will have your eye fixed on eternity, and it will shine so brightly that your troubles are placed into the far off corner until they completely disappear. He will wipe away every tear and make all things new.

In the concept of knowing God, most understand that the Ten Commandments are for our safety and protection, true, but their most important function and purpose is to establish and protect our relationship with Him and others. We know people because of a relationship we have with them, and God wants a great relationship with us. Love God. Love others. All the law is based on those two commands (Mark 12:30-31).

On God's part, He gives you the Holy Spirit to wash your mind, to make you a new creation. He will restore purity. He will help you with discernment and bring all things to your remembrance. This is how God gets to know you. Of course, God knows everything, but knowing everything about someone doesn't mean you have a relationship with that person. God wants the relationship and the Holy Spirit is how He does it!

Remember, to blaspheme the Holy Spirit is to eliminate your belief system—undo your relationship with God. (See Ch. 10- The Unpardonable Sin). There is no power in unbelief, no relationship at all. But with the Holy Spirit, you establish a connection with God that allows you to speak things as though they already were. You will speak truth about others. You will see them as God sees them, not as man sees. And because of your connection and relationship with God, you will help others grow into everything they were created to be—their true identity. Your relationship with God will edify and speak blessings over others, bringing God's kingdom here on earth. You will speak out and proclaim the good news of Jesus Christ. You are speaking God's language of faith—a love language. Angels go out to make it happen.

Truth overcomes the lie! Keep speaking it out. Speak what you want to happen.

This knowing of God should bleed over into our other relationships. If we love God, we will love others!

> *"Whoever does not love does not know God,*
> *because God is love."*
>
> — 1 John 4:8

There's that combination of words again, 'love' and 'know.' Love is a result of knowing God. And if you have that relationship, you will love others. Loving others doesn't force change in their lives. We will love them, even if they do not change. After all, isn't this how God loves you? They will be loved into the light in God's timing. Trust Him. Love covers a multitude of sins (Proverbs 10:12). Your love will cover them, just as God's love covers us, even if they never change.

We must love others to the cross, not judge them to the cross. God's love is what made the cross possible and it is the only thing that will keep it available for everyone. God is all about love and freedom.

The Love of the Cross Will Not Be Mocked

There can clearly be no greater act of love than what Christ did on the cross for you and me.

> *"For God so loved the world, that he gave his only begotten*
> *Son, that whosoever believeth in him should not perish,*
> *but have everlasting life."*
>
> — John 3:16 (KJV)

> *"Greater love hath no man than this, that a man lay down his*
> *life for his friends."*
>
> — John 15:13 (KJV)

Love is an extension of an action. If you change the action, you change the love associated with it. If someone gave you a gift of money to meet a need, you would probably consider that an act of love on their part. But, if later, they came to you and demanded their money back, it would change your perception of the level of love behind the action.

If Jesus died on the cross for you and then said that you must do this and that to get to Heaven, it would change the way you saw the cross. You would see it less as an act of love and more as a debt you owe. There is very little love in a debt. Changing the cross from anything other than what it was, is an act of mockery...and God warned us that He would not be mocked.

"Be not deceived; God is not mocked: for whatsoever a man soweth, that shall he also reap."

— Galatians 6:7 (KJV)

When we add rituals and ordinances to salvation, we are making a mockery of the cross—and watering down the love of God in the process. The cross gave each individual access to God through Christ Jesus (John 14:6). We don't need to go through man anymore. Jesus is forever our High Priest—a position earned on the cross. We can now come boldly to the throne of grace (Hebrews 4:16). God's love made it so that each and every person can come to Him at any time and in any place (John 4:19-24). Anything else is a mockery of Jesus' death and of God's great love!

God will not be mocked! When you sow to the flesh—and this can range from anything evil and sinful, to fleshly and prideful 'spiritual' service to God—you will of the flesh reap corruption. If there is something that we can do in the flesh to get ourselves to Heaven, it would, by definition, be a corruption of salvation. This is why we must turn to Jesus and Jesus alone for salvation.

Instead of singing, "We Thank Thee, O God, for a Prophet," we should be singing praises to our God for what *He* did on the cross for us!

The Single Three Cords of Love—The Trinity

Mormons do not hold to the idea of the Trinity. They have failed to see the love of God manifested in the Trinity. Without the Trinity, we would have no true way to relate to a God who can step out on nothing and create everything. The Trinity is an incredible way to express love to us!

Unfortunately, Mormonism has excommunicated the love of God by abolishing the Trinity from their doctrine. Take a look at these quotes by Mormon authorities:

- "God—We believe in God the Eternal Father, and in His son Jesus Christ, and in the Holy Ghost (Articles of Faith,1) This cannot rationally be construed to mean that the Father, the Son and the Holy Ghost are on in substance and in person."[85]

- "There are three gods...separate in personality, united in purpose, in plan, and in all attributes of perfection."[86]

- "God is an organized being just as we are who are now in the flesh. He is a progressive being, and possesses the capacity of eternal increase—perhaps once a child and mortal like ourselves."[87]

- "God is not omnipresent...cannot be physically present in more than one place at a time."[88]

- "Every man who reigns in celestial glory is a god to his dominions."[89]

---

85 Talmage, *Articles of Faith*, p.40

86 Bruce McConkie, *Mormon Doctrine*, p. 270.

87 *Gospel Doctrine* p. 64, *Articles of Faith* p. 259, *Journal of Discourses* 1:123.

88 Talmage, *Doctrine and Covenants*, p.48.

89 Bruce McConkie, *Mormon Doctrine*, p. 322.

- "Jesus-By obedience and devotion He attained to the pinnacle of intelligence which ranked him as a God, even in his preexistent state."[90]

- "Elohim is literally the Father of the Spirit and of Jesus Christ, and also of the body."[91]

- "Holy Spirit–The Holy Ghost is 'a personage of Spirit,' He does not have a body of flesh and bones, like the Father and the Son."[92]

- He "can only be in one place at one time although he 'emanates from Deity'...like electricity, or the universal ether...which fills the earth and the air, and is everywhere present."[93]

By taking a single, all powerful God and reducing Him to three gods with distinctly human qualities, Mormonism has made the love of God into a joke. No longer is the cross about God's love, now it has become a power play between godlike beings—just the natural process of eternal progression.

The Trinity is a manifestation of three aspects of one God—not three. We are made in God's image and are therefore a trinity in our own right. We have a body, soul, and spirit—three aspects of a *single person*. The family is a trinity with a mother, father, and children—all three make up a *single family unit*. Water can manifest itself in liquid, solid and gas, but they all are the same *single* element. An egg is made up of three parts, the shell, the white, and the yolk. Nevertheless, it is a *single* egg.

The concept is difficult to grasp because we don't have the power of God. Our three parts (body, soul, spirit) are bound to our body while God is not bound to a body of flesh. God is a spirit! When you take the three different parts of the Trinity and put them all together, you get a *single* God.

---

90 Ibid. p. 192.

91 Talmage, *Doctrine and Covenants*, p.466.

92 *Doctrine and Covenants 130:22*

93 Bruce McConkie, *Mormon Doctrine*, pp. 359, 753.

But when you compare what the Mormons believe to the following Scriptures, a different picture emerges:

God the Father:

- **Proverbs 8:23** – "I was appointed from eternity, from the beginning, before the world began."

- **1 John 1:1** – "In the beginning was the Word, and the Word was with God, and the Word was God."

- **John 1:3** – "God created everything through him, and nothing was created except through him."

- **John 4:24** – "God is spirit, and his worshipers must worship in spirit and in truth."

God the Son:

- **Hebrews 7:3** – "Without father or mother, without genealogy, without beginning of days or end of life, like the Son of God he remains a priest forever."

- **1 John 1:14** – "The Word became flesh and made his dwelling among us. We have seen his glory, the glory of the One and Only, who came from the Father, full of grace and truth."

- **Ezekiel 37:27** – "My dwelling place will be with them; I will be their God, and they will be my people."

God the Holy Spirit:

- **John 14:16** – "And I will ask the Father, and he will give you another Counselor to be with you forever."

- **John 14:26** – "But the Counselor, the Holy Spirit, whom the Father will send in my name, will teach you all things and will remind you of everything I have said to you."

- **John 15:26** – "When the Counselor comes, whom I will send to you from the Father, the Spirit of truth who goes out from the Father, he will testify about me."

These are just a few of the Scriptures that teach of a Trinity. Satan wants to limit God to a man like us—the Trinity makes Him so much more! At the foot of the cross, there is a welcome for every broken heart, outcast, lonely person and rejected individual. Our hope is a life spent with Him. Come to Him, and call him your God. He is King!

We will never know how much it cost the Lord to take our sin upon Him. This is not some knee jerk reaction that takes place among trillions of gods on trillions of worlds. This is the action of a single God who loves us greatly. Without the Trinity, we would have no way to relate to God. We could not love Him, because we would not know how to love Him. The Trinity allows us to see that love on a level that we can comprehend and therefore reciprocate.

As Addison Road says in their song *What do I know of Holy?*, "I think I made you too small." None of us will ever know how great or how big our God is. He is mighty to save and He can do anything! The only sure way of knowing His character and His will for your life is to know His Word. What do I know? I know His word. I know He is love, and He does not want anyone to perish. Let us live in great reverence and respect for our great, holy and pure God. I can assure you, He will not be mocked.

God is Omnipresent, Omnipotent, Ruler of All, Father of All, Beginning and End, and Without sin. Every beautiful thing in this world is a finger pointing back to God.

What Can You Do?

What are we to do now that we know all these things? It's a good question. Hopefully, you've read through this book with a prayerful attitude. Still, this is only a book written by a human. You need to go to God's Word for every answer you need.

Take courage. God will be with you as Isaiah 41:10 says, "So do not fear, for I am with you; do not be dismayed, for I am your God. I will strengthen you and help you; I will uphold you with my righteous right hand."

Here is what I recommend you do:

1. Begin praying. This is always a good place to start!

2. Read God's Word, the Bible, daily. I suggest you read a translation that is easy for you to understand such as the NIV or NLT and then compare the message to other translations. The most important thing for you to get out of your reading is the proper context and meaning. As with all foreign languages, often we need to have things restated several ways so we can understand. This does not mean however that the Bible is open for your own interpretation. We are to walk in God's commands and His will. So constantly search with an open heart to learn from God himself.

3. Find a Bible believing church that stresses the free gift of eternal life.

4. Find fellow Christians for encouragement and support.

5. Tell others about your new life in Christ and share the gift of eternal life that belongs to all who believe in Him.

I would love to hear from you myself and learn how your relationship with Christ has grown even deeper.

A Healing Prayer

"Thank You, Lord Jesus, that You are the God of hope and healing. I praise You, and I live in great awe and respect of Your majesty. I pray for all those that do not know You. I pray that we can all learn to trust that You are a good God and You are our one and only Shepherd that keeps watch constantly. I pray that we will all rely on Your Word, the Bible, to guide us safely back into Your presence. I pray that the truth of how perfect and holy You are will be revealed to those seeking to know You. I pray all will come to understand the sinless and great sacrifice that You have made for each and every one of us in order to conquer death and to save us from Hell. Thank You, Jesus! Thank You for everything You have done. I love You. Amen."

"The grace of the Lord Jesus Christ, and the love of God, and the fellowship of the Holy Spirit, be with you all. Amen."

— 2 Corinthians 13:14

"Religion that God our Father accepts as pure and faultless is this: to look after orphans and widows in their distress and to keep oneself from being polluted by the world."

James 1:27

Charities I support:
World Vision
http://www.worldvision.org
Samaritan's Purse
www.**samaritanspurse**.org
Voice of the Martyrs
http://www.persecution.com

Additional Resources
Mormonism Research Ministry
http://www.mrm.org/
Christian Apologetics & Research Ministry
http://carm.org/mormonism
Utah Lighthouse Ministry
http://www.utlm.org/

To receive a weekly newsletter or to receive further information on Loved into the Light Workbooks, World Wide Studies, wholesale prices and additional CD's by the author go to:
www.YourKingdomInheritance.com

Notes

Notes

Notes

13199297R00184

Made in the USA
Charleston, SC
23 June 2012